I0287984

Drawn & Engraved by C.C.Mitchell.

AFFAIR ON THE BUFFALOE HEIGHTS.

Published by Henry Colburn, 13, Great Marlborough Street, 1837.

NARRATIVE

OF A

VOYAGE OF OBSERVATION

AMONG

THE COLONIES OF

WESTERN AFRICA,

IN THE FLAG-SHIP THALIA;

AND OF

A CAMPAIGN IN KAFFIR-LAND,

ON THE STAFF OF THE COMMANDER-IN-CHIEF,

IN 1835.

By JAMES EDWARD ALEXANDER, K.L.S.

Captain 42nd Highlanders; and Lieutenant-Colonel, Portuguese Service.
Author of " Travels in the East," " Transatlantic Sketches," &c.

ILLUSTRATED WITH MAPS AND PLATES

By MAJOR C. C. MICHELL, K. H.

Surveyor-General and Civil Engineer, Cape of Good Hope.

IN TWO VOLUMES.

VOL. II.

The Naval & Military Press Ltd

in association with

The National Army Museum, London

Published jointly by

The Naval & Military Press Ltd
Unit 10 Ridgewood Industrial Park,
Uckfield, East Sussex,
TN22 5QE England

Tel: +44 (0) 1825 749494
Fax: +44 (0) 1825 765701

www.naval-military-press.com
www.military-genealogy.com
www.militarymaproom.com

and

The National Army Museum, London
www.national-army-museum.ac.uk

In reprinting in facsimile from the original, any imperfections are inevitably reproduced and the quality may fall short of modern type and cartographic standards.

CONTENTS

OF

THE SECOND VOLUME.

CHAP. XVIII.

PAGE.

The Governor takes Measures for the Safety of the Colony and Punishment of the Kaffirs—Cobus the Hostage—Missionaries saved—Board of Relief—Captain Armstrong's Arrangements at Kat River—Noble Conduct of young Groepe—Disaster at Fort Willshire—The Kaffirs assemble in Force in the Fish River Bush—Colonel Smith marches to dislodge them—Action of the 12th of February — Operations and Incidents of four Days — The Troops return to Graham's Town—Attack on the Kat River Settlement—Anecdote of Van Wyk—Author sets out for the Clusie—Exposed Situation—How to keep a sharp Look-out—Surprise and Defeat of the Port Elizabeth Yeomanry—Kaffirs again occupy the Fish River Bush—Lead Field-commandant Rademayer into an Ambuscade—His gallant Stand and valorous Exploit—How to look for Spoor—Visit a Vineyard—Love and War—Excellent Conduct of two Kaffir Queens—Colonel Smith pursues a Body of the Enemy into Kaffir-land, and returns to Graham's Town... 1

CONTENTS.

CHAP. XIX.

PAGE.

An Invading Force organized—Comparative State of Troops in 1819-20 and 1834-35—Why the War should be carried into the Enemy's Country—Hottentot Cavalry and Infantry — Character of Hottentot Levies — The Dutch Burghers—Bush Ranging—The Corps of Guides —The Regulars—Official Return of the Invading Force— The first and second Lines of Defence—Hintza's Duplicity—Behaviour to Piet Uys—Thinks the Colonists can be easily blinded to his Acts—Field-commandant Van Wyk's Mission and Message to Hintza—Distribution of Troops—Camps of 'Assembly—Intended Movements— Favourable State of the Weather—Mr. H. Fynn's Mission to Faku—His Answer to a Kaffir—Skirmishes—Kaffir Bravery—Magnanimous Conduct of Major Gregory— " Saddle up" to cross the Border—Author's Misfortunes —Leave Graham's Town for Kaffir Drift—Cavalry Camp on the Clusie—Chiefs Pato and Kama—A Rouse—Fort Willshire—Again under Canvass in the Field 33

CHAP. XX.

The British Field Force enters Kaffir-land—A Kaffir Beldame—Anecdote—Kabecca—Absurd Accident—Capaai attacks the Tambookies—A Farmer outwitted—The Deba and T'Slambie's Kop—Reconnoissance—An Alarm —Operations of the Third of April—A Scramble—Spy shot—Commatje Flats—Geological Phenomena—A Scientific Guide—Missionaries have sometimes short Memories—A Breakfast—Encamp between the Spruits of the Buffalo—Movements of the Second, Third, and Fourth Divisions—Affairs with the Enemy on the Seventh of April—Highland Spirit, (not Glenlivet)—Capture of a

CONTENTS. vii

PAGE.

Deserter—Affairs on the Ninth of April in the Mountains of the Buffalo—Sutton's Escape—The Camp by Moonlight 57

CHAP. XXI.

Effects of the Campaign on the Enemy—The Commander-in-Chief thanks the Troops—Further Arrangements — Head-Quarters "en Route" — Glen of the Cahoon — Tunglalaba — Simpson's Station — Prepare to enter Hintza's Territory — Kaffir Herald — Cross the Great Kye River—Shaw's Fountain—Visit of Amapakati —Receive a Message — A Gallant Company — Short Account of the Fingoes—Instances of Kaffir Oppression —Adventure in a Garden—Butterworth Mission Station —Agreeable Bed-fellows—Lieutenant Bailie's Sermon— Author and his Friends practise Witchcraft — The Second Division — A Fatal Accident — A Murder — Sergeant Howison's Adventure—Couba the Counsellor —Fingoes become British Subjects—Their Warriors arrive in Camp—Their Rejoicings and Bivouack—Final Message to Hintza—Declaration of War 89

CHAP. XXII.

Summary of Operations near the Frontier—The First Division marches—A Tornado—Encamp on the Kamega —Kaffir Women in Danger—March to the Izolo— Interesting Prospect—More Kaffir Women—Jock Maclaughlin—Colonel Smith's Operations—Attack Hintza's Kraal—Successful Operation by a Medical Officer— Gallantry of Driver—Results of Colonel Smith's Activity —The Cattle Mania—Instance of Carelessness—Three of Hintza's Counsellors arrive in Camp—Author's Opera-

viii   CONTENTS.

                                                    PAGE.
tions—Advent of Hintza to sue for Peace—Interesting
Conference and Treaty—A most barbarous Custom—
Hintza and his Son Crieli remain as Hostages—Hintza's
Appetite—His Opinion of the Bagpipes—Kaffir Revenge
—Pyramid erected—First Division returns towards the
Kye—Bookoo—Fingo Massacre—Dabakasee Camp—
Captain Warden's Return—His skilful Management—
What we suffered in the Field............................117

CHAP. XXIII.

Flight of the Fingoes out of Kaffir-land—First Division marches to Bombanee—The Author's Child—Camp on the Kye—Cunning Baboons—Camp at Night—An important Day in the History of the Colony—The General proclaims the Kye to be the New Boundary—His Declaration to Hintza—The Kaffir King offers to show Colonel Smith the Colonial Cattle—Behaviour of Crieli—Colonel Smith, with Hintza, marches towards the Bashee—Short Review of a Change in Sir Benjamin D'Urban's Sentiments—The Policy of extending the Colony—Duplicity of Hintza—Fatal Effects of a Blue Morœa—Camp at Impotshana—The Valley of Death—The Construction of Warden's Post—Return of Colonel Smith's Corps—Its Proceedings—Death of Hintza—Colonel Smith crosses the Bashee, and marches towards the Umtata—Captain Bailie's Proceedings—Death of Major White—Alerts in Camp 144

CHAP. XXIV.

Treaty with Crieli—Bookoo and Kinki retained as Hostages—Kaffir Characteristic—The Second Division creditably concludes its Services—Colonel England—

CONTENTS. ix

PAGE.

Gallantry of the Bowkers—Mr. Collett again Attacked —The Third and Fourth Divisions—The Queen Regent of the Gaikas — Mysterious Occurrence — Lieutenant Granett's Mission to Macomo and Tyalie—They meet Major Cox—The General's Message—The War continues—Capture of Macomo's Horses and Recapture of Prize Cattle—Death of Jan Greyling—Head-Quarter Division marches from Warden's Post—Death's Doings—Canine Fidelity—The Heights of Wellington—Rapid Construction of Fort Wellington—The Adelaide Spice Tree—Glen Aberdeen and the Valley of Peel—King William's Town—Buffalo River—Captain Beresford sent to England with Despatches — Hostages attempt to Escape—Jock Maclaughlin "no sae saaft"—Honourable Conveyance of Prisoners—Lieutenant Williams, R. E.—Construction of Forts Hill, Hardinge, Beresford, Murray, and White—Herbert Taylor's Hill — Botany of the Buffalo—The Lictor Insect—Expedition to clear the Country towards the Mouth of the Buffalo—The Surveyor-General—The Curiosity Hunter—Expedition to clear the Buffalo Mountains—Kaffirs harass the Fingoes—Expedition to clear the Banks of the Keiskamma—Fatal Accident 176

CHAP. XXV.

The New Province left in Charge of Colonel Smith—The Troops are thanked—First and Third Divisions discontinued—The General arrives at Fort Willshire—Conference with Suta, the Great-wife of Gaika—Arrival at Graham's Town—Employment there—Panics—Successful Patrols in the New Province—Valley of the Cowie—Anecdotes of Settlers—Bathurst—Forbes's Redoubts—Schemes of the Philanthropists to defend the Frontier—Kaffir Drift—Hortus Siccus—Fredericksburg

x   CONTENTS.

                                                              PAGE
—An Ostrich Hunt—The Gualana—Py the Counsellor
—Line Drift—Fingoes on the Iquora—The Queen No-
nubé—Escape of a Prisoner—Conference with the Fingo
Chiefs—A Beauty—The Age of Cant—March to Forts
Willshire and Beaufort—Block Drift—Fingo Location
—Ride up the Kat River—A Lion Hunt—The Beaufort
Stot—The Kat River Settlement—Camp Adelaide—Abo-
minable Plot—Andries Stoffel, *Esquire*—Balfour—The
Vagrant Act—A New System—Ride towards the Chumie
—Magnificent Prospects—Fort Beaufort—Return to
Graham's Town 206

CHAP. XXVI.

Concluding Events of the War—The Health of the
Troops—Patrols harass the Enemy—The New Town—
Kaffir Revenge and Cunning—Their Women take a part
in the War—Captain Stretch's Success—Bloody John
Bull—Fate of Lieutenant Bailie's Party—Fingo Bravery
—Bookoo released—Death of Captain Lingard—The
Kaffirs in Despair, resolve to pour again into the Colony
—Successful Result of Operations under Major Cox—
Captain W. Alexander brings the Chiefs to bay—They
submit and sue for Peace—Hostilities cease—Brigade-
Major Warden and the Author sent on a Mission to the
Amatola—Meet the Chiefs at a Grand Conference—Kaffir
Superstition—Plaatché, the Kaffir Adjutant-General—
Renewed Conference—The Governor's Message—Inter-
esting Debate on the Terms of Peace—The Result of the
Conference—The Governor meets the Chiefs at Fort
Willshire—Negotiations unexpectedly broken off—More
Fighting—Treaties of Peace and Settlement finally made
with the Gaikas, T'Slambies, and Congoes—Importance
of the Arrangements now concluded 244

CONTENTS.

CHAP. XXVII.

Results of Peace—Board of Relief—A Contusion—The Governor leaves Graham's Town for Cape Town—Unpleasant Adventure—Salem—Uitenhage—Our future Policy—A Word in Favour of Cape Town—Uitenhage Water and Widows—Bethelsdorp—A Word on the Missionary Schools—Port Elizabeth—Good out of Evil—The Christening of the D'Urban Lighthouse Rock—Steam Navigation—Captain Gardiner arrives from Natal—The British Territory there—Dingan and the Zoolahs—Uitenhage—Vanstaden's River—Human's Farm—Moolman's—Needy Hottentots—Meeding's—Rademayer's—Goose Kraal—Cradock Pass—George—Pakelsdorp—The Cayman's Hole—The Zitzikamma Forest—Mossel Bay—Muller's—Lombard's—Swellendam—A Comparison—The Patriarch Lindé—Caledon—De Kock's—Monuments to the Surveyor-General—Character of the Böers—Somerset—Sandfleet—Arrival in Cape Town 286

APPENDIX:—

Conference with the Kaffir Chiefs on the 15th of August, 1835..335

Conference with the Kaffir Chiefs on the 6th of September, 1835..339

Minutes of a Conversation between Colonel Smith and Guania on the 8th of September, 1835 343

Elucidation of the Cause and Manner of the breaking off the Treaties of Peace, from the 13th to the 17th of September, 1835 350

LIST OF ILLUSTRATIONS.

VOL. II.

	PAGE.
Part of the Great Fish River	1
Poorts of the Buffalo	57
Affair on the Buffalo Heights	79
Kaffir Warrior Caterpillar	89
Conference on the Great Kye	95
Scene of Hintza's Death	144
Departure of the Fingoes	ib.
Spider of the Impotshana	175
The Adelaide Spice Tree	243
Conference with the Kaffir Chiefs	262
Three Plates of the Drawings of the Aborigines	316

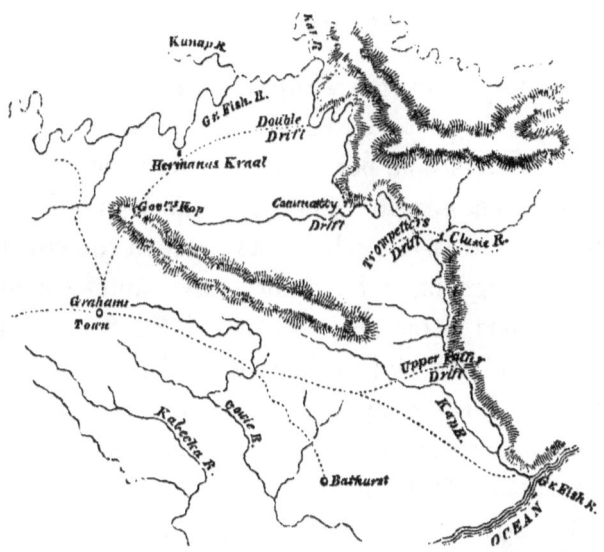

CHAPTER XVIII.

The Governor takes Measures for the Safety of the Colony and Punishment of the Kaffirs—Cobus the Hostage—Missionaries saved—Board of Relief—Captain Armstrong's Arrangements at Kat River—Noble Conduct of young Groepe—Disaster at Fort Willshire—The Kaffirs assemble in Force in the Fish River Bush—Colonel Smith marches to dislodge them—Action of the 12th of February—Operations and Incidents of four Days—The Troops return to Graham's Town—Attack on the Kat River Settlement—Anecdote of Van Wyk—Author sets out for the Clusie—Exposed Situation—How to keep a sharp Look-out—Surprise and Defeat of the Port Elizabeth Yeomanry—Kaffirs again occupy the Fish River Bush—Lead Field-commandant Rademayer into an Ambuscade—His gallant Stand and valorous Exploit—How to look for Spoor—Visit a Vineyard—Love and War—Excellent Conduct of two Kaffir Queens—Colonel Smith pursues a Body of the Enemy into Kaffir-land, and returns to Graham's Town.

MAJOR-GENERAL Sir Benjamin D'Urban having arrived, in the middle of January, at Algoa Bay, in his majesty's ship *Trinculo*, came immediately by Uitenhage to Graham's Town with the 72d Highlanders; and personally directed the arrangements necessary to remedy, as far as practicable, the great disasters which had befallen the colony, and to organize a force for active and extended operations in the field. Colonel Smith and the officers of the civil and military departments laboured incessantly and cheerfully to carry his excellency's measures into complete effect. The confidence of the inhabitants was now fully restored. The arrival of the governor and reinforcements, and some successes over the enemy, roused them—" dolores obliviscere et animos renovare." Although, as I before mentioned, six thousand of the colonists would have starved, if it had not been for the government rations, yet now they only desired to be led against their merciless foes.

Amidst the horrors which this barbarous enemy had committed, it was satisfactory to think that the chiefs Pato, Kama, and Cobus, of the Congo family, with Jan Tzatzoe, proved themselves to be faithful to the colony, saving the lives of some missionaries and traders. Cobus remained as a hostage in town; and having thrown aside his kaross, he dressed himself in a blue surtout, wearing also a black hat and gloves! His attendants appeared in all their pastoral simplicity.

The missionaries left in Kaffir-land now contrived to send messengers into the colony, stating that they were in very great danger; that the Kaffirs had murdered some traders even under the protection of their roofs; and had threatened them that their lives would be taken next. They therefore earnestly implored for assistance; and strong parties, under the command of Major Cox, were accordingly sent immediately to the Buffalo River, to Burnshill, Pirie, the Chumie, &c. &c. These detachments succeeded in rescuing the missionaries and some traders from their danger; and whilst returning with them to Graham's Town, recaptured a large herd of colonial cattle, slaying twenty Kaffirs.

The head-quarters of Macomo and Tyalie were now understood to be among the mountain fastnesses of the Amatola: the thick woods, precipices, and ravines of which are impracticable to horsemen. Arms and ammunition having arrived from Cape Town, they were distributed through the country; and the inhabitants of Port Elizabeth, Uitenhage, Bathurst, Somerset, Cradock, &c. were organized into corps of volunteers. Two boards were at the same time formed: one for agricultural relief, to supply in part the losses of the farmers, and place them in a condition to resume their occupations; the other for relieving the destitute. Shelter, clothes, and medicines, were furnished to the distressed; and every thing was done to alleviate their great calamities. At this time, besides the murder of their friends and the destruction of their houses and crops, their losses were estimated at one hundred thousand head of cattle, fifteen hundred horses, and many flocks of sheep and goats. The Kaffirs having swept the country from the Fish River round Uitenhage up to Somerset, and across by the Bavian's River, at length disappeared for a time.

Captain Armstrong had now concentrated the five thousand coloured settlers of Kat River in a rocky peninsula, which was named Camp Adelaide. By his great exertions and judicious management, he had caused a complete breach between those Hottentots who were wavering in their allegiance and the Kaffirs; and the enemy at last fell on the settlement, and burnt and destroyed what they could not carry off. A noble instance of courage, worthy of the best times of the Romans, was here displayed by a youth, the son of Field-commandant Groepe,—one of the most loyal and trustworthy men of colour on the frontiers. Young Groepe went out with his uncle to look after some of his father's cattle, and prevent them from falling into the hands of the enemy. They had gone four or five miles from Camp Adelaide when it began to rain, which prevented their seeing far: they therefore unsaddled; and, sitting under shelter, allowed their horses to graze in an open spot, surrounded with bush. They had sat some time conversing, and then rose to " saddle up:" when in an instant twenty Kaffirs, who had been watching them, appeared from the bushes round them. " Now," said young Groepe to his uncle, " we must stand back to back, and reserve our fire." They did so, and retreated. The Kaffirs hesitated a little; but at last one sprang forward and launched an assegai through the lungs of Groepe, who immediately fired, and the Kaffir fell. Groepe cried to his uncle, " Now fire, and escape; save the cattle if possible; and don't let my father lose them and his son on the same day: never mind me!"

The uncle accordingly fired, and jumped through an opening made among the Kaffirs. Their party then divided: half going after the uncle, who escaped, and half pursuing young Groepe. He presented his empty gun; they skulked aside, but continued to dog him; he tried to pull out the assegai which had passed through his right breast, but could not succeed; and in the act of putting the powder-horn to the muzzle of his gun to load, another assegai passed through his left arm, and one through his hat. He pulled these out, and hurled them at his assailants; and then, exhausted with loss of blood, he staggered on till he got near to his father's herdsmen driving off the cattle. The Kaffirs then retired; and Groepe sank down beside a rock facing the enemy, and called to the herdsmen to leave him to his fate, but to save themselves and his father's property. They drew the assegai completely through him, and carried him into Camp Adelaide. I saw him some time afterwards, recovering slowly; though the air was still passing out from the lungs between his shoulders. The governor presented him with a handsome double-barrelled gun, and a Dutch bible, for his heroic conduct.

A disaster now occurred in the neighbourhood of Fort Willshire. Three hundred Kaffirs, mounted and on foot, armed with guns and assegais, suddenly attacked a small cattle-guard, about a thousand yards from the fort; slew and stripped a corporal and three privates of the 72nd Highlanders, and two Hottentots, one of whose bodies they mutilated; and carried off all the sheep. The fort seemed to be closely invested by the enemy. Colonel Somerset returned after effectually scouring the bush of the Zuurberg, and Oliphant's Hoek, at the mouth of the Bushman's River, and of the Kowie; and Colonel

England with Major Gregory arriving in town from the Fish River, reported that they had had some skirmishing with the enemy: who had in great force taken up a strong position there, having with them a large herd of cattle for their subsistence. It appeared evident, therefore, that the Kaffirs had lodged themselves in the woody fastnesses between the Great Fish and Keiskamma rivers : awaiting, as in the war of 1819, the ad vance of the troops into Kaffir-land; and intending, after having suffered them to pass, again to fall on the colony, to take the troops in rear, or to interrupt their communications.

But a military chief of long experience was not to be outdone by savages; the paramount importance of expelling them from their fastnesses was immediately seen; and it was forthwith resolved by Sir Benjamin D'Urban to clear the ground between the Fish and Keiskamma rivers, before he should advance from the latter to retaliate on the enemy, and carry the war from our country into theirs. Accordingly, a force of about eleven hundred men, and consisting of detachments from the 72d and 75th regiments, Cape mounted rifles, artillery, burghers, and Hottentot sharp-shooters, was placed under the orders of Colonel Smith; who left Graham's Town for the Fish River, where he was delayed some time by a flood.

Colonel Smith's force was distributed into three divisions: the centre, or head-quarter division, to cross at a ford called Trompeter's Drift; the right, under Colonel Somerset, to cross at Kaffir Drift; and the left, under Colonel England, at Commatty's Drift. Thus, the flanking corps tending inwards and co-operating with the centre, would embrace the whole position of the enemy, and drive him out of it: the skilful nature of the movement being obviously such, as would in a great degree intercept his retreat over the Keiskamma.

The ground occupied by the enemy was a chain of woody heights of several hundred feet elevation, extending on the eastern bank of the Fish River, between the three fords. The heights were every where intersected with dark and deep *kloofs*, or ravines; full of nearly impenetrable bush; and affording excellent concealment to the enemy, and the cattle which he had collected there. The scene was grand and impressive. Silence reigned over the large features of a country on which there were no marks of the industry of man: the hills and woods had remained untouched since vegetation began to cover them, after the subsiding of the waters of the Deluge. The Great Fish River rolled in a turbid stream— though it looked clear at a distance under the influence of a summer sun; and in its course to the sea, laved the trunks of yellow wood and willows of Babylon. A signal-smoke occasionally rose from the bosom of a kloof; and a faint and far-off lowing of kine: whilst the plaintive and wild note of the golden cuckoo would occasionally be heard from the thorny mimosas.

On the night of the 11th of February, the river fell; and Colonel Smith, with Major Gregory and a corps of the head-quarter division, crossed it, ascended the hills without a check, and took up a position on the summit in rear of the enemy: the guns under Lieut. Levinge, royal artillery, pointing down the kloofs. To make a decided impression on the enemy, it was necessary to attack him in front at various points at once; and accordingly, two other corps of the head-quarter division, under Major Maclean of the 72d and Captain Halifax of the 75th regiment, when they had crossed the river, turned to the left, and at the respective distances of one mile and a half and four miles, lay on their arms till daylight.

When day dawned on the 12th, the enemy were observed in scattered masses in the kloofs: but immediately they saw the troops, they set up a shout of alarm; ran from their temporary huts; and rapidly drove the clumps of cattle, kraaled in various directions, into the bush. The action commenced by a six-pounder and a howitzer playing with round shot, grape, and shells, into the kloofs below. The troops, under Major Maclean and Captain Halifax, then penetrated the bush, and ascending the rugged hills, scoured the thickets. The enemy showed great determination with both musquet and assegai, in endeavouring to stop the advance of the British force, in ground which was so favourable for their defence: but our people overcoming all opposition, and driving before them the cattle, which (frightened with the firing and shouts) poured in great numbers from the ravines, the two corps joined Colonel Smith on the heights.

Colonel Somerset, with a three-pounder and four hundred and fifteen cavalry, having with great labour and difficulty ascended from Kaffir Drift, turned to the left, and also attacked the enemy with success, capturing many hundred head of cattle: whilst Colonel England, with a six-pounder and a mixed force, crossed Commatty's Drift, and, turning to the right, likewise engaged the enemy vigorously. The results of these combined and successful operations were, seventy-three of the enemy left dead, and a great many wounded, who, as usual, easily concealed themselves; two thousand five hundred head of cattle captured; and several flocks of sheep and goats, numbers of musquets, and bundles of assegais taken: our loss amounted to thirteen, viz. five killed and eight wounded. One of the killed on this occasion was a fine young man of the name of Goodwin, a volunteer, who descended into the bush, and getting separated from his companions was never seen again: his bloody jacket only was found pierced with assegais.

The troops bivouacked, much distressed with the heat, want of water, and encumbrance of cattle: however, officers and men were all on the alert, and anxious to be again engaged. Having recrossed the Great Fish River, Colonel Smith, on the 14th, directed corps of infantry, under Major Maclean and Captains Halifax and Bagot, to march up the eastern bank a considerable distance (six or eight miles). The cavalry crossed at a narrow and rugged pass, called Sheffield's; and above them again, Colonel England's corps at Commatty's Drift.

At daybreak, a six-pounder gave the signal for a general advance; the troops dashed into the ravines; and, scrambling by elephant paths, and tearing through the underwood, ascended the kloofs. The enemy had now left few men to defend the cattle; the main body of them having disappeared after the action of the 12th: but those who were seen were pursued vigorously, and many of them destroyed. On the 16th, the enemy had entirely disappeared: leaving one hundred slain, and probably five or six times that number wounded. The great guns did fearful execution among their dark masses; and a chief was seen running across the river, having lost both his arms with grape-shot. Thirty women and children of the T'Slambies fell into the hands of the troops; and they were fed, treated with every kindness, and released. Four thousand head of cattle were captured during the four days' operations; also horses, goats and sheep, arms and ammunition; and numerous huts and kraals were burnt. Our loss amounted to twenty-three, viz. twelve killed and eleven wounded.

Two or three incidents occurred during these affairs, which are worth recording. One evening, Colonel Smith, Major Cox, and some other officers were sitting round a fire, after refreshing with *karbonatje* and the contents of their canteens, when a party of Kaffirs crept towards them, and fired on them from a thicket. The bullets whistled past without taking effect; and the Kaffirs precipitately retired, eluding the search of the soldiers who dashed into the thicket after them. A disaster occurred one night among the 72d Highlanders. Two companies were sleeping on their arms near each other, and in the immediate vicinity of the enemy; one of the men, a young soldier, hearing a noise in the bush, started to his feet, called out "Kaffirs!" and discharged his piece; the rest awaking suddenly and thinking they were attacked, commenced a fire on each other; and four fine men fell mortally wounded, before the officers could put a stop to the firing.

An Englishman of the name of Wainright was pushing down a kloof, when a huge Kaffir started up from behind a bush, and brandished his assegai: the Englishman had no time to bring his gun to his shoulder, so making a rush at the Kaffir, he grappled with him; and they both rolled over together. The contest was doubtful; when a burgher running up, put the muzzle of his piece to the Kaffir's side and destroyed him. A party of Dutch burghers, under the charge of two officers of the regulars, rode to the top of a kloof, and saw Kaffirs below. The officers immediately dismounted, and ordered the böers to follow them into the bush. "Nay, mynheer," was the answer, "you are paid to do that: we are not; and we have *vrouwen en kinderen* (wives and children) at home." It appeared to be quite an unusual thing to many of the Dutch to go into the bush at all. Some went in, however, very readily: but others had only been accustomed to "*skeet de Kaffirs*" when they found them in the plain; and it was a new feature in Kaffir warfare, to make all our people scour the bush as they were now ordered to do. Perhaps the best way to destroy Kaffirs would be to rest concealed all day, and at night to dash on them at their fires in the bush.

Two Hottentots came over from the enemy's ranks with their arms. They said that some of their countrymen had gone over to the Kaffirs; and that others had been made prisoners: but that all of them now were dispirited, and wished for an opportunity to effect their escape. The troops resumed their cantonments in and about Graham's Town, with the exception of Colonel Somerset's corps of five hundred cavalry: which continued to occupy the ground from whence the enemy had been driven, extending from Fort Willshire to the Guanga on the eastern bank of the Fish River, and communicating with the friendly tribes of Pato and Kama on the right. A general order was then issued to congratulate the troops upon the complete success which had crowned their recent operations, and by which the necessary and important object had been attained of driving the hostile tribes from the woods and fastnesses of the Great Fish River.

" This enterprise was one of no ordinary difficulty. The enemy was numerous, well armed with musquets, and determined to hold his ground; which, from the rugged and thickly wooded ravines, was singularly favourable to his peculiar mode of fighting. The heat of the climate was suffocating in the woods; the unavoidable scarcity of water distressing; and the movements necessarily laborious and fatiguing. Nevertheless, the able dispositions of the officer commanding; the prompt and exact execution of his orders by those who led the different columns; and the unswerving and persevering energy of the officers and troops, triumphed over all obstacles; and the enemy were routed every where, and driven from their strong-holds and over the Keiskamma with heavy loss."

Reinforcements of burghers and Hottentots now daily arrived in Graham's Town. Among the former, were five hundred Swellendamers: stout fellows in high white hats, duffle jackets, and leather crackers; carrying long guns, four and eight to the pound; and riding, three and three, on ambling horses. The field-commandant of these was a fine old Dutchman, M. Linde: seventy-five years of age, hale and active, with a face like a hatchet; and who had been five times before engaged in border warfare. The Hottentots who marched into town from Port Elizabeth, Uitenhage, &c. were clothed in red worsted caps and moleskin clothes, and well armed.

During this time Captain Armstrong, at the Kat River Settlement, was fully employed. One day two Kaffir women visited some of their old acquaintances on the peninsula of Camp Adelaide, and incautiously let fall that a large force of Hintza's and Tyalie's Kaffirs were in the neighbourhood. Accordingly, on the 19th of February, Captain Armstrong sent out strong patrols of observation, with orders also to cover and protect the cattle of the settlement, which were obliged to be sent out to a distance daily, to graze. Large bodies of the enemy soon showed themselves from various defiles; and with loud shouts and whistling, repeatedly attacked the Kat River Hottentots, and attempted to drive off the cattle. Major Blakeway and Field-commandant Groepe, with the people under them, gallantly met and repulsed the enemy, and brought in the cattle at sunset, taking also some Kaffir horses. Sixty-seven bodies of dead Kaffirs were counted after this attack. The loss to the settlement was two men killed, and a man and a woman badly wounded. Field-commandant Van Wyk arrived during this attack; and bringing up a force of mounted burghers, he pursued the flying enemy, and prevented them from renewing their attack on the settlement.

In general orders, the foresight of Captain Armstrong in anticipating the attack, the able dispositions which he made to meet it, and his cool determination throughout its progress, were stated to have been alike conspicuous. The courage and firmness of those under him were also deservedly praised. An anecdote may here be given of Van Wyk, who so ably assisted on this occasion: as it shows, better than many paragraphs, the system which the pseudo-philanthropists had caused to be introduced on the frontier, previous to the grand foray of the Kaffirs. Soon after the invasion of the colony, Van Wyk arrived at Graham's Town from the Tarka for orders, and received them from Colonel Smith; who directed him to collect his burghers instantly, and repel the enemy. "I must have a license, mynheer," says the field-commandant. "A license for what?" cries the colonel. "A license to shoot Kaffirs, mynheer."—"The devil! Has not the war begun? I tell you, you are to shoot as many Kaffirs as you can."—"I know better than to do that," replied the sturdy Dutchman, turning to Major Michell, then quarter-master-general. "I may get myself shot by the government if I do that, and all my property confiscated."—" That's all nonsense," cried the colonel: "go and shoot immediately."—" Ja, mynheer, dat is goed; ik wil so doen: verdoem de Kaffirs! But I must have all that in black and white before I draw a trigger;" and again appealing to Major Michell, he got him to write out a license to shoot Kaffirs, wherever he could find them, and had it regularly signed by Colonel Smith.

Being desirous to see what was going on in advance, I took charge of some orders for Colonel Somerset at the Clusie; and set off, in the midst of violent rain, with eight mounted Hottentots. The party had a very bandit appearance, with their slouched hats, drooping ostrich feathers, long black cloaks, and guns carried across their shoulders; and we galloped and splashed on at night to Honey's Farm under Governor's Kop. The farm was occupied by a party of burghers, who comforted me with tea and sausages; and then we all lay down to sleep in sheep-skin karosses on the floor.

Next day, it continued to rain incessantly; and I was joined by a part of the Port Elizabeth yeomanry, headed by a dashing-looking young fellow, Mr. Calvert: in plumed hat, carbine in hand, a pistol in his breast, and a naked sword in his girdle. To get the men accommodated in houses near at hand, and to look after some provision-wagons which required escort, it behoved me to kick off my shoes, pull my trousers over my knees, and bustle about ever and anon during the day through mud, stones, and wet grass. Little attention is required to brush clothes or polish boots in a seat of war generally: therefore "the liberty of the field" is most pleasant.

It still rained; and though the wagoners declared they should make little or no progress, yet it was necessary we should attempt a start. Accordingly we moved off, ascending Governor's Kop; and Captain Harries and the remainder of the Port Elizabeth yeomanry, English and Dutch, now coming up, we formed altogether a party of fifty men: with four provision-wagons, and a small flock of sheep for karbonatjes. We rode along a ridge for some time, with vast plains below us to the left, and beyond them the rugged and lofty range of the Winterberg. There was scattered bush over the waste: but though our view seemed to embrace a hundred miles, we saw no water glancing in the light, and no smoke of fires arose. A solitary vulture soared aloft from a deep kloof; and on the right, and in the far distance, was the sea.

We "out-spanned" for the night in a hollow among the hills; ate our supper beneath the bushes; and lay down in our sheep-skins under the lee of the saddles. In the night we were attacked by wild beasts: not Kaffirs, but leopards, which scattered the horses and sheep, and destroyed many of the latter. In the morning, we pushed on to an open and elevated spot called Frazer's Camp; where I left Captain Harries, who was to remain there for some time, to keep up the communication between head-quarters and Colonel Somerset. I went on eight miles, with a small escort to the Great Fish River; and saw, at some distance, the white smoke of Southey's kraal, the manure of which had been burning for weeks. The river was up again, and rolled past like liquid mud, twenty or thirty feet deep. Four provision wagons and a guard of ten böers were waiting to cross; and here I sent back my escort, and remained with the wagons.

Two nights we lay at Trompeter's Drift, near the remains of traders' wagons, broken, scattered about, and partly burnt by the Kaffirs in January. The people with me said, " We shall get our throats cut here; for it has always been a bad place. There have been many skirmishes here; and there are bones of white men and Kaffirs lying under the bushes." I said, that the lesson which the Kaffirs had lately received here, would be likely to prevent their returning soon again. However, I set double sentries: but at two in the morning they did not answer, and were found asleep on the ground. They pretended that they had lain down to see the enemy's approach the clearer between the sky and the ground; and certainly this is the best way of holding watch in the field, if the eyes can be kept open.

As there was no likelihood of getting the wagons over soon, the only means of communicating with Colonel Somerset, far behind the hills, was by swimming the river. There was nothing moving in front: so getting the colonel's answer, and returning to town with an attendant, I recommended that Captain Harries's party should be moved to Trompeter's Drift, with orders to construct a raft out of the broken wagons, and thus to send across supplies to the cavalry in advance; and, above all, that immediately the party got to the Drift, they should surround themselves with a strong abattis, and keep a vigilant look out, as the situation was certainly much exposed. Harries's party was accordingly moved to Trompeter's Drift; pitched their tents; and drew up their wagons on the level plain on the right bank. But from want of military experience, they did not surround themselves with an abattis. A square of bushes with the four wagons at the corners, or a citadel of wagons in the centre, would have been a capital defensible post.

On the morning of the 7th of March, an alarm was given to this unprepared party, that a body of Kaffirs had fallen on the wagon oxen grazing on the opposite bank of the river, which was now low; and that the enemy were driving them off, after killing the Hottentots with them. Some of the burghers, who had been out buck-shooting in the neighbourhood, immediately hurried towards the wagons; and the captain ordered twenty men to catch their horses, "saddle up," and pursue. They did so: but failed to recover the cattle. A large body of Kaffirs, who had been watching the post from the opposite green and shrubby hills, seeing that the attack on the cattle had been successful, and noting a hurrying to and fro in the camp below, now looked over the bushes and determined on an assault. Accordingly, in several black lines, in Indian file, they moved stealthily and swiftly down the heights, and crossed the river at several points, in numbers perhaps a thousand.

The burghers now galloped from one side to the other, fired some shots, and did some execution.

But seeing the enemy closing in upon them, instead of rallying at the wagons, and endeavouring to save the lives of the unfortunate wagon drivers and leaders, who had no horses, the main body of the burghers retreated rapidly by the road to Frazer's Camp; and left the tents, wagons, and baggage in the enemy's hands. Two Englishmen and a Dutchman, Bance, Bilson, and Van der Kemp, nobly stood their ground, and refused to follow their comrades. Bance endeavoured to cover the retreat of two men, Titterton and Clark. The saddle of the former had turned with him; and he was running about with an assegai through his back, trying in vain to catch his horse. Clark had also got a heavy fall, and was so completely paralysed by fear, that Bance, after firing several rounds and keeping the Kaffirs off, could not induce the unfortunate man to mount behind him.

Bilson,—formerly of the Blues, and wounded at Waterloo,—a man of great size and strength, treating the Kaffirs with contempt, was determined to make a stand at a bush; but was quickly surrounded and assegaied; as was also a fine young man named Shaw, a wagon-owner and driver, the main support of his aged parents, who had lost another son a few weeks before at nearly the same place. Van der Kemp saved the life of another wagon-driver Randall, who was pursued by three Kaffirs. The Dutchman coolly fired and brought down the first; the other two retired; and Randall was carried off on Van der Kemp's horse.

A Hottentot servant had a narrow escape. Being hotly pursued through the bushes, he jumped into a porcupine hole, and lay there for several hours; having destroyed his own spoor, or track, by a bush which he pulled over him: the dust from the feet of his pursuers fell on his face; and he overheard them talking and "at fault" close above him. Of Captain Harries's party eight were killed, and some men and horses wounded. The enemy lost nine killed, but perfectly succeeded in their spirited attack. A detachment which went to the scene of this disaster shortly after, found the huts and wagons burning; and the enemy, having completed the work of destruction, had retired.

It was now evident that the Kaffirs in force had eluded the patrols of Colonel Somerset, and had passed between them into the bush of the Fish River, having come across the Keiskamma, and passed towards Commatty's and Trompeter's Drifts. Captain Jervis and Lieutenant Simonds, 72d regiment, from Fort Willshire, with Field-commandant Rademayer, a burgher force, and a three-pounder gun, following the Kaffir spoor, came upon a body of the enemy in a ravine near Commatty's Drift; slew some, and dispersed the rest: capturing one hundred head of cattle. This happened on the same day that Captain Harries was defeated. To secure the colony against another irruption of the enemy, and whilst the preparations for the organization of the invading force were drawing to a close, a battalion of Hottentot infantry, with a six-pounder, was ordered to reinforce Colonel Somerset on the Clusie; and another battalion, with some burgher horse, to occupy the Waay Plats and Kap River, and prevent the enemy from making an attempt to carry off the recaptured cattle grazing near Salem.

On the 9th of March, Field-commandant Rademayer performed an exploit of intrepid determination, which completely effaced the tarnish occasioned by the discomfiture of our people on the 7th. The commandant, with one hundred and seventy-five of his mounted burghers of George and Uitenhage, was returning to his camp on the Clusie from scouring the line between it and Trompeter's Drift; when in Trompeter's Poort, or pass, on the eastern bank of the river, he observed the spoor of horses and cattle, followed by that of Kaffirs into the bush. Seeing a fire in a kloof below, he dismounted forty of his men, and descended with them by a narrow path to examine the fire. They reached a spot where rocks and trees overhung the path on both sides, and further advance seemed impracticable; when a savage yell, and a volley of musquetry poured on them, were the first intimation which they had, that they were surrounded by a large body of the enemy, from ten to fifteen hundred in number, who had thus led them into an ambuscade.

The commandant, conspicuous with his athletic figure and black bushy whiskers, called to his men to stand firm and fight back to back. The Kaffirs showed themselves every where; and one immense fellow in particular, the rain-maker of Umhala of the T'Slambies, called to the swarthy warriors from a pinnacle of rock, "that the white dogs were now in their power, and to finish their work quickly." On the burghers thus hemmed in, the Kaffirs made a desperate rush, led by a chief with a musquet in one hand, and an assegai in the other; but they were met by a volley which staggered them. They, however, renewed their attacks repeatedly, and in a most determined manner, firing well-directed shots, and stabbing with broken assegais. It was a close hand to hand combat; and the want of "the cold steel" was much felt by the burghers. They, nevertheless, maintained their ground most manfully; and each burgher who fell was immediately covered with a heap of the enemy. Rademayer, striding over the body of a wounded comrade, brought many Kaffirs to the ground with his elephant gun. The enemy made several attempts, in the heat of the combat, to drag off their wounded, but thus exposed themselves to the more deadly fire of their antagonists. " Fire away, carles!" cried Rademayer: " there's help at hand."

The party above, hearing the firing and shouting of the contest below, detached twenty of their number to assist, led by Field-cornet Muller. They joined Rademayer, and created a powerful diversion in his favour after the fight had lasted a considerable time; and the Kaffirs at last retired, leaving upwards of seventy dead, besides many wounded, who crawled off from this field of slaughter.

Six burghers were slain and eight wounded severely; many more, among whom was the gallant commandant, had gun-shots and assegais through their clothes; and all were begrimed with blood and powder. Prepared for another attack, and carrying off their wounded, with the guns of their own and the Kaffir dead, they rejoined their comrades above, and then returned to their camp. In general orders, the intrepidity, able conduct, and personal prowess of the field-commandant, and the corresponding gallantry of his people in the affair of Trompeter's Poort, were stated to be beyond praise.

About this time the Hottentot Ensign Piet Low, who had been with a party escorting commissariat and ordnance wagons, reported to me that he had seen the spoor of three hundred Kaffirs crossing the road between Graham's Town and Hermanus' kraal. Accordingly, I was allowed to go with Captain Ross and forty of the Cape mounted rifles in pursuit. We reached the spot, and it was interesting to see the sagacity of the Hottentots in looking for the spoor. The grass was examined to see if it had been pressed down by the foot, and if twigs had been broken off the bushes; and stones were carefully lifted to note if they had been moved. All, however, that we could make out was, the impression of the great toe of a man who had passed two days before. We made a wide sweep by Jointje's kraal and Fish River bush; were out two days; did not get a shot at a Kaffir; and were half roasted by the sun:—as indeed was Piet Low by the other Hottentots, for being the cause of such a fruitless expedition.

Amidst the horrors of conflagration and bloodshed which we had lately witnessed, I may be permitted to record the pleasing contrast which we enjoyed about this time in a scene of cultivation and peace. The general and staff rode out on a beautiful evening eight miles to visit the vineyard of one of the most enterprising and intelligent farmers on the frontier, Mr. T. C. White, late 25th regiment, and we found an oasis in a dull part of the country. A comfortable house and much cultivation by the banks of a stream, which had three strong dams across it, proved what a little labour and pains will do in the way of irrigation. Garden-grounds and fields were watered at will, and the produce was most extraordinary. The *haanen-poot*, muscadel, constantia, and other vines, were trained on espaliers; and the delicious clusters of large size and delicate bloom hung most invitingly, and in the greatest abundance, ready to hand. Nor were ripe peaches and pears wanting. I am ashamed to think of the desperate attack which we made on this garden of delights, led on across a wooden suspension-bridge by the excellent proprietor himself, now, alas! no more. Sleeves were pulled up, and feats of *gourmandise* ensued among the young officers of the party, which I have rarely seen equalled. They revelled in sweets; and each variety of fruit seemed more luscious than that which had been tried before.

It was evening, and we saw five large clouds of dust on the neighbouring hills. We thought of a surprise by the enemy, but it was only "innocent sheep." Mr. White had no cattle to tempt the kine-loving Kaffirs; and had kept his fine-wooled merinos on his farm with trifling loss. Five flocks of a thousand each now came from different points bleating towards the shelter of the kraals, and driven by armed Bechuana shepherds, who were paid ten dollars a-month. Mr. White found this a better system than the usual one of giving them a few head of cattle annually, and allowing them to accumulate a herd inconveniently for the farmer. We rode home rapidly in the dark, and it was said we escaped falling into the hands of the Kaffirs, a party of whom visited the farm shortly after we left it.

I wish I could introduce a tale of love to awaken the sensibilities of my fair readers, already, I fear, tired of war's alarms. Ladies there were in plenty in Graham's Town at this time: unfortunates driven from their comfortable homes, now laid waste and desolate, subsisting on commissariat beef and brown bread; and lucky in getting even such food, in confined and unfurnished quarters. The marriage of many a fond pair had been interrupted by this too cruel war. We had no leisure now to breathe our vows at ladies' feet; and lovers, instead of leading the fair to the hymeneal altar, were leading, or being led, on patrol in the field;

instead of sharing in marriage feasts, were snatching pieces of karbonatje off a forked stick, and washing it down with the muddy water of *vleys*, or pools; and instead of a downy pillow, were resting their heads on a stone or a wooden canteen, nestled in a couple of sheep-skins under a bush, and embracing a carbine instead of a bride.

Let me, however, here record the excellent conduct of the two chief ladies of the Cis-kyean Kaffirs. Suta, the great widow of Gaika,—when a hundred and fifty Kaffirs rushed at a trader at Burnshill to murder and plunder him, and when their assegais were uplifted to pierce him,—interposed her body between the deadly weapons and the Englishman; and declared that they must pass through her first before they reached him. She then led him off safely. Nonubé, the regent of the T'Slambies, also acted in a similar manner, and showed herself equally adverse with Suta to the attack on the colony. They told their people that the English had done them no harm: both of them by their influence saved missionaries and traders, and much property; and showed that all Kaffirs are not equally bad. Many men, in fact, were compelled to fight against us by their bloody-minded and marauding countrymen; and as the excellent missionary Boyce remarked, " It was a cause of deep and heartfelt sorrow that these first should suffer the evils of war, in common with those who had provoked it, and brought the scourge on their own heads."

Colonel Smith had been sent to the neighbourhood of Fort Willshire to prepare a central camp of assembly for the troops about to advance; and after the affair at Trompeter's Poort, pursued a retreating body of the enemy some distance into Kaffir-land. He shot some of them, though the main body escaped, owing to the fatigue of his horses; he burnt huts and cattle-kraals; and then returned to Graham's Town with twelve hundred head of cattle.

Don't sneer at cattle, gentle reader; they are the chief wealth, yea, and strength of the natives of South Africa; and they feel the loss of their herds more than that of home and family.

CHAPTER XIX.

An Invading Force organized — Comparative State of Troops in 1819-20 and 1834-35 — Why the War should be carried into the Enemy's Country — Hottentot Cavalry and Infantry—Character of Hottentot Levies—The Dutch Burghers—Bush Ranging—The Corps of Guides—The Regulars — Official Return of the Invading Force — The first and second Lines of Defence — Hintza's Duplicity — Behaviour to Piet Uys—Thinks the Colonists can be easily blinded to his Acts — Field-commandant Van Wyk's Mission and Message to Hintza—Distribution of Troops—Camps of Assembly —Intended Movements—Favourable State of the Weather— Mr. H. Fynn's Mission to Faku—His Answer to a Kaffir— Skirmishes—Kaffir Bravery—Magnanimous Conduct of Major Gregory—"Saddle up" to cross the Border—Author's Misfortunes—Leave Graham's Town for Kaffir Drift—Cavalry Camp on the Clusie—Chiefs Pato and Kama—A Rouse—Fort Willshire—Again under Canvass in the Field.

In the middle of March, after great exertions had been made, a "force was organized and arranged at once for entering Kaffir-land, and for leaving behind an adequate defence for the frontier." To show what limited means were placed for protection and retaliation in Sir Benjamin D'Urban's hands, on the occurrence of the Kaffir invasion, it will here only be necessary to give a comparative state of the force at the Cape on the breaking out of the last Kaffir war, and on this more appalling crisis:—

	In 1819-20.	In 1834-35.
Companies of Royal Artillery	2	1
Regiment of Light Dragoons	1	—
Cape Corps of Cavalry	1	1
Battalions of Infantry	5	3
Royal African Corps	1	—
Cape Corps of Infantry	1	—

the infantry being eight hundred strong each battalion, at the former period, and only five hundred at the latter. Cape Town could not be left with less than one battalion: so that there were only one thousand bayonets and two hundred mounted rifles left disposable for the frontier.

It was imperatively necessary to finish the war by an invasion of Kaffir-land to a certain extent: because Hintza, the main though distant spring of the border Kaffirs' aggression, and the receiver of their plunder, would have otherwise escaped with impunity; and because the border tribes, and in fact the whole of the natives of South Africa, would have concluded that the British possessions could at all times be assailed with comparative impunity. They might otherwise, also, well entertain the hope of ultimately expelling the white men from South Africa entirely:

after which the tribes, falling on one another, would repeat the desolating horrors committed by the monster Chaka.

The general decided that three thousand troops of all descriptions, burghers and others, would be necessary for carrying the war into Kaffir-land; whilst to secure Graham's Town, the frontier posts, and the line of the eastern border, two thousand men were indispensable. The colonial forces were accordingly increased by such means as were at his excellency's disposal. These consisted of Hottentots, of whom there were embodied two provisional battalions of four hundred bayonets each; and three provisional companies of seventy-five men each were also added to the mounted rifle corps. The officers of these new levies were gentlemen on half-pay and respectable settlers. The Hottentot infantry were dressed in claret-coloured jackets and trousers, of whatever material, in fact, was nearest at hand; with broad-brimmed black hats, and cartouch boxes strapped round their waists; and they were armed with bright-barrelled musquets, and as many bayonets as could be found. The mounted rifles wore in the field a green forage-cap and jacket, and leather trousers; a pouch, haversack, and canteen hung from their shoulders; the double-barrelled carbine was covered with a sheep-skin case, or holster; and a large blue cloak afforded excellent shelter in bivouacking.

Hottentots have a natural aptitude for war. They are a reckless people, light hearted, light made, and hardy. With their high cheek bones, narrow eyelids, projecting chin and lips, and smoke-dried complexion, they are far from being a handsome race. But, to use a homely phrase, they have a "rough and ready" look about them; march and fire very well; have an uncommonly keen sight; rival North American Indians in tracking an enemy by his marks, though several days old, on the ground and on the bushes; are indifferent to the shelter of tents; can eat six pounds of meat and two of bread at a sitting, and then, with the assistance of a girdle, go three days without food; and, in short, are excellent materials for light troops, and are rapidly trained to war, whether on foot or on horseback.

The Dutch burghers are generally very tall and lusty men, subsisted from their youth upwards on mutton, and living in one of the healthiest climates in the world, which is totally free from marsh miasma and contagious disorders. When called out for the defence of the colony, they go into the field usually with a couple of horses, one of which they ride, and the other they lead. On this last is strapped a *vel kombaars*, or sheep-skin blanket, to sleep in, some trifling change of raiment, and some *biltrng*, or dried meat. Many burghers have a little Hottentot boy, called an *achter rijder*, perched like a monkey, with a handkerchief round its head, on a third horse. This attendant carries on the march the long *roer* of his *baas*, or master, and hands it to him when he desires to bring down a buck or Kaffir. From early and long practice, the Dutch burghers are excellent marksmen; and though they prefer fighting the Kaffirs out of the bush to exposing themselves, under every disadvantage, in it, having no arms for close combat, yet we have seen that they *can* fight, and desperately too, in the bush. With the addition of the chief of weapons, the sword, in their hands, and the knowledge how, and inclination to use it, they would be most formidable antagonists any where.

It is certainly no child's-play tracking through the dense bush by a narrow path in Indian file, having a volley of musquetry suddenly poured on the party from above, and stalwart and naked warriors rushing with yells and stabbing assegais from the elephant grass around; and though one is constantly liable to this in Kaffir warfare, yet, strange to say, neither the sword nor short lance had been thought necessary for troops liable to be exposed to these emergencies, and very few of the *arme blanche* were found in the Cape armoury. Though all the musquets issued to the

Hottentots had bayonets, yet they absurdly threw them aside as useless incumbrances.

There was a sprinkling of English settlers among the burghers who crossed the frontier; and one body of burghers, the corps of guides, was composed entirely of British farmers of Albany, whose homes had been destroyed. All of them were deadly shots, active and useful in the field. The guides wore bands of leopard-skin round their white hats.

> "And now, good yeomen!
> Whose limbs were made in England, show us here
> The mettle of your pasture: let us see
> That you are worth your breeding."

The royal artillery and regular infantry were, as usual, highly pleased with the prospect of more fighting, and of retaliating on the ferocious invaders of the colony in their own country: the regulars were prepared for the field by broad peaks being added to their forage-caps before and behind, and leather trousers for the nether man. White cross belts and black cartouch-boxes were laid aside; and light hairy pouches were attached to the brown waist-belt, from which also hung the bayonet in a frog. A knapsack with very few necessaries, a blanket, haversack, and canteen, completed their equipment. It is a pity that the red jacket is so easily seen at a distance: still it has its *effect*, after a short experience of the gallant breast which it covers.

OFFICIAL RETURN.

Return of the Forces upon the Eastern Frontier, assembled for the purpose of advancing into Kaffir-land.

Head Quarters, Graham's Town,
25th March, 1835.

Regulars.	Guns.	Mounted	Infantry	Total.
Royal Artillery . . .	3 3-lbrs. 2 6 ,, 1 5½-howitzer.	,,	25	25
72nd Highlanders . .	,,	,,	371	371
Cape Mounted Rifles .	,,	358	,,	358
1st Provisional Battalion of Hottentot Infantry .	,,	,,	411	411
2nd do do .	,,	,,	350	350
Total . .	6	358	1157	1515
Burghers.				
George	,,	310	,,	310
Graaf Reynet	,,	242	,,	242
Somerset	,,	532	,,	532
Swellendam	,,	453	,,	453
Beaufort	,,	62	,,	62
Corps of Guides . . .	,,	40	,,	40
Total . .	,,	1639	,,	1639
General Total . .	6	1997	1157	3154

(Signed,) H. G. SMITH, Colonel,
Acting Deputy-Adjutant-General.

This force was distributed into four divisions. Colonel Smith, C. B., the second in command, continued at the same time in the performance of his duties as chief of the staff to the united regular and burgher forces. The first division, with which were the head-quarters of the commander-in-chief, was commanded by Lieutenant-Colonel Peddie, K. H., 72nd Highlanders: (2 six-pounders, 434 cavalry, 837 infantry, total 1271).

The second by Lieutenant-Colonel Somerset, K. H., commandant of the frontiers of Kaffraria: (1 three-pounder, 1 howitzer, 715 cavalry).

The third by Major Cox, K. H., 75th regiment: (2 three-pounders, 309 cavalry, 438 infantry, total 747).

The fourth by Field-commandant Van Wyk: (500 cavalry).

Return of the Troops on the first Line of Defence.

Head Quarters, Graham's Town,
19th March, 1835.

Regulars.	Guns.	Mounted	Infantry	Total.
Royal Artillery	3 6-lbrs 1 24-howitzer.	,,	3	3
Sappers and Miners	,,	,,	21	21
75th Regiment	,,	48	413	461
Cape Mounted Rifles	,,	20	11	31
Total	4	68	448	516
Burghers.				
Graham's Town Volunteers	,,	30	355	385
Albany Burghers	,,	120	,,	120
Beaufort ditto	,,	80	21	101
Fort Beaufort Levy	,,	57	102	159
Kat River Legion	,,	115	387	502
George Town Volunteers	,,	44	,,	44
Uitenhage Burghers	,,	138	,,	138
Port Elizabeth Yeomanry	,,	36	,,	36
Total	,,	620	865	1485
General Total	4	688	1313	2001

(Signed,)   H. G. Smith, Colonel,
Acting Deputy-Adjutant-General.

LINES OF DEFENCE.

To Colonel England, 75th regiment, was entrusted the important charge of the first line of defence: his head-quarters were fixed at Graham's Town. This line extended in its front from the Winterberg, including the Kat River and settlement thereon, Camp Adelaide, and the Chumie and Keiskamma rivers, with the forts Beaufort and Willshire, to the sea. The want of a regiment of light dragoons was now very sensibly felt, among other purposes, to keep up the communications: it was therefore necessary to mount a number of the 75th regiment, and arm them with carbines. They made very smart troopers, *tooraloos* as they called themselves, corrupted from *tirailleurs*, and did good service. The Graham's Town volunteers were brought into excellent order under Lieutenant-Colonel Sparks, captain 38th regiment, on leave from his corps in India.

To Colonel Cuyler, late landrost of Uitenhage, the charge of a second line of defence was entrusted. He had under his command the local force and posts of defence of Uitenhage, including those of Zuurberg, excepting Port Elizabeth: which, being the *place d' armes* and sea-port of the eastern province, both the place and district were under a separate commandant, first Colonel Thompson, royal engineers, and afterwards Major Tripp, 98th regiment.

The above officers were directed to communicate with each other, and with the civil commissioners of Albany and Somerset, Graaf Reynet, and Uitenhage; and mutually to assist and co-operate with each other: observing a few heads of general instructions, but otherwise acting according to their own judgment and discretion, as particular occasions might require.

Hintza, the king or paramount chief of the Amakosa, had all this time been playing a double game. He had received the plundered cattle into his territory; for it was well ascertained that fifty thousand head, besides one thousand horses, had passed the mission station of Butterworth; he had sent many of his people to join the forces of the border chiefs; and his counsellors (*amapakati*) were undoubtedly hostile, *but he himself professed not to be so:* thus waiting the turn of events, and thinking that his designs and acts could not be penetrated and ascertained.

A Dutch böer, Piet Uys, of the Kromme River, a fine specimen of the manly character, was returning to the colony from Natal; and, ignorant of the war, arrived at the kraal of Hintza, now established on the T'Somo. Hintza received him in a friendly way, and informed him of the rupture between the colonists and the Kaffirs; declared that he was averse to it, and that he had accepted no share in the plunder; and having, as he imagined, made the desired impression, he suffered the farmer to depart.

Now all this was after he had instigated his countrymen to the murder of the trader Purcell; to the plunder and cruel treatment of the other traders; to the destruction of the mission station at Butterworth; to the inroads and murders committed within the colony; after he had approved and sanctioned the project of the border chiefs to invade the colony; and even after he had received a large share of colonial plunder. Truly, he must have imagined that the colonists could be easily cajoled into a belief of his friendly disposition; and he must have supposed them so blind, that aggressions might be made on them at any time without their discovering that he was the prime mover and adviser on the occasion.

Field-commandant Van Wyk was sent on a mission to Hintza shortly after the commencement of hostilities in February, and again in March, to ascertain if he was our friend or foe. When Van Wyk announced his approach, the amapakati advised a message to be sent to him, that Hintza would receive him if he came with not more than twenty men: but Van Wyk at the same time had private and certain information, that a plot was laid to get rid of such a determined leader of borderers as he was known to be; and that if he came with a few men they could easily be distributed in different huts at night, and the whole be destroyed. Accordingly, the field-commandant suddenly appeared with two hundred men at Hintza's kraal, when the chief, though actually present, was said to be out hunting; and both on this occasion and that of his second mission, Van Wyk returned without seeing him. Tyalie at this time sent to Hintza to say, that he had killed so many of the colonists that the air was polluted with their dead.

His excellency now directed Van Wyk to send a message, as before, to Hintza, to ask whether he was at peace or war with the colony; and, if the former, to prove it by separating himself openly and at a distance from its avowed enemies: who, since their recent reverses, were occupying the fastnesses at the sources of the Buffalo, Chumie, Keiskamma, and Kabousie, and thus in immediate contact with Hintza, and falling back on him for support. He was also exhorted to show his recollection of his having been saved from the destructive inroads of the Fitcani by the colonial forces in 1828, by sending back the plunder which had been driven into his territory; to prove by his actions, not by his protestations, that he was our friend and ally; or else be confounded with our enemies, and treated like them.

Nothing resulted from this message; and the general made his arrangements accordingly. The defensive line and posts being provided for, his excellency determined to advance into Kaffir-land by the following general distribution of his troops for this operation. They were divided into a central force and two strong flanking corps: the Keiskamma and Chumie rivers formed the base of departure; the main depôts of provisions and the hospitals on this base being at forts Willshire and Beaufort. The object was to advance eastwards beyond the Great Kye, and perhaps to the Bashee; and thus to include in the operations the country of Hintza: bringing up either shoulder a little, as occasion might require.

It being requisite for preparation to take up camps of assembly, the central one (head-quarters) was accordingly established on the right bank of the Keiskamma, near Fort Willshire; where many roads of communication meet. The camp of the right flanking corps, under Colonel Somerset, was formed near Mount Somerset, opposite the Line Drift, or ford; that of the extreme left, under Van Wyk, about the Klip-plaatz River; and the left centre, commanded by Major Cox, at Fort Beaufort, opposite Block Drift, on the Chumie River.

It was intended, in the first instance, that the centre corps should move straight forward towards the Buffalo and Kye; that the right flanking division, composed entirely of mounted riflemen and burghers, should advance rapidly by the lower Buffalo, and sweep round towards the left by the Gonubee; and that the extreme right, consisting also wholly of burgher cavalry, should move towards the Kabousie and Kye: the left centre meanwhile occupying a central position between the Keiskamma and Kye, to keep the country clear behind the troops in advance. Such were the general outlines of the arrangement for the advance into Kaffir-land. The great heats of summer were now over; and the weather was very propitious for the march of the invading force. The rains had kept the streams flowing for some time past; and had covered the face of the country with abundant pasturage, to maintain the horses and cattle required for service in the field.

At this time Mr. H. Fynn, long a resident at Natal, and lately employed as interpreter with the troops, was sent on a mission, in the cutter *Circé* by way of Natal, to Faku the chief of the Amapondas, to prevent his joining the Amakosa Kaffirs against the colony, and to bring him down on our enemy's rear if required. Mr. Fynn had lately occasion to communicate with a Kaffir of the hostile tribes, who said to him, " The commando is all over now."—" Oh no," replied Mr. Fynn; " we are only now going to begin."—" That's very strange," says the Kosa: "when a dog steals a bone, you give him a kick and let him go." " Yes, that's true : but if the dog goes mad, we shoot him."

There had been various skirmishes with the Kaffirs lately, who, in small parties, were hovering about the borders for plunder, and to give information to the main body of the Gaikas in the mountains, and to the T"Slambies occupying the lower Gonubee and Kye. Hermanus, formerly a counsellor of Gaika's, but now having committed himself with his people and being a friend of the English, did good service with a few men in leading the Kaffirs into snares and destroying them. But some more colonial farmers at this time were surprised and slain.

A considerable body of the enemy received a severe lesson from some Tarka böers below the Winterberg. They had come on a marauding expedition; and were tracked out and followed by a party under two brothers, Greyling by name, field-cornets: who hemmed them in at a kloof, from which there was only one outlet. Ninety Kaffirs were here shot by the long guns of the farmers; and their bones are now lying in a great white heap in the bottom of a ravine.

Individual instances of great bravery were sometimes displayed by the Kaffirs. Among these, may be recorded the hardihood of a single Kaffir, who jumped in through the window of a frontier house, in which there were two or three Dutch farmers with their families, waiting for an opportunity to fall back into the colony. The Kaffir hurled an assegai at a farmer, but missed him; but before he had time to draw another, one of the Dutchmen snatched up a rifle and levelled it: when the Kaffir covered his head with his kaross, and received the contents of the piece through his brain.

I mentioned before, that a single Kaffir, if surrounded, would stand up and throw his assegais to the last. This determined spirit of " no surrender" is to be admired; as much as the spectacle of a dozen stout fellows galloping after and " shooting down" a single foe is calculated to excite only disgust and contempt. But I here give a trait of an opposite description. Major Gregory of the 98th regiment, whose activity and zeal at the commencement of the war are deserving of every praise, noticed one day in the field a Kaffir dashing across an open spot. He galloped after him, quickly covered him with his gun, and being one of the best shots in the colony, would certainly have destroyed him: but upon seeing that the Kaffir was a solitary straggler, the gallant major threw up the muzzle of his piece and said, with the characteristic humanity of the man, and with the spirit of the true soldier, "I can't shoot that poor devil."

It is now high time to mount and cross the border. We had all been, for some weeks, feeding and nursing our horses into condition, and getting every thing ready for the field: when lo! on the second night before we started, I found that two strong horses, out of three, had disappeared from my small stud. Maané of Bethelsdorp, the very worst servant I ever had—lazy and sulky, but with a capital voice for singing hymns,—had allowed them to stray away from the kloof where they were feeding. I mounted before daylight next morning; rode all about the hills and ravines in the neighbourhood of Graham's Town; and then, with a Bechuana well versed in spoor, ran about on foot all the afternoon behind the gardens and among the broken ground: —but the search was fruitless. I could not have accompanied the general into the field at the time, if a kind friend had not interposed: this was Dr.

Ambrose Campbell, who lent me a horse; and I fortunately found another for sale.

At twelve, noon, on the 26th of March, the general and staff, with an escort of rifles, rode out of town: putting, as the Persians say, "the lucky foot first," for it rained heavily. The officers attached to his excellency on this occasion consisted of Major Dutton, military secretary; Captain Beresford, Mr. Charles Somerset, and myself, aides-de-camp; Lieut. Wade, 72nd regiment, commanding the escort; Major Michell, surveyor-general, in charge of the topographical department; and Dr. John Murray, deputy-inspector-general of hospitals, who had "smelt powder" with his excellency a quarter of a century before. There was very little of "the pomp and panoply of glorious war" about the party. The general wore an oil-skin chako, plain blue surtout, and trousers strapped with leather: the rest, forage-caps of various kinds, and long-backed blue or green jackets and trousers of cloth, or leather crackers. Telescopes, hairy ammunition-pouches, and guns carried on the thigh, or in leopard and buck-skin covers, gave our appearance a dash of the picturesque.

Guided by Colonel Somerset, and having forty miles to go to inspect the line of the Kap by Governor's Kop and the Clay-pits to Caywood's, near Kaffir Drift, we set off at a gallop; splashed along the wet roads; and were soon soaked above and muddy below. We reached Mahony's place in its dismal dell; and the ruins of his house still standing roofless and black with fire. I turned aside, but for a minute, to look for the body of Mr. Brown, said to be still unburied: it was under a heap of stones. I next looked for the general: his excellency and staff were rapidly disappearing across the face of a hill. I looked back for the rifles: their horses were showing the effects of much patrolling, and knocking up far in the rear. I essayed to follow his excellency: but it was at a slow pace; for corn and my new horses had not been intimately acquainted of late. I was thus left alone with my amiable black, to struggle on in the best way I could.

It rained in pelting showers; the dark and dangerous Fish River bush was below on the left; and we rode along green hills. It fell dark; and we dismounted and looked in vain for spoor. I knew somewhat about the general direction which we had to go: but neither of us had been on the road before. We listened: no noise of the approach of the escort was heard; only the damp night wind sighed over the waste; and we continued to ride on in uncertainty along a ridge which we thought would have no end. A strange dog which had accompanied us, pushed forward whining into the obscurity; barked angrily; and ran back to us howling. We looked to our arms; again the dog went on and barked, when a rustle as of a bundle of assegais was heard: but it was only a porcupine angrily shaking its quills at the dog.

We were at fault in the bed of the Kap River for some time; confused among the rocks, stones, and brushwood. But at last, after a diligent search, we found a broken and muddy path, and followed it. Neither ourselves nor our horses had had any thing to eat since morning; it was now ten o'clock at night; and we had not once unsaddled. In compassion to the poor animals it was becoming necessary that we should at last give in: when, from a little eminence, I discovered a star of the first magnitude in the horizon. I watched it, and found that it remained stationary: it was therefore either a Kaffir fire, or the light of our bivouack. We urged on the unwilling steeds; and in half an hour found ourselves under the bushes with his excellency's party: the escort came in an hour afterwards. It was an odd beginning this:—but it was all right; "rain being a sign of luck."

Next morning we crept out of our sheep-skins,

—the old campaigners having covered theirs with a tarpaulin,—shook ourselves, and attacked some coffee and karbonatje; and mounted and rode off leisurely. We approached the Kaffir Drift post, and found all the buildings roofless and scathed with fire; and boxes and iron bedsteads broken and scattered about. This was rather humbling to our pride. Looking westwards, we saw the great round hill, Mount Donkin; and several hundred feet below us, towards the east, was the Great Fish River winding through its deep bed, past bright green spek-boom and naked euphorbia. Lilaceous plants, with umbels covered with pale pink flowers, waved beside us.

We descended to the river by a very steep road of broken schistus; saw the spoor of buffaloes, and the great prints of hippopotami in the clay at the bottom; and crossed Kaffir Drift up to the girths. This ford has a bad reputation, and is believed to be the haunt of a water sprite. The Kaffirs, to propitiate it, enclose occasionally meat in a hide, and sink it with stones to the bottom, that the kelpie may feed on it, and not on them.

> " Under yon rock the eddies sleep,
> Calm and silent, dark and deep,
> The kelpie there rests in his fathomless pool,
> Till he lights his candle of death and dool.
> Look! now, look! and thou'lt shudder to see
> How he gapes, and glares with his eyes on thee."

After the long and steep ascent—strewed with bones of bullocks and horses—had been accomplished, we rode over undulating and grassy plains with scattered bush; saw great herds belonging to the friendly Kaffirs, the Congoes; and ever and anon pursued small troops of that noble buck, the *haartebeest*: the size of an ordinary horse, dark brown, with thick and black horns curved backwards. Two or three were shot and brought along on led horses. Quaggas and ostriches are not unusual on these plains. After a ride of thirty-five miles, we reached Colonel Somerset's cavalry camp on the Clusie. A square of wagons, with two light field-pieces at opposite angles, enclosed the tents: the horses and oxen grazed near.

The chiefs Pato and Kama came here with a few followers, to wait on the general. The former is a stout made, yellow, and roguish-looking man, of middle age, and dressed like a böer, with a broad-brimmed hat, jacket and trousers. The latter is a fine-looking young Kaffir (Gonaquabie). On ordinary occasions he wears a hat and white shooting-jacket; and when among European officers, a lancer uniform, blue with red facings, and silver lace. Pato has several wives; Kama only one, and is believed to be really a convert to Christianity:—thanks to the exertions of that worthy and noble man, the Rev. Mr. Shaw, of the Wesleyan mission.

In the middle of the night I was awoke by some young officers, suddenly roused "to boot and saddle," cursing their own carelessness, and that of their servants, in mislaying parts of their dress or munitions of war. Haversacks were then filled with biscuit; holsters with pistols of brandy; and hairy cartouch-boxes were strapped round the waist, amidst many oaths and "*verdoem de Kaffirs!*" One hundred and fifty rifles and burghers rode off with a field-piece at day-break, to scour the country towards the sea.

We saddled up after breakfast; and with occasional galloping reached Petrorius's camp of Graaf Reynet boers, on the ridge between the Keiskamma and Fish River. Next descending to the beautiful banks of the former, we were refreshed with an unusual sound in Africa: bright and sparkling water leaping over rocks into long deep pools; and then rushing impetuously and gladly past, over a broken bed. We tarried a short time at Fort Willshire in its low, hot, and commanded site; and at last, a few miles farther on, at an old kraal of Macomo's, we found, in a well wooded and watered hollow, the tents and wagons of the head-quarter camp. Bowers were woven among the bushes for some of the officers; and an eminence above the camp afforded a glorious prospect of mountain scenery, from the village of Somerset to the summits of the Amatola, the head-quarters of the hostile chiefs.

It would have surprised an oriental campaigner, accustomed to tents of vast size, with double flys and walls, gilded tent-poles, silk curtains and luxurious couches, Indian mats and Persian carpets, all carried on elephants with gaudy trappings, to have seen the simple way in which Sir Benjamin D'Urban was lodged in the field. A small, green-lined, bell tent covered his excellency, with only room inside for his iron camp bed, and a small writing table. Externally this tent was only distinguished from the others by some blue and red stripes at the top of the pole, and by a single sentry moving about. Major Michell and myself spread our karosses on rushes under the same canvass, and strapped our arms, instruments, and drawing materials to the same pole: to me a source of great satisfaction.

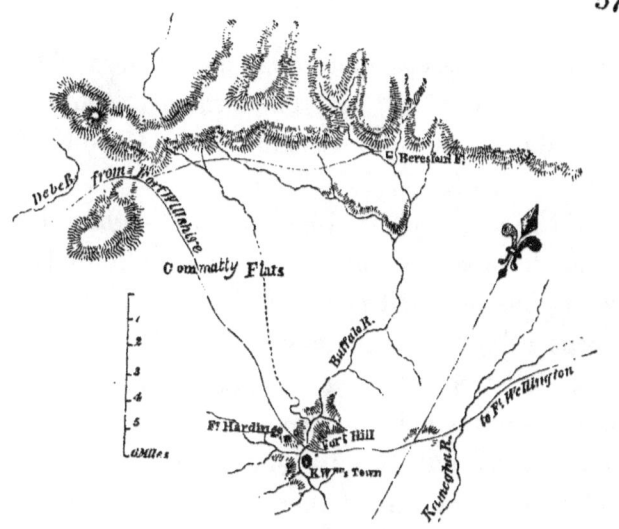

CHAPTER XX.

The British Field Force enters Kaffir-land—A Kaffir Beldame—Anecdote—Kabecca—Absurd Accident—Capaai Attacks the Tambookies—A Farmer outwitted—The Deba and T'Slambie's Kop — Reconnoissance — An Alarm—Operations of the Third of April—A Scramble—Spy shot—Commatje Flats—Geological Phenomena — A Scientific Guide — Missionaries have sometimes short Memories—A Breakfast—Encamp between the Spruits of the Buffalo—Movements of the Second, Third, and Fourth Divisions—Affairs with the Enemy on the Seventh of April—Highland Spirit, (not Glenlivet)—Capture of a Deserter—Affairs on the Ninth of April in the Mountains of the Buffalo—Sutton's Escape—The Camp by Moonlight.

At day-light on the 31st of March, the bugles roused the troops of the head-quarter division to get under arms; tents were quickly struck; the wagon oxen "inspanned;" and the lengthened column of march, under Colonel Peddie, 72nd regiment, who had lost one arm at Salamanca, moved towards the Kciskamma to cross into Kaffirland.

Field-commandant Linde's Swellendam burghers led the way : a Patagonian race, formidable with guns like wall pieces, and immense powder-horns swinging at their hips. The Cape mounted rifles followed under a redoubted old soldier of many foreign fields,—Major Lowen: their dark green caps and jackets relieved by their brick-coloured " crackers ;" their short and thick double-barrelled carbines on their thighs; every second man smoking a little pipe ; and all peering over the country with their keen and restless eyes. Next marched actively Major Bagot's Hottentot infantry in sad-coloured raiment, relieved by their white haversacks and hairy gun-covers. The mountain pibroch announced the approach of the 72nd Highlanders under Major Maclean ;—and what northern heart could be unmoved on hearing the wild notes of our native hills, and seeing four hundred Caledonians under arms, swarthed by the African sun ; but whose eyes brightened under the influence of the inspiring strains, and whose breasts glowed with the hope of returning with honour from their country's service! Two six-pounders, under

Lieut. Levinge, followed the Scots, with attendant artillerymen; grim with the dusty way, and impatient to give further proofs of their terrible arm on the savage hordes. The mounted corps of guides under Captain Southey next showed their spirit of defiance, by their hat-bands of leopard-skins; and a train of seventy provision and ammunition wagons brought up the rear, which was strongly guarded.

The general galloped down to the ford, and saw his force pass over in safety; though the water was high, and the bottom rocky. We were now in Kaffir-land, but not a Kaffir was to be seen: they were all in the fastnesses of the Amatola; but with scouts hanging, doubtless, on our flanks to watch the progress of the troops. The beauty of the country increased as we advanced. Clumps of trees and bushes diversified the landscape; there was abundant food for man in large fields of maize and millet, waving ripe and unreaped in the fresh morning breeze: and sweet pasturage for beast was indicated by the presence of thorny mimosas. "Why were the Kaffirs not content with this fine country of theirs?" several of us simultaneously exclaimed: "that they must needs carry the firebrand and assegai into ours; and vain of their fancied strength, and urged on by an indomitable thirst for plunder, incur the risk of a severe retribution?"

We passed some huts burnt down by Colonel Smith in his late dashing inroad; only one hut having been left standing, for an aged and decrepid woman. There was a halt and an " off saddle ;" and several of us went to see the old Kaffir. She was sitting at the wicker door of her large beehive and very neatly thatched dwelling; several folds of cloth stained with red clay were round her crisped hair; and the lower part of her body was concealed by a kaross of softened hide. She drew in her stomach as we approached; and clapping it with her skinny hand, called out " *Lambëlli, lambëlli!*"—" I am very, very hungry." Haversacks were immediately searched, and biscuit given to her. She leant forward and kissed the hands of the donors; soaked the biscuit in a little pot of water beside her; and rapidly munched it, still mumbling " Lambëlli."—" Where are Tyalie and Macomo?" was asked. She stretched out her lanky arm, and arching it, pointed to the mountains northwards, and drawled out the word " Amatolee."

We did not find out until after we had been some time in Kaffir-land, that it was customary with the Kaffirs to leave an old woman at their deserted kraals, to give information to the warriors, who stole back at night to communicate with her, and supply her with food. Of course, *our* old woman said she had been left by all her people, and was dying of hunger. Doubtless she must have laughed heartily,—not in her sleeve, because she had none,—but at our simplicity, when we left her with a great pile of biscuit and *biltong*, (dried meat,) and clapping her belly with hollow sound for more. She pretended deafness too, and would answer nothing but " Amatolee," and " Tamboochānee," (in the bush of the mountains,) reminding me of the master of the good ship *Tyne* hailing a schooner on the coast of Brazil, " Where are you from?" Answer, " Bahi."—" Where are you going to?"—" Bahi."—" Did you see the English admiral?"—" Bahi," (roaring with hands on each side of the mouth). " We took you for a slaver."—(Louder still,) " Bahi!"

We halted for the night on a slope of the river Kabecca; and when foraging for melons and pumpkins in the millet fields, a disagreeable smell directed my attention to an open spot among the high grain. There Driver, the athletic and hard-featured elephant-hunter, was seen resting on his rifle, and contemplating the dead body of a Kaffir, lying stripped before him, and with one leg pulled off by the wolves. The Kaffir had been shot in the recent skirmish with Colonel Smith's party;

and had been dragged out of the concealed spot in the bed of the river—where, soaked in blood, he had crept to die—by the ravening beasts, which in nature and habits Kaffirs so much resemble.

Very heavy dew fell at night, and an absurd accident happened to Major Michell and myself in consequence. Our bell tent became so taut with moisture, that, on a little breeze springing up, the pegs were pulled up in a moment; and the tent was carried some distance from us with a loud crack. On looking out like turtles from our karosses on the ground, we could not make out for some time what had become of our canvass. "Oh! quel plaisir d'être soldat."

We now heard of more disturbances in South Africa unconnected with the Kaffir war. Capaai, the son of a Zoola chief, who had revolted from King Chaka, had fallen, with his wild Fetcani mountaineers,—living to the north-east of the Amapondas of Faku,—on the Tambookies about the station of Clarkeburg: whither the missionaries of Butterworth, Morley, and Buntingville had fled. He had routed and dispersed the Tambookies; killed an English trader; and carried off two thousand head of cattle. Vodana, of the Tambookies, now prayed the governor for assistance; and the missionaries and traders applied for an armed force to remove them in safety to the colony. Thus the whole of South Africa, from Delagoa to the Cape, seemed to be in commotion: the Zoolas having attacked the Portuguese; the Fetcani the Tambookies; and the Amakosa the English.

The Kaffirs tried now to create a diversion by entering in small parties the colony behind us: however, the general's excellent defensive arrangements, and Colonel England's activity and vigilance, soon put a stop to their proceedings; but not before the " slim carles " had played Mr. Collett, of the Koonap, an ugly trick. He had just published rather a vaunting letter in the newspapers, stating " that if the farmers of the frontier had remained, like him, on their places, they might have saved their property:" for, in fact, the Kaffirs seeing his place rather strongly guarded, had left it at first, and " swept clean" all round and beyond it. But returning upon it when Mr. Collett was a little off his guard, they carried off his horses to prevent his pursuing, and then murdered his herdsman and *lifted* his cattle.

Our next march was in the direction of T'Slambie's Kop,—Intabakandoda, or hill of man, of the Kaffirs: we crossed the Deba River, and encamped on its right bank four miles from the base of the remarkable hill. It is a long ridge, the flanks of which are covered with forest trees; and in the centre, a craggy summit springs up, a favourite citadel of the Amakosa. Their huts were seen at the edge of the bush on the plain below; the woods were known to be full of them; and on the bare parts of the ridge we saw, through our glasses, several bodies of them sitting and watching us.

Colonel Somerset now joined us with the second division, after making a wide sweep from the Clusie, by the Beeka, to the Deba. His circular camp of wagons and tents was formed at some little distance from ours. Major Cox also, who had crossed the Chumie at Block Drift, rode in with an escort for orders.

On the 2nd of April, the general rode out to reconnoitre the enemy's strong position. He proceeded to a lower hill opposite T'Slambie's Kop, when the bush at the top was found to contain Kaffirs: but Colonel Smith with the escort drove these off, killing some of them. After a reconnoissance there, his excellency went to another double-headed hill, the Icanda, or Eggs. Here he found Major Michell and myself: the one with a red shawl over the cap and a blue shirt over the clothes, on account of the heat, with two guns on shoulder á la Robinson Crusoe, and keeping a look-out; while the other took bearings. The general was vexed at our being thus at a distance from the camp, among scattered bush, near creeping Kaffirs; and we promised to conduct ourselves more cautiously for the future.

In the evening, the troops were ordered to be in readiness to march at midnight. We had just finished a simple meal at the small round table of his excellency's mess tent, and were proceeding to prepare our saddle-bags and karosses for the morrow; when a sharp firing commenced at Colonel Somerset's camp. Bugles blew loud to call in pickets; bullets whistled about for some time; and it seemed that the enemy had made a desperate attack on the second division, entrenched behind the wagons. All was again quiet for a while: when more flashes and more " chattering of musquetry" were seen and heard; then " cease firing" was rung out from the brazen throats of the bugles; and the general sent Captain Beresford to learn what was the matter.

It appeared that Kaffirs had been seen about; a musquet or two had been fired into the camp, and some assegais had been thrown; when the böers immediately commenced and kept up a furious fusilade. One lying on his back beside a wagon, determined not to be behind hand, fired off his piece in the air; and the great *coegel* made a hole in the tilt above, about the size of a child's fist. Two of Colonel Somerset's picket were killed on this occasion.

At midnight the troops got silently under arms; the tents were struck and packed; the two squares of wagons were strongly fortified with mimosa bushes drawn in between them; and the wheels were also linked with chains. The wagons were left in charge of one hundred and fifty men. His excellency then saw in the obscurity, the main body of the first division pass towards T"Slambie's Kop with heavy tread, rattle of pouches, and roll of cannon wheels. The march was conducted in the greatest silence; and, as we passed the second division, we heard the guns and horsemen of it also moving off their ground stealthily.

Kaffir fires were noticed among the woods of T"Slambies Kop; we heard the long howl of dogs; plovers flew up singly at our feet with strange screams; and then a wild halloo of alarm, apparently two miles off, indicated that our movements had been closely watched, and that the enemy were not asleep in their mountain fastnesses.

The column of the first division reached the bottom of the ascent at three in the morning; the priming of the fire-arms was felt; and the files closed up in anticipation of a stout and determined resistance in our attempt to penetrate into the heart of the enemy's position. A broad cattle path led between woods; and we toiled up this, but gained the summit without opposition. A dog only ran out of the bush and howled at us. The men lay down at the top of the ridge,—the castellated and remarkable summit of the Intabakandoda rearing its head above us,—and tried, a very difficult matter, to keep themselves warm until sunrise. The old campaigners stood by their horses, and leant against them to get the benefit of their heat.

When light broke on the scene, we renewed our march; passing magnificent woods on either hand, over pasturage of the richest kind, and across many streams. The mountain glens through which we wound were picturesque and beautiful to a degree far beyond all power of expression. Forgetting bullets and assegais, I halted and gazed round continually in a silent transport of emotion and delight. Nor was it possible to refrain from breathing a fervent hope, that the period might arrive when, throughout the favoured land of the Amakosa with its heavenly climate and noble prospects, peace might dwell in its valleys, and in the wild breasts of the race which inhabits them: when its people might neither dread foreign nor domestic oppression; but, cultivating the soil, and tending their flocks and herds, might dwell in joy and gladness under the influence of wise laws and of our holy religion!

In a hollow we passed a burnt trader's house, in which the owner had been murdered. Then the column filed along hill-sides where wheel had never gone before, but where now the artillery bullocks did wonderful service. We opened great valleys bounded by noble mountains; scattered wood was every where seen; and clear water leapt from rock to rock. While brown and deserted huts, six and seven together, were seen sometimes perched high on a commanding plateau, at other times far beneath us,

"Low down in the broom."

There was a conference among our chiefs. The colonists' property had been pillaged and burned; it is invariably the custom in war to retaliate to a certain extent; and now it was necessary that an example should be made to show our superiority in arms, to drive the enemy to submission, and thus speedily to stop the farther effusion of blood. The firebrand was therefore applied; and hut after hut sent forth a dense smoke, sparks, and red glaring flames. The clear atmosphere and the beautiful colours of the landscape were marred by the conflagration; but it was necessary and unavoidable.

The Kaffirs now showed themselves. On the opposite hills, and beyond cannon shot, the tall dark figures moved in their flowing mantles, grasping their arms. They halted, looked towards us, and shouted to their people concealed in the woods below. We passed on, and took some black and white goats from the skirts of the bush. I entered some of the huts before they were burnt; and found in them broad shields, baskets of corn, and cooking vessels. A heavy firing of great guns and musquetry was then heard: this was Colonel Somerset with the second division, and Major Cox with the third, commencing their attacks on the positions of the enemy.

Colonel Somerset had been directed to move after midnight towards the sources of the Buffalo, and to clear the hills to the right, or eastern extremity of T'Slambie's Kop; firing, when it was light, into the kloofs. He did so; drove the enemy, out of them; and they, assembling on the crests of the hills, loudly abused the troops. Major Cox moved from Block Drift, the ford of the Chumie, clearing the lesser Amatola to a ford of the Keiskamma below Burnshill. Captain Jarvis, also of the third division, with one hundred and thirty red jackets and Hottentots, made a detour round the lesser Amatola, and descended to the Keiskamma. Captain Warden, of the Cape mounted rifles,—of whom the Kaffirs had said, that such was their esteem for him, in consequence of his excellent and impartial conduct towards them at all times on the frontier, that he might pass unharmed through them, even after the war had begun,—moved with one hundred mounted burghers and a company of Hottentot infantry to the left of T'Slambie's Kop, clearing as he went, towards one of the fords of the Keiskamma. Thus, the horns of the force were swept round and through the strong ground of the enemy.

The head-quarter division continued its advance. We reached a neck of land joining opposite heights; and looked down on a rich valley bearing traces of Kaffir cultivation, and beyond it the majestic Amatola mountains. It was now difficult to get the guns any farther; so that the artillery with the infantry were ordered back to camp: on which an old Hottentot sat down on the ground, pulled off his shoes, and swore with a round oath (*almagtig*) that he would not go back; for that he had not been allowed to enter the bush, and had not taken even a calf that day!

The cavalry moved down a slope towards the banks of the Keiskamma: where we unsaddled for a time; and, under the bushes among unburied Kaffir skulls and bones, we refreshed with a little biscuit and biltong. We then saddled up and pushed on again, following the river's course until some cattle was seen on a wooded slope. Böers and riflemen were sent to bring them out and engage the enemy: and the old Commandant Lindé, who became quite excited on seeing the "*beestjes*," leading his men up the hill, soon drove a herd out on the plain. We crossed the Keiskamma twice; and our rear was then attacked by the Kaffirs: who fired from the bush on both sides, and seemed determined to recover the cattle. Their fire, however, was briskly returned, and they sustained some loss in men and arms: the böers acting according to the American naval maxim, " Don't give up the ship."

Captain Warden descended a hill to meet us in a beautiful plain beside the river. He had been hotly engaged; and having driven the enemy, who opposed him with musquet and assegai, up the hill, he had slain some of them with trifling loss to himself. One Kaffir was struck whilst shouting at the top of a crag: he rolled over, and crashed into the trees below. Captain Warden's party then came suddenly upon a cave, in which there were carpets, tables, chairs, mirrors, and other European articles; and here Suta, the great widow of Gaika, and eighteen female attendants were also found. The queen and her maids of honour were treated with all courtesy, and were allowed to remain in their mountain grotto.

We crossed the Keiskamma, in all four times; and some of the fords were strong and difficult. We captured horses, cattle, and goats; passed Burnshill; and were lighted on our way after nightfall by the fires of kraals burning in every direction. As we approached the camp, a sharp firing commenced from a party of böers in front, who said that they had been attacked; and a fine young man, a guide of the name of Lloyd, received a mortal wound through the spine. At eight o'clock P. M., we rolled off our horses, after having been, with little intermission, since midnight, or twenty hours, in the saddle, with only a mouthful of food, and having accomplished a distance of between forty and fifty miles. We had a good deal of excitement to sustain us; the poor horses, indeed, wanted this; but they endured the fatigue of the broken ground, ascents, and descents, wonderfully.

The above movements were all made with great exactness, and served to show the Kaffirs the nature of a combined operation. From the traces of the enemy, and the intelligence received, it was now evident that the main body had retired and concentrated at the *pcorts* of the

Buffalo, where we hoped to give a good account of them. On the 4th of April, men and horses of the first and second divisions recruited their strength on the banks of the Deba; the third division taking up a new encampment at Burns-hill. Meanwhile, it was very gratifying to see the commander-in-chief, notwithstanding his toils, rise with the sun, as usual, and ride through the two camps in excellent health and spirits. It was certainly a great trial of the strength and endurance of his excellency, after being confined to a desk for months, then suddenly to mount and undergo long and hot marches for days together. But he seemed rather to benefit than suffer by the change.

Horace says, " Pallida mors æquo pulsat pede," &c.

> " Pale Death (my honoured friend) is sure
>   His prey to seize in every place;
> The tented field or rustic bower,
>   He visits with impartial pace:
> But it is meet, around the head
>   Or myrtle green or flow'rs to twine,
> And sacrifice a lamb or kid
>   In shady grove at Faunus' shrine."

We now complied in part with the latter recommendation: for an immense flock of captured goats being driven into camp, a general scramble ensued. Red jackets, burghers, and Hottentots, rushing upon their prey, tumbled in among them; and each man carried off one or more struggling captives on his shoulders: determined by means of karbonatje to keep "pallida mors" off as long as possible.

On the 5th, we prepared to move forwards. At night the dogs howled considerably; and there was a good deal of shuffling about his excellency's tents. A couple of shots were fired by the nearest sentries; and in the morning a stout young Kaffir was found dead within fifty yards of us, with a bundle of assegais and a bag of honey beside him. He was one of the spies who had been creeping about us in the night.

On the 6th of April we were again under weigh; and passing the Deba neck, we came upon a plain full of strange holes, like large basins: hence this plain is called Commatje Flats. One of the guides, old Holder, explained the cause of these scientifically: "The earth here," he said, "had been once much soaked with rain, and had got the shivers: *argal.* them holes and cracks had been made!" On our left was a glorious mountain, on which the woods and grassy slopes were arranged and alternated in the most delightful manner, reminding me of the beloved Ochills about Alva, in "the north countrie." We passed the missionary station of Pirie: now levelled to the ground; but occupying the richest soil, and amongst the finest pasture which I had seen for a long time.

Some people in England imagine that, when a missionary comes to South Africa, " he immediately sacrifices every worldly comfort for the Gospel's sake;" wanders about in the wilderness; and perhaps subsists, like St. John the Baptist, on locusts and wild honey. This is neither the case, nor should it be so: all missionaries should not be erratic and moving about with the Nomade tribes; but as many as can should live in fixed habitations, and show the advantage of civilized habits to the heathen.

God forbid that I should undervalue missionary labours, undertaken for the most beneficent of all purposes. Nevertheless, though I know well that he who attempts to scrutinize even the working of the system, runs the risk of being charged with infidelity and a spirit of persecution, yet I cannot here accord indiscriminate approbation. I said before that I did not consider the system perfect: as little care is taken at home in the selection of the instruments, for a great and a most important task; and certainly we had little cause to be satisfied with some of the missionaries, (not Wesleyans,) who were rescued at their earnest entreaty from Kaffir-land. After they had been a little time in safety, they turned round on the military and said; " We were in no danger among our flocks; we might have stayed longer in our vineyards, and in the field of our labours;" and this after they had declared that their lives were in hourly peril, and after great trouble and risk had been incurred in extricating them!

With one fat and lazy fellow, the tool of a political party, I was much provoked. To hear him talk, you would imagine that his labours were endless, and that his only fare was a crust of bread, and the pure element; but the Black Knight of Ivanhoe's address to the jolly Clerk of Copmanhurst would have applied well to our frontier preacher:—" It seems to me, reverend father, that the small morsels which you eat, together with this holy, but somewhat thin beverage, have thriven with you marvellously."—" I was convinced that there was better food in the cell, holy clerk, since you first doffed your cowl."

We looked about for a stream to prepare our morning's meal, and found one in a shady dell: out of which a party of the enemy appeared, and sat down for awhile on the height above us. We may be said to have breakfasted with a carbine in one hand, and a karbonatje stick in the other: but a few shots kept the Amakosa from disturbing us, whilst desperately attacking the meat and soaked biscuit with appetites of the finest edge for wholesome provant. We rode on; crossed that beautiful river the Buffalo, rushing clear and bright over its rocks and pebbles; and encamped between the *spruits,* or sources, of the river.

The head-quarter division was on very beautiful ground here; in a park gently sloping towards the river, and within a mile and a half of the mountains of the Buffalo, one thousand feet in height. Two *poorts,* or openings, into these, filled closely with forest, which extended along the face of the mountains, formed the sources of the river. The second division separated from us at the mission-station of Pirie; and proceeded down the Buffalo to observe the enemy in that direction, and to sweep the country between the Buffalo, Chalumma, and Keiskamma.

The third and fourth divisions now made a movement towards us. The fourth division had had some skirmishes with the enemy in approaching the sources of the Keiskamma from the Klipplaat's River: in one of which, Field-commandant Van Wyk was wounded by an assegai in the hand. Some Kaffirs had been killed by this division; and two thousand four hundred head of cattle had been captured.

At two o'clock in the morning of the 7th of

April, Colonel Smith with four hundred men (72nd, Hottentot infantry, and burghers) moved towards the eastern spruit of the Buffalo, to intercept any of the enemy who might be retiring with their cattle before the third and fourth divisions, which were advancing higher in the mountains. Not seeing these divisions,—for they had been delayed by the rugged nature of the country which they had to cross,—and observing cattle grazing in considerable numbers on the open plateau of the summit on his left, Colonel Smith immediately concluded that a body of the enemy was not far off; and detached Captain Crause, with three companies of the Hottentot provisional battalion, to penetrate the bush, ascend the mountain, and prevent the Kaffirs from retreating with their herds in a westerly direction. Sharp and continued firing commenced on the sides and summit of the range; we in camp became excited and anxious to participate in the attack; and the general mounting his horse, we joyfully followed him toward the mountain.

On the summit of the range, as at T'Slambie's Kop, there is a high detached rock, bare and naturally scarped. Here Zyolo, a son of Dushani, had taken post with six hundred chosen warriors. Captain Murray, with Ensign the Honourable C. Stewart, advanced with a company of the 72nd regiment to attack this citadel; the points of the assegais were seen bristling over the rocks; and then the defenders stood up, cheered, fired and hurled assegais and stones on the Highlanders clambering up from below. The gallant captain drew his men up after him, and had musquets handed to him, to fire wherever he could see a head above him. Five of the Scots were wounded; and the captain himself received some assegais through his cap and clothes: but in his excitement he was not conscious that he was wounded, until one of the men behind him said, " There's ane of them things stickin' in ye, sir ;" and drew an assegai out of his body below the ribs.

It was found that the *crantz*, or rock, was inaccessible at the point first attempted; and after a severe but ineffectual struggle to ascend it, a detour was made to assault it in another direction. Captain Murray, though faint with loss of blood, would not leave his men; and having hit on the proper place for the ascent, and being joined by Captain Gilfillan with a company of Hottentots, he caused the enemy to abandon precipitately their citadel: leaving several killed among the rocks, and countless assegais, which were immediately broken over the knees of the Highlanders.

The sharp "ping" of round bullets, and strange

whistle of long Kaffir lead continued over-head. One of the 72nd was carried in a bearer past the general with a bad assegai wound through his lungs; and then came a train of women and children out of the bush, begging to be sent to a place of safety. Thirty of them were sent to camp, where they received a tent and food.

Reinforcements were ordered up; and the companies of provisionals who had gone into the bush westwards, being hotly engaged, Captains Murray and Gilfillan moved towards them. Horsemen also being now posted in the open spaces on the side of the mountain, the cattle began to pour out from the forest, bellowing and running wildly down the slope, and driven before the Hottentots with the greatest spirit. The Kaffirs followed closely and threw assegais from the lowest skirts of the wood, but could not save their cherished herds. Many of the enemy were killed and wounded, with small loss to our people; and four thousand head of cattle, with many goats, were secured and sent into the camp, which became a vast Smithfield of lowing kine.

In getting the two last assegais that had been thrown, from some Hottentots who were lamenting the loss of one of their serjeants, I saw a strange figure among them: dark, tall, and strapping, and covered with a 42nd plaid. "What! another of the Black Watch here?" No; it was Louis Arnoldus, a Hottentot deserter to the enemy, who had served many years in the Cape corps. He had now been surrounded in the cleft of a rock; and his immense elephant gun, carrying four bullets to the pound, having received a shot in the stock which had disabled it, he himself had been secured. He was brought into camp, tied neck and heels, laid down beside a picket-fire, and threatened with a noose if he did not reveal all that he knew about the Kaffirs. He said that Macomo, Tyalie, Eno, &c. were all in these mountains; and promised to show some of their fastnesses if his life was spared. The compassionate Highlanders fed him like a sparrow, and stuck a pipe in his mouth.

There had been constant skirmishing all day; after night-fall a heavy firing was heard for some time at the eastern poort; and at length a party of Van Wyk's burghers galloped up, escorting Dr. Ford, 72nd regiment, who had been sent to dress the field-commandant's hand. It appeared that this party, after entering the poort, and whilst riding along a narrow and rocky path, had been attacked by the Kaffirs: who intimated their presence by driving an assegai through a horse; then running about the rocks in and beside the road; and trying to cut off the party. This had occasioned the firing which we had just heard. Some of the enemy had been left dead on the road.

On the evening of the 8th, the troops were again drawn round the enemy in the poorts of the Buffalo; and on the 9th, there commenced another concentric attack which lasted all day. Colonel Peddie was sent with a strong corps towards the eastern poort; and from him Major Maclean was detached to circle round the mountain range, and descend through the bush by the western poort of the river. Lieutenant Granett, of the 98th regiment,—one of the most valuable officers employed in this war, active, daring, and intelligent,—guided by Louis Arnoldus, led a party towards the western part of the range. The commander-in-chief and staff, with an escort of mounted rifles, a party of the 72nd regiment, and the guns, advanced up the western poort of the Buffalo; and, for some time, took up a position on a small knoll commanding all the forest below.

We were now in the midst of a glorious and most impressive scene, which it was impossible to contemplate, circumstanced as we there stood among some of the most gigantic features of nature, without feeling powerfully moved. The sublimity of the spectacle consisted in its vast extent of primeval forests; where, in many places, there were not even Kaffir paths: so thick and entangled were these ancient woods, so solemn and silent their recesses:—

> "Far as the dazzled eye can glance,
> Spreads the broad land one glorious bower
> Where Amakosa shake the lance,
> And still defy a conqueror's power."

Looking up the glen of the poorts, its bottom and sides were seen to be closely set with dark, pale, and bright green foliage; and to our right and left, the great forest stretched far and wide across the mountain side. The *els, sneeze,* and yellow wood trees, assegai and Kaffir broom, (*erithrina corallodendron*) bearing papilionaceous flowers like bunches of coral, were linked together with *baviaan's tow,* or wild vines; and many aged "sons of the forest" waved hoary with long tufts of grey moss. The bare summits of the range, on either hand, were composed of green pastures, or of naked precipices.

The woods were known to be full of Kaffirs; the six-pounders awoke echoes among the trees and rocks, until then unknown; and rounds of spherical case, smoking and hissing through the air, and loudly bursting and scattering two score bullets, were fired into the hollows. The third round was followed by a far-off death-scream; and we afterwards found that the chief Eno there narrowly escaped destruction, seven of his men falling dead by his side. He precipitately fled, leaving his leopard-skin kaross, which was afterwards brought into camp.

Armed Kaffirs were seen on the craggy summits high above us; they brandished their assegais, and apparently dared us to reach them: but a round shot or two, " with rush of anger," crashing against and splintering the rocks, caused them speedily to conceal themselves. We moved higher up the poort with one of the guns, and established ourselves for some time in an open triangular space surrounded with thick forest. There we lay for a season listening to the firing in other parts of the range; and the extended ranks, with ready-cocked musquets, pointed towards the bush. I assisted to take a horse and some goats from the skirts of the wood; and some months after this, in speaking to a minor chief of Kaffirs, he said, " You remember the field at the poorts of the Buffalo, where you lay for some time?"—" Yes." " You took a horse and goats there: but we got them all back again. I was close to the edge of the bush then, with many warriors."—" Why, then," I asked, " did you not show yourselves and fight?"—" We did not like your fire-wagons, (great guns): for just before this, a ball had struck a rock below me; and thinking that the next would strike a little higher, I ran down into the bush. We wished to make peace then."—" Well; why did you not call out from your cover, and say so?"—" That would have been strange indeed, and given you a good direction where to fire. No, no; the Amakosa are not fools altogether."

At last moving, like a scene in a play, across a neck above the source of the river, appeared to our eager expectation the third division, with dark lines of horsemen, and infantry with glancing arms. A couple of guns were opened by Major Cox; the shot plunged into the kloofs in our direction; and he was answered from our side. After some more firing, the third division moved on to another point.

Lieutenant Sutton, field-adjutant of the third division, had now a narrow escape. Riding with some officers along a wet and narrow path, where they were carrying a three-pounder on men's shoulders, a Kaffir fired a long ball at him with deliberate aim from behind a rock. "The leaden passport to eternity" brushed past the adjutant: who instantly brought his double-barrelled gun to his shoulder, and shot the Kaffir through the right arm. He fled; the second barrel broke his thigh; and he fell. The Kaffir had a good gun, a horn of powder, and three dozen of bullets with him.

Lieutenant Granett, after a march of eight

miles, penetrated into the steep and broken ground where the enemy lay. They opened on him with musquetry, and threw assegais; and some of his people were disabled : but the fire was sharply returned; and the lieutenant himself shot a famous huntsman, Barber by name, who has been known to go up single-handed to a wild buffalo in a thicket, and throw an assegai into him. Granett was now dragged violently to the ground by Louis Arnoldus. He at first suspected treachery : but Louis said, " Down for a moment ; I see you marked out." His keen eye had watched the enemy, and perhaps saved the lieutenant's life. After a struggle for the mastery for some time, the Kaffirs fled, leaving two hundred and fifty head of cattle in the possession of the party ; but, in driving them off, a great number of them fell over a *crantz*, or precipice, and were destroyed.

In the evening, into camp—which again lowed with some thousand head of cattle—we all returned except Major Maclean : whose party of three hundred strong, were occupied for ten hours in cutting a clear way with axes ; and the men were compelled to stand to their arms without sleep or food, until daylight showed them how to extricate themselves from the forest of the western poort. "Damn this wark!" said Jock Maclaughlin, of the

72nd regiment, to his comrade, "I didna care aboot the want o' the bit or sup; but the Kaffirs are like eels, and we hadna a gude feight ava!"— "Ye needna fash yersel," cried his comrade: "ye'll hae a wamefu o' that too, afore aa's dune."

Next day was one of rest, and I strolled in the evening with Major Michell to sketch, and to note the birds, insects, and plants which occurred by the banks of the Buffalo. Black and yellow sugar-birds were chirping about the orange flowers of their favourite plants; beetles, with white spots on their black coats, were clustering about the delicate leaves of the mimosas; and among the branches were seen that strange parasite the *cassina capensis*, or Cape misletoe.

At night it was very agreeable to wander out alone in the clear moonlight, when the sounds of the camp were all hushed; and to gaze on the clean-looking tents and white squares of wagons, and the various coloured cattle now quietly reposing and leisurely chewing the cud. Near a tree a watch-fire, surrounded with slumbering and wrapped-up figures, would send its glare among the branches; displaying knapsacks and canteens hung up; musquets resting against the trunk; and horses picketed close by. The last light burning was in a small tent, near which walked slowly to and fro a cloaked horseman, with his carbine in a loose white sheep-skin cover, for protection against the dews, but ready to slip off at a moment's notice. This was the general's sentry. The river was heard hoarsely rushing below; dogs barked occasionally; hyenas howled in the distance; and then a Kaffir would set up a shout of derision and mockery from the bush.

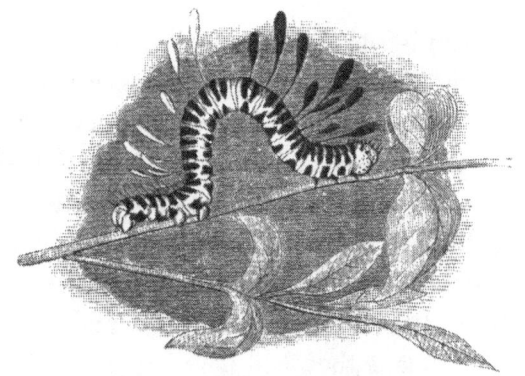

KAFFIR WARRIOR CATERPILLAR.*

CHAPTER XXI.

Effects of the Campaign on the Enemy—The Commander-in-Chief thanks the Troops—Further Arrangements—Head-Quarters " en Route "—Glen of the Cahoon—Tunglalaba—Simpson's Station—Prepare to enter Hintza's Territory—Kaffir Herald—Cross the Great Kye River—Shaw's Fountain—Visit of Amapakati—Receive a Message—A Gallant Company—Short Account of the Fingoes—Instances of Kaffir Oppression—Adventure in a Garden—Butterworth Mission Station—Agreeable Bed-fellows—Lieutenant Bailie's Sermon—Author and his Friends practise Witchcraft—The Second Division—A Fatal Accident—A Murder—Sergeant Howison's Adventure—Couba the Counsellor—Fingoes become British Subjects—Their Warriors arrive in Camp—Their Rejoicings and Bivouack—Final Message to Hintza—Declaration of War.

THE border chiefs and their followers,—as was learnt from their women and the Hottentot de-

* The front or foremost feathers, of a velvet black : the rear one of a snowy whiteness. The head, rump, and hind feet, orange yellow. The rest of the insect milk-white ground, and jet black spots, arranged as in the above sketch, which is of the natural size.

serters, who left them with their arms,—were now completely disheartened and dismayed by the vigorous manner in which they had been recently attacked; and they dispersed through the glens of the Buffalo and Amatola, seeking shelter where they could best find it. Their losses in killed and wounded were very great; fifteen thousand head of cattle had been taken from them, and sent into the colony; and they had been taught what they did not seem to have contemplated: that, however thick the woods, or rugged the mountains, among which they might conceal themselves, our troops, patient of fatigue, would unhesitatingly penetrate to their fastnesses; close with them; and drive them before them wherever they were to be found.

The commander-in-chief, in general orders, declared his high gratification at the gallant conduct of the troops; congratulated them on the result of the indefatigable and well-disciplined exertions with which they had executed the combined and successive operations since they had entered Kaffir-land; and expressed his particular satisfaction, that their success had been effected with small loss in killed and wounded, and without a sick list.

His excellency now directed the third division, under Major Cox, to continue on the theatre of the recent operations, and incessantly to pursue, attack, and harass all the straggling parties of the enemy; to allow them no repose; and to prevent them from banding together for mischief towards the colony, or in the rear of the advancing force. The fourth division was to co-operate with the third from the Chumie; and the second had gone down the rivers Chalumma, Buffalo, and Cahoon, towards the sea, and was eventually to join the first at the Gonubee.

The head-quarter division was again " en route." On the 11th of April, we crossed the Buffalo, its bed composed of compact green stone; and took the direction of a fine valley, in the midst of which there was a convenient " outspan," called the yellow wood trees, on the banks of the Nameka River. Here we halted for an hour or two, and again " progressed." Many huts lined the bank of the stream on our left, said to have been inhabited by very bad Kaffirs; and out of these had rushed, on the commencement of the war, three men, who attacked with clubs a luckless trader (Stamford) while quietly walking along the road in company with a Hottentot woman, and beat in his head. One of the Kaffirs had the impudence to go with the woman next day to Mr. Brownlie's mission-station on the Buffalo, and to ask for a reward for bringing her in.

In order that the enemy might not harbour in our rear, we consigned all the kraals to the flames; and after a march of eighteen miles, we established our bivouack in a beautifully wooded glen of the Cahoon River, at a place classically named by the Kaffir traders, " Hangman's Bush." Here it was said that a Kaffir was strangled by his chief for a strange act of witchcraft, in milking a cow into his own mouth: which is not allowed in Kaffir-land, as it is supposed to occasion misfortune to another party.

Our next march was to the Gonubee River, where we breakfasted; and then up the Gonubee Hill, from which a very grand and extensive prospect was obtained. The country near appeared open, undulating, and with scattered bush; the mountains were to the north; and the sea was seen in an opposite direction. We passed Hoole's trading station in ruins. The owner stated that Kaffirs from a distance had commenced plundering him; when the Kaffirs among whom he lived carried him up into a hill behind his station; and concealed him in the bush for twelve days, until they could send him off in safety. After a march of fourteen miles, we encamped on the side of a hill in a valley called Tunglalaba. Here the thermometer was seventy degrees at noon; and we had afterwards thunder and lightning with much rain. But at night the thermometer fell to fifty-seven degrees; and we felt it bitterly cold. In the valley was a chain of *vleys*, or pools. We halted a day here, waiting for the second division; and in the evening, the Kaffirs came near and howled and laughed at us like wild beasts.

On the 14th, the march was resumed; and Major Michell and myself, having pushed on in advance to have time to reconnoitre the country a little, had nearly shot what we took for a Kaffir spy, moving off two miles from the camp, refusing to stop or answer a challenge, and making for the bush. He turned out to be a reckless Hottentot, following the spoor of a lost horse. After a march of fourteen miles, we encamped at Simpson's burnt station. The Kaffirs were lurking about some kraals below; and while I was busy collecting some cocks and hens for the table—which foraging tricks I had learnt from the Cossacks—Hermanus, the interpreter, crept along the ground into a bush: from which "breathing of sudden death," he pulled out by the neck of his kaross a Fingo herdsman of the enemy, rejoicing in the name of Doobooloo.

The 15th of March was an important day for the troops. The column moved at daybreak, and passed near some deep and remarkable kloofs on the left: at the side of which were fantastic precipices of rock. We commenced a long descent towards the bed of the Great Kye River; and saw through our glasses parties of Kaffirs sitting round fires on the opposite banks, there about four hundred feet high. When we reached the broad river, then fordable and flowing over rocks and stones between high crantzes, projecting and receding in a picturesque manner, the general halted under the willow trees,—the heat was most intense, and the flies most annoying,—and calling to him the commanding officers of corps, he told them that they were now entering the country of Hintza: who, though believed to be a most ungrateful dissembler, still professed friendship for the English. That, in consequence of these amicable professions, and in order now to give Hintza the opportunity of proving his sincerity, the general ordered that plundering fields, burning huts, and shooting Kaffirs should be rigidly prevented by officers; that if firewood or vegetables were wanted, an officer appointed for the purpose was to take care that these were procured under proper regulations; that commanding officers were held responsible that these commands should be strictly obeyed; and that if eventually Hintza did not give satisfaction, by returning the colonial cattle, the whole country

CONFERENCE ON THE GREAT KYE.

Published by Henry Colburn, 13, Great Marlborough Street, 1840.

should be scoured. A general order to the above effect was also issued here, before the troops crossed the river.

I was directed to bring up the infantry and wagons, halted some distance in the rear; and then the whole prepared to move across the river: when a loud and long shout was heard from the wooded slopes on the opposite side; and a tall and robust Amagaleka, his kaross thrown back to display his noble figure, appeared on the hill side. "Ho! Mangesee!" he cried: "Ho! English! do you know what river this is?" The interpreters, Hermanus and Klaas, laying aside their arms, went to the front, followed by Colonel Smith, on some stones leading over the river; and answered, "We do know what river this is: the Neiba or Kye."—"Why have you come here?" Answer: "To speak with Hintza." "We don't want to fight with you."—"Very well: but we must see your king, Hintza, and must cross into his country:" on which, looking towards the top of the ridge, we noticed a large body of Kaffirs with musquets and assegais, preparing, apparently, to dispute the passage of the river.

Nothing could persuade the messenger to come over to us. He retired, after receiving a *distinct* message to Hintza and Bookoo, as is afterwards noticed; picked up his bundle of assegais, which he had left behind a bush; and joined his comrades at the summit. The troops, guns, and wagons crossed and ascended the long winding road on the other side, without opposition; the Kaffirs having unexpectedly disappeared. We encamped on the heights ten miles from the Kye at Shaw's Fountain: where the trader Purcell had been murdered at his own door, as formerly mentioned. It rained excessively, and the bugle rang out the glad sound of a *zoopje*, or dram, for the troops. Highlanders and Hottentots answered with a shout.

Large bodies of Kaffirs now sat on the eminences about three or four hundred yards from us, seemingly in deep consultation. After half an hour's delay, a party of them took heart of grace, rose, and advanced towards us. These were some of the *amapakati*, or counsellors, of Hintza, accompanied by those of his brother Bookoo; who has charge of the country about the lower Kye. The amapakati came to us without assegais, walking close to each other, and carrying high their walking staves on their shoulders, in token of peace. Several of them had their hair dressed with close-set balls of red clay; and one of them resembled Lord Brougham, both in nose and wig. One or two wore tufts of jackal's skin;

their karosses were handsomely ornamented with sugar-loaf buttons variously disposed; and they glittered with brass rings and belts. They shook hands with the general, and then sat down on the ground with sage and cunning looks; drawing their karosses about them to hear attentively his excellency's intentions.

The general told them, as he had before told the herald, to send immediately this message to Hintza:—that no satisfactory answer having as yet been returned to the communications made through his officer, Van Wyk, he would not now stand still, but go on till he met Hintza himself; that in the mean time he would refrain from doing any violence to his people; and that it rested with Hintza now to prove himself a friend or foe of the English, by giving an answer in five days. The counsellors said little in reply, but that his excellency's message should be given to their great chief. After receiving a warning that any Kaffirs approaching the camp after dark would be fired at, the amapakati retired.

Our next march led over a strange saddle of land with two wooded ravines, running up to it on either hand. Many hamlets were passed, at which women were beating out heads of millet, and otherwise peacefully employed; also much cattle was seen: all which were left in quiet, though much to the annoyance of the Hottentots and burghers. A chief of the Fingoes lately attached to a mission-station joined us, Macalema by name: who said, that the Fingoes were on the eve of rising on Hintza when we entered his territory; and that they would willingly join us against their masters and oppressors. Macalema was directed to remain with the camp to see what turn events would take; and accordingly he marched on in front of his excellency, in a blue jacket and white trousers: followed by four of his people, with cock-tail head-gear and flowing karosses; and carrying their commissariat on a stick on their shoulders in the shape of ribs and belly of beef. The dark and stout Hermanus, conspicuous with his white hat and small black feather, guarded them. Truly we were a gallant company!

It is now a proper place to say a few words regarding the Fingoes. Wanderers, or outcasts, is the meaning of this name; and in Kaffir-land it is a term of reproach. But the people who bear it, although not so tall, nor so handsome as the Amakosa, yet are a fine straight-made and active race of men; and some of them have even European features, though all are very black, and have crisp hair.

In Hintza's country there were the remains of

nine tribes who formerly lived in the country about Natal, and were attacked and scattered by the Zoola chief Chaka, and by Matuana, from fifteen to twenty years ago. The survivors of the tribes fled, and became herds and "hewers of wood and drawers of water" to the Amakosa. The names of the nine tribes are,—

Amahlubi	The tearers or strippers.
Amazizi	The people who bring.
Amagobizembi	The crooked axes.
Abasékuneni	Those who are in the truth.
Abaswawo	The people who curse.
Amantozaki	Those who are his things.
Amabile	The people of the women's breasts.
Abayunani	The united people: and the
Amakledwani.	

These broken tribes had each a chief in Hintza's country: but the greatest among them was Umklambiso.

The dress of the men and women of the Fingoes had a general resemblance to that of the Kaffirs; the softened hide kaross forming the covering. There is, however, one great distinction between the Kaffirs and the Fingoes. The tips of the ears of the Fingoes have usually very large openings in them; and these they always showed when there was any doubt as to their identity.

It was impossible to ascertain the exact number

either of Hintza's people between the Kye and towards the Umtata, or of the Fingoes: but we may roughly estimate it at eighty thousand of the former, and twenty thousand of the latter, of all ages. Besides the Fingoes in Hintza's country, however, there were Fingoes among the Gaikas and T'Slambies: but fewer in number. I have given an instance of Kaffir oppression and barbarity towards these last; and now it may be said generally, that the state of the Fingoes under the Amakosa was that of *grinding slavery*, and that the wrongs inflicted on these poor, scattered, and despised people, loudly called on Heaven for vengeance on their task-masters.

The pseudo-philanthropical party at the Cape, for their own political purposes, and without the slightest regard to truth, wished to make it appear that the Kaffirs did not oppress the Fingoes. We, who saw the state of the Fingoes among the Amakosa, know better; and, in proof of what we assert, we bring forward these few facts. The Fingo herdsmen lived in hamlets near those of the Kaffirs; accumulated a few cattle; and men and women equally tilled the ground. If a Kaffir wished for a new kaross, he would watch for some days a Fingo braying and preparing a hide; and when it was ready, he would seize on it without payment. If a Kaffir took a fancy to one or more Fingo cows, he carried them off in the same way; and if a Kaffir wanted a hand-maid, he would take by violence any Fingo girl that pleased his fancy, in spite of the remonstrances of the parents, and of the girl herself. Finally, any of the Amakosa could wound or kill a Fingo with perfect impunity. We dare the religio-political clique of the Cape colony to the proof, that what we have now stated is not strictly true.

We continued our march; saw many herds of cattle by the way-side in charge of Fingo herdsmen; and the burghers stole off the road to look for colonial marks: but the colonists' cattle had not been left in such exposed situations. Accompanied by two of the amapakati, perhaps as spies, a thin old man Soocho, and a tall strapping fellow called by us Longtombolo, we halted to breakfast in some gardens of maize and melons. Here we found some Fingo women, to whose *children* one of our gentlemen was accused of being very attentive; and the old maxim of "playing with the child for the sake of the nurse," was invidiously quoted against him. One of the ladies took a three-feet pumpkin from her head, and presented him with it for his civility!

We passed over some green slopes, and then saw below us in the valley of the Gona, and in the bosom of verdant hills, the mission-station of

Butterworth. It was strange, but very gratifying, to see so far in Kaffir-land two white buildings, one of which was a chapel, neatly thatched, with a few out-houses beside them, and twenty Fingo huts round: seated on a knoll with a large garden behind, and with a beautiful clump of trees on the banks of the river in front. The station had been for some time abandoned: but fire had not been applied to the roof, though the windows were broken; furniture and books were scattered about; and the chapel bell had been knocked to pieces on a stone.

The ways of Providence are often dark and mysterious; and it does not become the ignorant and short-sighted creatures of a day to attempt to penetrate or scan their ends. The people to whom the Gospel had been carried, and whose best interests the Wesleyan missionaries in particular had laboured to promote, rose up against them, compelled them to flee for their lives, and destroyed the stations from the Bashee to the Keiskamma. None of the tribes of the Amakosa had nationally received the Gospel: for the mild control of Christianity was irksome to these wild and untamed children of Kahabe and Galeka. Its influence, however, was just beginning to be felt among scattered portions of the people; and we trust and believe that, though there has been

AGREEABLE BED-FELLOWS.   103

a suspension of missions in parts of Kaffir-land, this will last only for a season; and that by renewed exertion, they will be re-established on a firmer foundation than they ever were before.

We rode down to the river, and pitched his excellency's tent in a field of maize, under the shadow of a spreading yellow wood tree, small leaved and dark, where also a bower was woven of green boughs for shelter from the noonday heat. A thick puff adder, beautifully mottled, but with large fangs conveying the most deadly poison, crawled up lazily from the river, and was seeking shelter in a holster, when he was discovered and killed. Besides flaming heat, occasional very heavy rain, and bitter cold,* we had to endure on this service the rather unpleasant idea of being liable, whilst sleeping on the ground, to have as a bed-fellow a snake or a scorpion. Let the campaigner or traveller in Southern Africa avoid trees: unless he is indifferent to finding in the morning coiled up for warmth by his side a serpent; or nestled under his cheek a scorpion. In the open field one is not so liable to the visits of these irritable bed-fellows; but near trees they are often to be found. An unfortunate and harmless *guana*, of large size, being

* The thermometer here was at forty-two degrees an hour before sunrise.

seen under some horizontal strata of rock, was mistaken for a puff adder; and we tried in vain for a long time by smoke, fire, a ramrod, &c., to get him out: at last out he crawled, resembling much a young crocodile, three feet long.

It was Sunday, and the surveyor-general and myself walked up the knoll to look at the mission-house, and to hear a discourse. We found the garden enclosed with a wall; it had been well kept; and there were many peach and fig trees in it, besides melons and potatoes, beans and peas. The Hottentot stomach, ostrich like, refuses nothing: ripe or unripe, all is digested; so that the garden was soon cleared of every thing but leaves and stems. A small but attentive congregation were assembled in the chapel, to hear Lieutenant Charles Bailie, of the 1st provisional battalion, preach. He was decidedly one of the best officers whom we had in the field, active, brave, and zealous: he was universally esteemed; and his death afterwards was very deeply lamented. The prayers, the songs of praise, and the discourse, were very impressive, considering the time and circumstances under which we were met. The preacher alluded to the scattering of the mission flocks, and the darkening of the religious horizon in Kaffir-land; and seemed to be inspired with as sincere a desire to do good spiritually, as he had often done excellent service with his Hottentots before the enemy. The sealing of his fate shall afterwards be recorded.

We remained some days on the Gona, waiting for the second division to rejoin us, and for Hintza's answer to the last communication. The officers walked about the country within two or three miles of the camp; and a small party of us one day visited the lately deserted kraal of Hintza, lower down the river. We found there the grave of one of his daughters, roofed over with boughs, and plastered with clay. A large royal hut stood some distance off, on the roof of which we sprung, and then performed a little witchcraft by dancing round it hand in hand. The effect of this frolic will be hereafter seen. As my worthy old instructor on that grand instrument of war, the bagpipe, (Donald Macdonald, pipe-maker to the Highland Societies of London and Edinburgh,) used to say, "The daftest folk in the world are doctors and offishers."

Some Kaffirs came in from Bookoo, and went to Colonel Smith: but he turned them away with scorn, and declared that none but those from Hintza himself could then be allowed to communicate with his excellency. Several expresses had been sent to bring up the second division;

and at last it appeared, descending towards the Gona. We thought at first that it had sustained a defeat: for men, horses, and wagons straggled along the road without order or regularity; and after continuing to pass us for hours, encamped two miles from us. We found, however, the enemy had not dealt severely with the division; but, on the contrary, that they had lost to it, after some skirmishing, between two and three thousand head of cattle in the Lower Buffalo, Gonubee, Cahoon, &c.; and that the cause of the disorderly march was, the knocking up of five hundred horses out of seven hundred. The second division thus became crippled. The artillerymen of the two divisions had a social meeting here; and an excellent man of Lieutenant Levinge's brigade, mistaking his road at night, fell over a small *crantz*, or precipice, between twenty and thirty feet high, into the bed of the river, lay there all night, bruised and bloody, and never spoke afterwards.

Some Fingoes came in and reported that a white man was lying not far from the camp, killed with assegais. Accordingly a wagon, with an escort, was sent to bring in the body; and it presented a ghastly spectacle, dressed in a blue surtout and white trousers, blood-stained about the nose and grizzled hair, and with assegai wounds in the chest and side. It was recognised to be the body of Armstrong, an elderly guide, who had thus met his death. A small party of Hottentots had been sent under his charge with the post-bag to the rear. Armstrong allowed his party to go on without him; remained behind drinking in camp; was probably beset with Kaffirs when half-drunk, among some rocks and bushes about three miles from the Gona; assegaied, and his horse, watch, and gun taken. All this showing the effects of intoxication and of Kaffir treachery; for there was an armistice with the Trans-kyean Kaffirs.

A pensioned sergeant of the 72nd regiment, of the name of Howison, now opportunely joined the division, freighted with tea, sugar, flour, rice, pipes, tobacco, and "other groceries." It showed extraordinary fool-hardiness in Howison thus to have pushed on without an escort from Graham's Town; but he nearly suffered for it. A small party of Hottentots fortunately happened to join him at the Deba. Kaffirs were seen in the gardens by the way-side, in twos and threes, gathering maize. They shouted to each other; ran off and collected in number about forty; and then made an onset towards the wagons: women and children turning out of some huts to share the expected plunder. Howison, anticipating the attack, pushed on with his men to meet the Kaffirs; and this bold front and a volley staggered the enemy, who were driven up a hill and gave no more trouble. Two wagons sent by a private speculator, without an escort, from Graham's Town to Fort Beaufort, were not so fortunate. The Hottentot drivers tapped some spirits; the Kaffirs watching their opportunity, rushed on the wagons, and assegaied one or two of the most incapable of the Hottentots, while the others fled; cut out the oxen; plundered and overturned the wagons; and secured six musquets.

A tall, reckless-looking fellow of a Kaffir, with handsome rosettes of beads about his neck, and arrayed in a leopard's skin kaross, now came into camp to hear the news, as he said. It was curious to see how he swaggered; to note the wild independence in his eye; and to watch his graceful attitude, and arrangement of his kaross for exhibiting his muscular limbs, " in all the pride of manhood." Nor was it less remarkable how he " pouted the lip of contempt, and upturned the nose of scorn," when he came near any of the Fingoes. These poor people, indeed, now began to flock to us in great numbers; thankfully eating the heads, tails, and entrails of the slaughtered oxen; hammering out the fresh marrow from a shin; and pleasantly licking it off a stone.

When Driver, the elephant-hunter, saw the proud Kaffir, his countenance kindled with wrath; and the finger of impatience itched to pull the trigger of destruction. "There's an infernal rascal!" he cried; "Couba, a counsellor and a spy of Hintza's: that's the villain that headed the party which destroyed my trading station on the other side of the hills. Only let me drill a hole in his jacket,—the gallows scoundrel!" Couba, leaning on his staff, merely sneered and grinned at Driver. "Yes, you know me," muttered the latter bitterly; "and a ball and your hide shall be better acquainted before long." Couba was now closely watched and prevented from leaving the camp; but civilly treated.

Hintza had been allowed five days to give an answer to the general's message: nine had now elapsed; and he neither sent nor appeared. His excellency therefore came to a decision accordingly. The chiefs of the Fingoes had been for some time negotiating with the British commander. They declared that they had long intended to leave the Amagaleka, whose oppression was intolerable; that they were resolved to seek another home as soon as they could escape with impunity; and they now entreated the general to become their father, to deliver them from slavery, and to give them a new country.

The murder of Armstrong had now in itself broken the truce on the part of the Kaffirs of Hintza; and he had disregarded the message sent him four days beyond the time fixed. Seeing, therefore, that it was useless to treat Hintza with further ceremony, and believing that, if the Fingoes were to be located between the Fish River and the Keiskamma, they would materially assist in the defence of the colony, besides affording a supply of hired servants, the governor agreed to take them under his protection; and said that they should now become subjects of the King of England. The deputies, on hearing this, were delighted beyond measure: "they threw aside sack-cloth and ashes; their faces were whitened; and their consequence was increased." Messages were immediately sent round to the Fingo kraals to collect the women and children, herds and moveables, and to come without delay to the British camp; and the men were also ordered to arm.

The morning of the 24th of April was to us one of exceeding interest. Dark masses of Fingo warriors were seen advancing down the hills; they drew near, and were found to be armed with shields and assegais; and their heads were variously ornamented with jackals' tails, feathers, and pieces of hide cut like horns, giving them an unearthly appearance. The doctors wore gallbladders among their long, matted hair; and the great doctor, who strengthened the people for war by gall, incantation, &c., wore on his head a large fur cap, and had his loins girt with various handsome skins disposed in stripes.

The Fingoes advanced in compact bodies of fifty. Holding their broad shields and assegais before them, and their staves in the air, they stamped the ground with their heels; sang, in a deep melancholy tone, "that they wanted a home, and would fight for one;" then broke into a more animated war song; struck their shields with their staves, uttered short cries, and whistled by making a strange mouth with their thick lips and inhaling the air. The whistling began low and faint at first, until it ended in resembling the sound which accompanies the flight of a thousand birds. The shields were shaken, too, and resounded like the wind rustling a few leaves; gradually increasing until it seemed as if a storm raged among the boughs of a forest.

Then the Fingoes opened out into large circles facing inwards, singing and stamping as before. One dashed into the midst, shouting and challenging with brandished assegai; the rest hooted at him, and touched his shield in derision with the buts of their weapons; a captain then sprung forward, his head fluttering with long plumes, and tigers' tails at his waist, leaping and bounding with extraordinary agility, and feigning to engage in combat: when the first fell back into the circle. They moved round singing, and ever and anon yelled and showed how they would destroy their enemies, by thrusting at the ground and uttering "*Ha-hoo-hoo!*" With several hundred thus engaged, the scene was one of wild excitement and animation; and it was difficult to resist enacting a part in the war game.

FINCO WAR SONG.

At night, circles of twenty or more sat round fires with their shields on edge to windward, roasting meat on the embers. Then one would snatch up a hot junk; transfer it to his mouth, ashes and all; saw off a piece with his assegai,—their noses were not much in the way,—and then hand the remainder to his neighbour, muttering and talking in a low tone, all the while, about his new country. Then a rude water-pipe went round, made of a cow's horn, into which, through a hole in the side, a reed was thrust. At the top of the reed was an earthenware cup, containing tobacco and what appeared to be the leaves of the intoxicating *dakka*. Holding the horn in the left hand between the knees, the smoker covered the opening of the horn with the fingers of the right hand, and inhaled between them the smoke which passed gurgling through the water. After two or three long whiffs, the pipe was passed on; and the last smoker "blew a cloud" into a reed, in which there was water, and ended by whistling on it. This was unaccountable, but very laughable: however, they all went through the same ceremony very gravely. When they lay down to sleep, they covered themselves with their shields, and nestled close to each other for warmth: reminding me of the Roman *testudo*, or tortoise of joined shields to secure assailants against an enemy's darts in attempting to scale a wall.

Captain Warden was sent off on the 22nd, with a detachment of cavalry, accompanied by three hundred Fingo warriors as guides, to assist in rescuing the missionaries and traders from their perilous situation at Clarkeburg on the Bashee, and to escort them to camp. Couba, the military counsellor, was then sent for, with two other Kaffirs, who had come into the camp, to have a declaration read to them by his excellency. Three or four Fingo captains came to beg their karosses and ornaments, supposing that the Kaffirs were about to be executed. The general, through the medium of Mr. Shepstone the interpreter, thus addressed Couba :—

That Hintza and his subjects, in imminent peril some years ago, had received from the British the greatest assistance which one people could receive from another; and had been saved by the colonial troops from the Fetcani : a service attended with much expense and inconvenience to the British government. That these great benefits had been duly acknowledged by Hintza : but what return had he now made for them ?

That when the governor was actually negotiating with the border chiefs, subordinate to Hintza, to confer on them greater advantages than they had ever received before, in annual presents, extension of grazing ground, &c., they, with the knowledge and consent of Hintza, were preparing to make a treacherous and most unprovoked invasion on an unprepared country. That Hintza, forgetful of the great obligations which he had received at the hands of the English, had given no notice to the governor of what was intended; but, on the contrary, had countenanced the atrocious conduct of the border chiefs: who, without previous declaration of war, had swept through the British territory, and ravaged it with fire and sword. That Hintza had assisted the invaders with men; and had received a very large share of plundered cattle and horses:

That, in February and in March last, the governor had sent messengers to Hintza, to propose mild terms to him, and that he might still continue to be an ally of the English by separating himself from the border chiefs, and giving up the plunder which had been sent into his territory; but that to these messages no satisfactory answer had yet been returned:

That, therefore, the governor had come into Hintza's country with the troops of the king his master, to demand an answer to the above communications; that still, though nine days had elapsed and Hintza was known to be not far distant, having received no apology, no return, no answer from Hintza, for these and for other reasons now to be stated, war was declared against him:—First, for the cruel murder of Willam Purcell, a British subject, by the connivance of Hintza. Secondly, though it was agreed that the soldiers of the one force should not harm the soldiers of the other, until a declaration of war was made, that a white man (Armstrong) had just been murdered by some of Hintza's people. Thirdly, for destroying without provocation, the mission houses and trading stations established by Hintza's permission in his country, and causing the missionaries and traders to fly for their lives:

Therefore were hostilities now to commence: for having provoked which, and for having brought down vengeance on himself and on his people, Hintza would ere long bitterly repent:

That the Fingoes had now been taken under British protection; and that any one who should molest them would be slain. Finally, that a communication had just been received from the Amaponda country, that Faku was ready to fall on Hintza the instant the governor should give the signal. That the Amatembies were also ready.

Couba and the others were now dismissed with their arms, having engaged to report faithfully to Hintza; Colonel Smith waved his cap; and war with Hintza was announced by firing eastwards a shotted six-pounder.

CHAPTER XXII.

Summary of Operations near the Frontier—The First Division marches—A Tornado—Encamp on the Kamega—Kaffir Women in Danger—March to the Izolo—Interesting Prospect—More Kaffir Women—Jock Maclaughlin—Colonel Smith's Operations—Attack of Hintza's Kraal — Successful Operation by a Medical Officer— Gallantry of Driver— Results of Colonel Smith's Activity — The Cattle Mania — Instance of Carelessness—Three of Hintza's Counsellors arrive in Camp—Author's Operations—Advent of Hintza to sue for Peace—Interesting Conference and Treaty—A most barbarous Custom—Hintza and his Son Crieli remain as Hostages—Hintza's Appetite—His Opinion of the Bagpipes—Kaffir Revenge—Pyramid erected—First Division returns towards the Kye—Bookoo —Fingo Massacre—Dabakasee Camp—Captain Warden's Return—His skilful Management—What we suffered in the Field.

HINTZA was now our declared enemy: it was evident that, conscience stricken, he had not ventured to appear before the general; and the great forbearance hitherto shown by his excellency towards this perfidious chief, was succeeded by a firm determination to inflict on him a severe and richly merited punishment for his base ingratitude and treachery.

118   SUMMARY OF OPERATIONS.

The troops near the frontier had not been idle during the late proceedings on the Gona. Captain Armstrong had sent out from Camp Adelaide on the Kat River, a patrol to recapture some cattle; and the party were returning from the Chumie Hoek with one hundred and seventy goats, when a band of Kaffirs showed themselves in strong ground, and defied the troops. Accordingly, on the night of the 10th of April, Captain Armstrong marched with a party of mounted men and a small field-piece; surprised the Kaffirs at dawn; shot six of them; and took thirty horses, eight hundred head of cattle, and two hundred goats: with which he returned to Camp Adelaide after "performing the service with his usual ability and judgment."

On the 17th of April, the third and a part of the fourth divisions had moved towards the poorts of the Buffalo; and on the morning of the 18th, three detachments of the third division having penetrated the precipitous and woody ravines, surprised and killed at daylight several of the enemy, and captured two thousand head of cattle. The two divisions continuing to pursue and harass the enemy on subsequent days, had scoured their fastnesses among the Chumie, Amatola, Keiskamma and Buffalo mountains; sent into the colony five thousand head of cattle; and ably and efficiently executed the instructions with which the commanders of the divisions were charged.

At ten o'clock on the morning of the 24th, immediately after the declaration of war, the first division broke up from its cold encampment on the Gona. The north-west wind had there rather astonished our bones; and one night a hurricane, accompanied with pelting rain, levelled our tents. Some luxurious gentlemen who chose to take off their clothes "on turning in," were compelled to look about for shelter in their shirts; the cold wind sorely disturbing their light drapery!

The commander-in-chief took with him part of the first division, and marched northwards; and Colonel Smith, immediately after the declaration of hostilities against Hintza, proceeded with three hundred cavalry, mounted rifles, burghers, and guides, to intercept the enemy; who were said to be passing rapidly with their cattle over the T'Somo. The second division was left on the Gona, to renovate and refresh the men; to maintain the communication by the ford of the Kye; to receive Captain Warden on his return with the missionaries; also to assemble the Fingoes under its protection; and eventually, be sent with the missionaries and the captured cattle into the colony.

We passed up and along hills of easy ascent,

covered with verdure and clumps of bush at considerable intervals; took some armed Kaffirs prisoners, hovering about us on foot and on horseback; were joined by some Hottentot deserters from the enemy, their firelocks in good order, and each with a little bit of paper over the priming to preserve it; and then descended after a march of a dozen miles, and encamped on the banks of the Kamega. Hearing a faint scream in the bed of the river, deeply shaded with trees and bushes, I jumped down into it, and found some of our Hottentots using rather roughly some Kaffir women and children, who were trying to conceal themselves with their few moveables. Without a little club-law it was not easy to make the provisional soldiers understand that the women of the enemy ought to be perfectly safe from all violence: but there was no instance of serious injury to any of them.

Next day we continued our march towards the T'Somo and Ameva rivers, in which direction Hintza and his legions were supposed to lie. A little army of Fingo warriors now accompanied us: running in long lines and single file across the hills; carrying their broad shields and assegais horizontally in the left hand; they bounded joyfully on a-head, and cleared some kraals full of cattle, the owners of which had fled to the bush.

We ascended some heights, and burnt the grass to show our track to Colonel Smith's corps of cavalry; heard a good deal of firing in the direction where he was supposed to be; marched on over a large grassy plain; and encamped near some Kaffir huts on the banks of the Izolo, a branch of the T'Somo, in a notch of a long line of green and bush-topped hills.

I went up the hill on the south of the camp; and from its rocky and woody summit, and from the midst of the orange-crowned heads of aloes, I could discern the long blue ranges and brown conical peaks of the mountains beyond the Bashee, even as far as the Umtata. I longed for wings to flee away and visit there the beautiful but neglected harbour at the mouth of the latter river; as well as the kaross-covered descendants of Europeans, one of whom is the queen regent Nonubé of the T'Slambies, already mentioned with honour. In that quarter the soil is of most extraordinary fertility; and there also is the remarkable hole in an iron stone hill, through and about which flow the waters of the Umpakoo.

There was a noise of struggling; and some Kaffir women appeared among the rocks and bushes below, who had been hunted out by our new Fingo allies, intent on plunder. One old woman tried to conceal herself by lying flat on her face, with hands and legs stretched out, and covered with her kaross on a rock, from which it was not easy to distinguish her. With the assistance of some of the gallant 72nd regiment, a stop was soon put to the rudeness of the Fingoes; and the Highlanders and Kaffir women were soon on friendly terms through the medium of tinder-boxes.

A roguish-looking young Fingo, who had ferreted out among the rocks some hides with colonial marks upon them, came up the hill, and wanted to get the women down among his people, " to take care of them :" but this " Jock Maclaughlin" would by no means allow. " We dinna come here to hunt oot women and children; ye maun noo consider yersels Mangesee, or Englishmen. Nae doobt the Kaffirs hae ill used ye, ye'r wives and bairns and aa; but ye mauna meddle wi their women noo: that's no alloo't !"—" But we want to be led on to fight the Kaffirs," said the Fingo, through a Hottentot interpreter. " It will be time enugh," cried Jock, " when the *Incosee Incoolo*, as ye ca' the general, leads ye on, and tells ye to feight :" so the Fingo returned from whence he came.

Colonel Smith in the mean time made a rapid and successful sweep with his cavalry force. After leaving the general on the 24th of April, he soon arrived in sight of the retreating enemy: when a Fingo came up and said, that the chief Maguay was near, and might easily be captured. Accordingly, Lieut. Balfour of the 72nd regiment, the colonel's aide-de-camp, was detached with some mounted rifles, and boldly and dexterously succeeded in securing the chief alive,—no easy matter —as well as one of his followers and eighty head of cattle. With part of the force, the best mounted, and after a gallop of an hour and a half, the Kaffirs and cattle being at speed, the brother of the chief Chopo was taken prisoner; twenty Kaffirs were shot; and four thousand very beautiful cattle were captured at the foot of Kamega-berg. At two the following morning, the Kamega-berg was crossed. The enemy was surprised again, more were shot, and twelve hundred head of cattle captured. Field-cornets Nel and Greyling were particularly forward and active on this occasion; and Colonel Smith also derived great assistance from his brigade-major, Captain Doyle, 72nd Highlanders.

On the 26th of April, the active and indefatigable chief of the staff again left head-quarters, with detachments of the Cape mounted rifles, burghers, 72nd Highlanders, provisional infantry, and three hundred Fingo warriors, to endeavour to secure the person of the Kaffir king. The force arrived at the T'Somo; and there hearing that Hintza was at his kraal on the Gongolocho, seven miles distant, the colonel pushed on with the cavalry. But a Kaffir vidette on the look out was seen to gallop rapidly in the direction of the royal kraal; and when it was reached, the huts were found empty. The Fingoes soon sacked and burnt them; and part of the dress and ornaments of the great wife were found here. The colonel then turned in the direction of the mountainous range between the T'Somo and Kye. The cavalry moved towards a mass of cattle; the enemy drove them off rapidly; but four thousand head fell into the hands of the infantry, disposed so as to intercept them.

The general and a part of his staff were out with a small escort at this time; and cattle being seen in a kloof, a disposition was made to secure them. A certain medical officer was on this, as on all other occasions, particularly active; and we used to jest afterwards about " three hundred head of cattle falling to the doctor's bow and spear on a Sunday." Cattle lifting seems natural to Scotchmen.

Four or five of the provisional Hottentots were surprised and assegaied in a kloof; and Colonel Smith's cavalry pursuing with rapidity, came up with the enemy in a deep ravine, running into the

Kye, called the Accalomba. Here the colonel ordered the burghers to dismount: Driver dashed down at their head; drove out the Kaffirs; and took two prisoners and twelve hundred head of cattle in a very spirited manner. One of the prisoners was frightened into directing us where to find more of the enemy; and after a most fatiguing and hot march of twenty-five miles, they were discovered in the bed of the Kye. Some were shot; and the rest fled, leaving in the hands of the troops three thousand magnificent cattle, twelve hundred of which were colonial. Also many horses, some of which died from excessive fatigue, after being a very short time in the possession of the captors.

The force returned to the head-quarter camp on the Izolo; and though the old peninsular campaigner may be amused with this account of a *grande chasse*, I beg to assure him that the difficulties just encountered were of no ordinary nature: in a most rugged country too, where there were no roads; where the distance marched was great; where the heat was excessive in the day; and where there was no shelter of tents at night from the chilling dews. The extraordinary exertions of the officers and men, deserving of every eulogium, were crowned with great success. Their loss was trifling, and that of the enemy considerable, during the last five days' arduous service; and the spoils of victory were fifteen thousand head of cattle, which to the South Africans are what money and goods are elsewhere. These herds were driven rapidly into camp, in apparently interminable columns, by Fingoes whistling and rattling their shields as they swiftly ran alongside the bellowing and dust-raising kine.

In the course of these several hard days' work, Colonel Smith was much indebted to Major T. C. White, assistant quarter-master-general of the burgher force, for the valuable assistance afforded by his ability and judgment. The colonel also thanked, in addition to those already named, Captains Murray and Craven, 72nd Highlanders; Captains Crause, Cowderoy, and Gilfillan, 1st provisional infantry; and Lieutenant Wade, Cape mounted rifles.

This campaign in Kaffir-land had infected us all with the cattle mania; we knew also a little of "spoor;" became judges of pasture; and in a short time we might have been figuring in karosses. Five Hottentots, and the same number of Fingoes, having only three guns in the party, left camp to search for firewood, and straggled on looking for cattle. They soon saw the *beestjes;* the Fingoes lent the two unarmed Hottentots assegais; the Kaffirs with the herd were attacked

INSTANCE OF CARELESSNESS. 127

and wounded; and seven hundred head of kine were driven into camp by these ten men. But here, on the other hand, we are bound, as faithful chroniclers, to condemn the carelessness of some Dutch burghers. Five thousand head of cattle were counted out to them to drive, with the assistance of a party of Fingoes, to Colonel Somerset's camp. The Dutchmen rode on a-head; neglected their charge, although so valuable for the plundered colonists; and in the course of two short marches, only half the number of cattle reached the second division.

Three of Hintza's counsellors now galloped into camp, and said that the great chief sued for peace, and wanted to treat with the general. " Why should Hintza die ?" said the amapakati. His excellency answered, that he had no wish to destroy Hintza; but that hostilities should be continued until the Kaffir king appeared before him; for that he would treat with no one else. The counsellors then rode off. I watched them through a glass from a hill as they pushed down the valley; and two miles off they joined a body of about forty horsemen. They then all dismounted; turned their horses to graze after " knee-haltering" them to prevent their straying; and sat down in a large circle on a rising ground, appaparently in deep consultation. One conspicuous figure was evidently Hintza himself. After a considerable time spent in this way, fires were lighted; a hasty repast was prepared and eaten; and then the whole mounted and disappeared at night-fall behind the hills.

Flesh without vegetables, we all know, is very heating: we had no want of beef and mutton; but *revenir toujours* to the same food was bad *pour la santé*. Following my old vagabondizing propensities next day, I took my trusty broad-sword under my arm; and with four or five Fingoes I went off quietly a few miles to seek for melons, pumpkins, &c. :—" something good for food," among fields which waved invitingly with maize and millet. We made a successful foray without accident; and on our return in the evening, in passing a tent a voice said, " His majesty has arrived."

A cloud of dust was seen over some dark horsemen approaching the camp up the valley of the Izolo. Major Lowen and Captain Beresford were sent out to see who they were. Hintza advanced from the rest and shook hands, pronouncing his own name; and the whole, to the number of forty, then galloped in, armed with assegais, on long-tailed horses, with sheep and buck-skins for saddles, and with their leopard-skin karosses, bull's hide mantles, and brawny limbs, looking like figures on a Grecian frieze.

Hintza, with a young and favourite counsellor, Umteenee, was led towards the general's tent. His followers remained on the ground at a little distance at their horses' heads. The great chief of the Amakosa appeared upwards of six feet in height, robust and fleshy, and about forty-five years of age. His skin was very dark, and might have claimed for him the title of another African king,—" The great black one." His crisp hair was without ornament, and he wore whiskers and a short beard. His nose was low and aquiline; his eyes and lips were prominent and large; though his carriage was dignified, he could not look any one steadily in the face; and he had altogether a most sinister expression of countenance. His ample mantle was of beautiful leopard-skin; and buskins of untanned hide covered his feet. His ornaments were a brass belt round his waist; many brass bracelets; an ivory ring above one elbow; and red and white beads round his neck, and in one ear. He grasped a bundle of well-made javelins in his left hand, and a *sambok*, or whip of buffalo-hide, depended from his right wrist. Such was the prime mover of the invasion of the colony.

The general received Hintza with his usual courtesy; and with Colonel Smith and Umteenee, they sat down on camp-stools in the open space between the tents; while we stood round to witness this interesting conference. The declaration which had been made to the counsellor Couba on the Gona, was now read to Hintza; and the effects of his conduct were pointed out to him in the loss of his people and cattle, and the preparations for bringing down upon him, not only the further vengeance of the English, but Faku of the Amapondas, and Vodana of the Amatembies. Hintza was then asked to explain himself.

He replied, with occasional gesticulation of the right hand, and thrusting out of the chin and elevation and depression of the eyebrows, that he now sued for peace; that he had not seen Van Wyk when he came with a message, having gone after some of our stolen cattle to restore it; that as to Purcell's murder, it was committed below the wagon-road; and that he had nothing to do with the people on the south side of it. "They," he continued, "go their way, we go ours: you may deal with them as you like. This is the first time that I have heard of Armstrong's murder: Soucho, the old counsellor, came to me with a message; but as we were not on good terms, I did not pay attention to what he said. I am on bad terms with the T'Slambies, and with the Jalousies: they will not obey me. It is true that I am the great chief of the Amakosa: but it is a mere title; I can't compel all the Amakosa to do as I wish. I can't restrain them."

The general answered, that Hintza must immediately send a message, and cause his orders to be obeyed, to Tyalie, Macomo, and the other frontier chiefs, to lay down their arms, under promise of personal safety; that he required of Hintza twenty-five thousand head of cattle, and five hundred horses now, and the same number at the end of twelve months, to make up the colonial losses; besides three hundred head for Purcell's widow, and three hundred for Armstrong's, and the murderers of these two men to be executed; and, above all, that the Fingoes, who had now become British subjects, should not be molested or injured in person or property. Hintza was given forty-eight hours to consider these terms: if he agreed to them and fulfilled them, leaving two hostages in his excellency's hands, there should be perpetual peace and alliance between the British and the Amakosa; if he rejected them, a bloody war would recommence, and would be prosecuted with vigour. In the meantime, and whilst Hintza remained in camp, which he had expressed a wish to do, he was promised that he should have no cause to complain of his treatment.

Hintza and his people now returned to tents which had been pitched for them, strongly guarded at a respectful distance by a circle of Highlanders. According to the South African custom, a fat ox was driven to the Kaffirs to slaughter; and we then witnessed a most strange and revolting spectacle, illustrative of savage customs. Half a dozen Kaffirs started up, laid aside their karosses, and approached the ox: one, with a noose of *riem*, or hide, on the end of an assegai, after a few attempts, slipped it over the horns; another held the tail, a third put a riem round the left fore-leg, and another round a hind-leg; the head and legs were then drawn together; and the ox fell bellowing to the ground. The animal was now secured firmly, and prevented from rising. The chief butcher then, with an assegai, cut open about a foot of the skin of the belly; and lying on the ground, amidst the groans of agony and helpless struggles of the unfortunate brute, he thrust his right arm up to the shoulder into the ox; gave a twist and a pull at the heart; ruptured one of the large arteries; and drew away the omentum: which was thrown on a fire, cooked and eaten, before the last convulsions of the victim had ceased!

We were all exceedingly disgusted; and some felt very sick on witnessing this barbarous sacrifice. Not so the Kaffirs: they were all alive, and immediately proceeded to flay the animal with their assegais grasped short; with an axe they broke in the ribs across the middle; the ox was in a pool of blood; and one fellow taking out the gall-bladder went off with it, and drank the warm gall "to make him strong." He evidently enjoyed the offensive potation: but making faces after it, like a Highlander after a dram, affecting reluctance to take what might not agree with him; and when it was all over giving vent to a hearty "pegh!"

The forty thieves—Kaffirs I mean—sitting round their fires, ate up a great part of the ox that night. Hintza was feasted by Colonel Smith: he also ate heartily, but would not drink any thing but coffee; he was thoughtful for some time, and then said after dinner, "We must now talk politics." Colonel Smith ended a long conversation by reminding him that the Tambookies and Amapondas were ready to fall upon him, on the general giving the signal, if he did not comply with his excellency's wishes; and the colonel warned him that it now rested with himself whether he was to continue to be the great chief of the Amakosa, supported by the English, or whether war, interminable war, was to be waged, and

"Thou know'st, great son,
"The end of war's uncertain."

Next morning, Hintza professing to agree to his excellency's terms, and offering, of his own accord, to remain with his son as hostages, came out of his tent into a large square formed by our varied force, drawn out for the occasion. Here, on his repeating to the general that he agreed to and would fulfil the terms of the treaty, they shook hands in token of amity; and three guns were immediately fired. In the afternoon, I had the honour of showing Crieli, (or Sihili,) Hintza's eldest son, the way to the camp. He is a good-looking, tall youth, about eighteen years old; and his appearance is very prepossessing. His mother is Nomsa, of the Tambookies.

The appetite of the Kaffirs is quite extraordinary: thus Hintza, after eating a very hearty dinner in Colonel Smith's tent, would go to his own, and his cook (naked out of respect) approaching him, would present the fatty omentum of an ox for the great chief's supper. A Highland piper was ordered to play for Hintza's amusement; and he strutted about in the usual consequential manner, "skirlin' like mad:" whilst the Kaffirs sat on the ground mute, and with their right hands on their mouths, uttering occasionally to one another a short "Oh!" Hintza was asked what he thought of the music. He answered, that he could not understand it properly; that some of it reminded him of his children at home, and made him cry; and that he supposed that the instrument had been invented by us out of regard for the general, to imitate his crying when he was a little boy; and to remind him of the crying of his children!

Hintza and his people were in great wrath one morning, and no wonder: for a favourite horse of his was found with its mane and tail cut and hacked, apparently to disguise it, for the purpose of stealing it. This was, in the estimation of the Kaffirs, a great insult: besides, it might be witchcraft, and was a bad omen. But it was revenged in their own way. The same night Field-commandant Lindé lost six of his best horses; and although the old gentleman raged and stormed, and wished to sacrifice every Kaffir indiscriminately on both sides of the Kye, all was of no avail: the horses could no where be found.

On the 1st of May, the beginning of the South

African winter, it was intensely cold in the morning and evening; hoar frost lay thick on the ground; and from off a table which had been left in the open air, there was as much of it collected as made a good sized snow-ball. There was also ice seen; and at sunrise the thermometer was at forty degrees. In the afternoon, wishing to mark the spot of the treaty with Hintza, the surveyor-general and myself, with Corporal Finlayson and four of the 72nd regiment, went up to one of the hills above the camp; and pulling off our jackets, erected with considerable labour a stone pyramid several feet high.

On the 2nd, we turned our heads in the direction of the colony, and marched back towards the Kye, Hintza and his suite accompanying us. In an ample red cloak, a present from the general, ornamented with gilt clasps and brass buttons, and made by the master-tailor of the 72nd regiment, the great chief himself was clad; and some of his men were equipped in ordnance blankets, which, with abundance of food, tobacco, &c., had been supplied to them. We halted to breakfast in a grove of yellow wood trees, in our rude and simple fashion: when occasionally there was something very much approaching to a scramble for the soaked biscuit and karbonatje, as we sat round a cloak or horse-rug spread on the ground, and ministered to by the general's faithful old servant, Cox.

The chief Bookoo, Hintza's brother, was announced to be approaching; and we saw about two and twenty colonial oxen driven on before the tall and lusty chief. He advanced on foot, in the midst of a crowd of followers; his head bald, and his nose upturned like that of a Calmuck. Colonel Smith received him, and he then sat down with a counsellor. I was curious to see the Kaffir mode of salutation: there is none. When Colonel Smith, brought Hintza to Bookoo, the latter did not get up to salute the great chief; and though the brothers were on good terms, and had not seen one another for some time, Bookoo merely looked at Hintza over his shoulder. The great chief then sat down on his hams beside Bookoo; and they remained talking together, keeping up a muttering conversation.

How different, I thought, was all this from the refinement and ceremony of the East! the slow approach to a great man; the taking off of slippers; the obeisance at a distance, and then nearer; the affected disinclination to sit in the presence of a ruler; and lastly the reverential feeling which considers it a high honour to be supplied with a place on the corner of his carpet. But such were the simplicity of manners, probably, in the days of Abraham and Lot: when "they were very rich in cattle," as appeared now among the Amakosa.

An express now arrived from Colonel Somerset to say, that, in violation of the treaty, the Kaffirs were falling on the Fingoes, and had destroyed thirty of them at one place. This, as may be supposed, highly incensed the British general; and he desired Hintza might be told that he was immediately to put a stop to this outrageous conduct, or else must take the consequences; that if the massacre continued, he would hang up two Kaffirs of Hintza's suite for every Fingo that was destroyed in future; and that he would begin on that very spot.

Hintza affected surprise at first. "Why is there so much made of the Fingoes," he said: "are not they *my dogs;* cannot I do with them as I like?" But afterwards getting alarmed, he sent speedy messengers, and desired his people to stay further violence. Bookoo was asked why he came on foot? "I am poor, I have no horses," said he; though it was well known that he had numbers. "What are these twenty-two oxen which you have brought?"—"All the colonial oxen that I ever had in my possession; and I now give them up for the sake of peace:" answered the crafty knave. But the day had gone by for these shallow artifices to have any effect.

We marched to a long valley through which the small river Dabakasee (excellent news) sometimes ran, and sometimes tarried in *vleys ;* and we pitched our tents opposite a grove of trees. Colonel Thompson, royal engineers, and his son, Mr. Alfred, here joined his excellency; and we remained some days at the Dabakasee for the fulfilment of Hintza's engagements: who with Crieli and Bookoo were allowed to walk about, but always of course accompanied with a guard of honour. On the 5th of May, we were much gratified on seeing the safe return of Captain Warden from his important mission to Tambookie-land. He came with a train of nineteen wagons; containing one hundred British subjects, missionaries and traders, with their families and effects, whom he had been instrumental in saving. Five hundred Fingoes, many hundreds of cattle and sheep, likewise accompanied the wagons; and the whole had been, without accident, brought across the entire breadth of the enemy's country, under the conduct of the escort with which the general had entrusted Captain Warden on the banks of the Gona. But this was not the only valuable service which Captain Warden had rendered on this occasion. He had communicated with the great chief of the Amatembies, (Tambookies,) Vodana, regent of the tribe since the death of his brother Vosanee; had confirmed him in his alliance to the British; and, but for some of his counsellors, would have brought him along with him also, to be located nearer British protection.

An important matter was to get the Tambookies to commit themselves with the people of Hintza: for, notwithstanding they professed enmity, many of Hintza's Kaffirs used to come and sit in a friendly way, feasting by the Tambookie fires of an evening. " You must prove that you are the ally of the English," said Captain Warden to Vodana, "by attacking the Amakosa." Accordingly, after some delay and difficulty, he got Vodana into the field on the 27th of April, with two thousand warriors fully equipped in their plumes and arms, and forty horsemen. Captain Warden led on his riflemen and Fingoes; the Tambookies hesitated a little about attacking the Kaffir kraals; the captain showed them the example; put spurs to his horse; broke the ice; and attacked the Kaffirs. The Tambookies immediately followed this good example; and poured into the kraals like a torrent. Several Kaffirs were killed, and one by Vodana's own assegai; and four thousand head of cattle were captured in this spirited affair: which, with the others of a similar nature, already described, combined to bring about Hintza's submission.

I had a good deal of conversation with the Rev. Messrs. Palmer, Ayliffe, Davis, and Satchell, of the Wesleyan mission; and they seemed very grateful to his excellency for saving their lives, and seemed highly delighted to find themselves sleeping among their families, for the first time for months, in perfect security. The poor Fingoes were also well pleased, and formed circles, and performed their war dances. On their way from Clarkeburg, one thousand Kaffirs had followed Captain Warden's party, threatening them with an attack; and one Kaffir found his way into the circle which had been formed of wagons, with Fingo shields and musqueteers between the intervals. But he was detected in the act of spying by the Fingoes; was tried next morning; and condemned to be shot. This, I believe, was Couba, the counsellor and spy, formerly mentioned on the Gona. Driver was thus saved the trouble of "drilling a hole in his jacket:" for his perfect skeleton was lying by the way-side not long ago.

Many armed Kaffirs were now in camp on pretence of seeing Hintza. They were ordered to lay down their weapons: but on their refusing, a company of Highlanders was suddenly called out, and ordered to prime and load. This hint had the desired effect; and the bundles of assegais were dropped in a moment. Hermanus, the interpreter, detected a plot to rescue Hintza, now detained as a hostage in honourable durance, until he should fulfil his compact. The camp was to have been attacked from without; and Hintza's suite would have risen within, and overpowered the guard. Nothing was said to Hintza; the sentries were quietly doubled; and two Kaffirs were shot approaching the camp in the middle of the night, to see if all was ready for the treacherous attempt, which now of course failed. The camp of the second division, over to which I galloped one day with Dr. Murray, had also been kept constantly on the alert, by the Kaffirs endeavouring to recover the captured cattle at night.

While thus encamped on the Dabakasee, we had some tremendous storms of rain, accompanied with vivid lightning, and the loudest thunder I almost ever heard: the echoes of which rolling up the valleys and round the hills, had a sublime and magnificent effect in the night. It was very wet and muddy on the Dabakasee camp-ground, owing to the frequent rain; and the cold was considerable. Besides which, I would entreat the compassionate reader to remember that we were in the country of lions, leopards, elephants, hippopotami, wild beasts of all kinds, and wild Kaffirs. But with a few rushes below our kaross at night, and a tin of hot tea, we made ourselves very cosey and comfortable; and we used to laugh when sipping our evening potation, whilst we read sentences like this from the colony: " Poor fellows, what they are suffering for their country!"

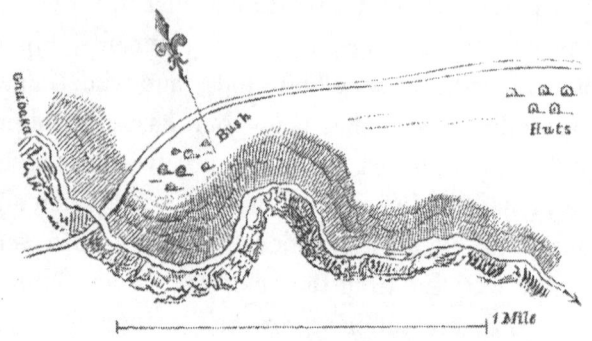

CHAPTER XXIII.

Flight of the Fingoes out of Kaffir-land—First Division marches to Bombanee—The Author's Child—Camp on the Kye—Cunning Baboons—Camp at Night—An important Day in the History of the Colony—The General proclaims the Kye to be the New Boundary—His Declaration to Hintza—The Kaffir King offers to show Colonel Smith the Colonial Cattle—Behaviour of Crieli—Colonel Smith, with Hintza, marches towards the Bashee—Short Review of a Change in Sir Benjamin D'Urban's Sentiments—The Policy of extending the Colony—Duplicity of Hintza—Fatal Effects of a Blue Morœa—Camp at Impotshana—The Valley of Death—The Construction of Warden's Post—Return of Colonel Smith's Corps—Its Proceedings—Death of Hintza—Colonel Smith crosses the Bashee, and marches towards the Umtata—Captain Bailie's Proceedings—Death of Major White—Alerts in Camp.

ON the 7th of May I witnessed a most interesting sight, and one which causes this day to be of great importance in the annals of South Africa. It was no less than the flight of the Fingo nation, seven-

DEPARTURE OF THE FINGOES.

teen thousand in number, from Amakosa bondage, guarded by British troops, and on their way across the Kye to find a new country under British protection.

The march of the second division presented an extraordinary spectacle. Passing near the first division, a mounted advanced-guard appeared; then long trains of white tilted wagons, including those of the missionaries and traders, lately saved, wound along the road and through the bushes; and next came many thousands of cattle. For not only were there ten thousand head which had been captured lately by the troops, but twenty thousand head of which the Fingoes had "spoiled the Egyptians" before the peace with Hintza. There were also numerous flocks of goats.

The Fingo males were all armed in readiness to defend their gains; and even the little boys had miniature assegais. It was not an easy task to get all the old, and infirm, and children along. Many, tired and foot-sore, tarried by the way-side; and though the wagons saved a great number, yet I fear that not a few helpless people were assegaied by the revengeful Kaffirs hanging on their rear.

The men, unlike Kaffirs, did what they could to assist the women, in carrying the children and household goods. But it was distressing to see how the poor females were overloaded. There was commonly a long roll of mat on their head; and about it were skins of millet, milk baskets, cooking utensils, and large wooden pestles for pounding grain : whilst, in the folds of their karosses behind, hung a child; and another, perhaps, was led in the hand. After the Fingoes, marched the mounted and dismounted men of the second division; and the rear-guard under Captain Forbes anxiously endeavoured to pick up the stragglers of the Amafingoe.

Certainly, this removal of the Fingoes from Amakosa slavery was a very happy event for these docile people; and a most severe blow for the proud Kaffirs, who disdained to work when they could get helots to till the ground, or to tend the herds. Nothing like this flight had been seen, perhaps, since the days of Moses; and it was a just retribution on Hintza, and on his people: who exercised the power of life and death over the Fingoes at will, and without appeal; and who regarded them in little higher estimation than beasts. Besides being a great benefit to the Fingoes themselves, their emancipation was likely to confer a great benefit on the colony. Located along its borders, under strict surveillance, they would be likely to assist in defending it well against their old oppressors; and would furnish also, what is so much required for the increasing prosperity of the Cape colony, additional hands for agricultural labour, herdsmen, and shepherds.

The head-quarter division likewise broke up on the 8th from its camp, and followed towards the Kye: halting among some rocks and bushes on a height called Bombanee; and having Hintza, Crieli, and Bookoo still with us. Their portraits were here carefully taken; and I made an ample oriental turban of striped shawl for the great chief, which he wore when he went to Colonel Smith. But, at other times, it adorned the head of the keeper of his greyhounds! Seventeen lean cattle were driven into camp, as part payment for the murder of Purcell; but were quickly driven out again, and the driver of them saluted rearwards for the mockery: Hintza having been overheard to direct the promised cattle to be driven towards the Stormberg and Bashee. I believe that a villainous attempt was made at this time to assassinate Colonel Smith. A Kaffir armed with a pair of pistols came to the colonel, and said he wished to be his servant, as he hated his own people. He was discovered to be Hintza's horse-stealer, and a great ruffian; and refusing to leave the tents, he was flogged out of camp.

We still marched westwards; and on the road saw a little Fingo boy, between three and four years old, sitting beside a kid, and thus left to the tender mercies of the wolves or Kaffirs. On questioning him where his people were, he replied, pointing beyond the hills, that his mother was "*ingapoo,*"—" over there." Probably overloaded, she had been obliged to leave him here; and I carried him off on my holster cover. He cried at first, but soon changed his tone on his mouth being filled with biscuit. He is now alive and well, and a child of great promise, under the care of very kind guardians; and as he is rather rotund, like a young Bacchus, he answers to the euphonous name of Gomesh, or Big Belly!

Some *friendly* Kaffirs fired at some of our officers as we were descending towards the bed of the Great Kye, and no wonder: for it must have been a most provoking thing for Hintza and his hordes, to see the removal of so many of the cattle of which they had audaciously made a prey, and which were most precious in their eyes. We reached the waters of the noble stream, and encamped on the eastern bank with high and bare precipices opposite to us.

CUNNING BABOONS.

> " Rushing on with mighty force,
> Rolls the Kye his glorious course;
> Flashing now with flaming red,
> O'er his jagged schistus bed;
> Now with current calm and wide,
> Sweeping round the mountain's side;
> Ever noble, proud, and free,
> Flowing in his majesty."

In places apparently inaccessible to human foot, we saw baboons with a flock of goats; and it was generally believed in camp that, like ants keeping the aphides insects for their milk, these cunning baboons kept the goats to supply their dairy. At night, the appearance of the camp was peculiar: its white tents and wagons in a dell enclosed by high walls of rock fringed with trees and shrubs, and the whole clearly revealed by the moon sailing above. There was deep silence around, save the rushing of the Kye; then baboons howled from their cliffs; and a fearful shriek of women was heard far up the river. This was afterwards ascertained to have proceeded from a party of Fingoes, who with their cattle had been surprised by some Kaffirs whilst asleep. Two of the Fingoes were assegaied, and their cattle carried off: but their countrymen followed in force, retook the cattle, and put to flight their enemies.

The 10th of May, 1835, is worthy of commemoration, as a day of great consequence in the history of the British possessions in South Africa. It was evident that some important step was to be taken: for in the morning the troops were drawn out to form a large parallelogram facing inwards; and the artillerymen stood beside their guns with lighted matches. Expectation was at its stretch; Hintza, his son, and his brother, with the counsellors, were brought from their tents; and stood in the midst, anticipating a crisis in their fate. They looked very grave, but showed no other symptoms of fear, than that of big drops of perspiration on their brows. The general and Colonel Smith stood facing the west; and there was profound silence, whilst a proclamation was read to the following effect:—

That in the months of December and January last, the chiefs of the Gaika and T'Slambie families, with the concurrence and consent of Hintza, paramount chief of the Amakosa, had, without just provocation or declaration of war, burst into his majesty's colony of the Cape of Good Hope; laid waste the eastern province, with fire and sword; and plundered and murdered the peaceful inhabitants. That with the troops of the king, his master, the general had defeated, chastised, and dispersed the border chiefs; had penetrated into

THE NEW BOUNDARY. 151

the country of Hintza; and had compelled him to sue for peace, and to ratify a treaty. That since it was absolutely necessary to remove the above treacherous and irreclaimable savages to a safer distance, to provide for the future security of the colony, the chiefs and people of the Gaikas and T'Slambies, as Macomo, Tyalie, Umhala, Eno, Botma, &c., were henceforth expelled beyond the Kye; and the new boundary of the colony was declared to begin at the Stormberg, proceed down the Ameva, and White Kye to its junction with the Great Kye, and from thence to the sea: thus adding a new territory to the colonial possessions of Great Britain, between the Keiskamma and the Kye rivers.

This proclamation having been made in the presence of the officers and soldiers of his majesty's forces, and of Hintza, his two relatives and counsellors, a royal salute of twenty-one guns was fired, the troops gave three cheers for King William IV., and were then dismissed to their tents.

His excellency then made this declaration to Hintza:—That twelve days ago, after an ineffectual resistance, Hintza had ratified a peace with the general; and of his own accord agreed to remain with his son and heir, Crieli, as hostages for its fulfilment. That his deportment then had apparently been so frank and honourable, that the general refrained from continuing further hostilities, which he had reserved to himself the power of doing until the first instalment of cattle and horses was paid, thus wishing to save the people of Hintza from the further scourge of war. But that in return for all this, Hintza had deceived the general throughout; had not fulfilled the stipulations of the treaty; and might therefore now be considered a prisoner of war, liable to be sent to Cape Town. Still, however, the general was inclined to believe his assertions, and that his presence in the midst of his people would better enable him to fulfil his solemn agreement. The general would not therefore remove him out of his own country : but as he (Hintza) himself proposed, would send him with a corps of British troops under Colonel Smith, the better to exercise his power as chief, and to collect the cattle and horses due. That Hintza therefore would be considered as a hostage, guide, and protector with Colonel Smith; while Crieli and Bookoo were detained as hostages with the general.

I watched the countenance of the great chief after this declaration; and there was an expression of exultation in it, as if he had succeeded in a favourite scheme. He then set himself busily about preparing to mount his horse, and took no notice of his son, who was now to be separated from him. The generous nature of Colonel Smith would not allow this; and taking Hintza up to Crieli, he made him shake hands and take leave. Crieli stooped down and tried to suppress his emotion, which Kaffirs are taught to do: but human nature was too strong for him; and when he held up his head, his eyes were filled with tears. It was impossible then not to feel much interested in him, or to abstain from a hope that he had not inherited the evil disposition of his parent.

Now the head-quarter camp was again a moving and a bustling scene. Pack-oxen were rapidly collected; and on them tents, provisions, and ammunition, were placed for Colonel Smith's corps of five hundred men: composed of mounted rifles, part of Field-commandant Groepe's Kat River legion, two companies of Highlanders, three of the provisional battalion, and half of the corps of guides. This corps marched again east- wards: whilst the general crossed the Kye, and entered the new province of Queen Adelaide.

Let us now shortly review the change which had taken place in the sentiments of Sir Benjamin D'Urban, with regard to the Kaffirs. Before he had come into personal contact with them, and before he had visited the frontier, he knew that they were a rude and a barbarous people; but at the same time he believed, that under the system of border policy they had been as much "sinned against as sinning." His excellency entertained the most benevolent views towards the native tribes generally: but all that he witnessed when he came to Graham's Town, the ferocious murders and heartless devastation which the savages had committed, and the continual distress of ruined men, widows, and orphans, taught him the real character of the Kaffir tribes. He gained further a personal knowledge, during the progress of the war, of their ferocity and treachery; and this experience finally dictated to him a necessity for a totally different line of policy, from that which he had desired and projected.

Moved by powerful and irresistible reasons, and feeling all the heavy responsibility which he incurred, without means of previous reference to higher authority, his excellency extended his majesty's colony to the Kye: thus adding seven thousand square miles of fertile country, originally Hottentot, and now fairly forfeited by the enemy, to the king's dominions. This was the only measure which could promise to repay the expenses of a war, on the part of the British most unwillingly undertaken: the only means of providing security for the future against the savage natives of South Africa, by fixing a safe and defensible boundary for the colony.

For years past, no frontier could be so insecure as the eastern one of the colony of the Cape. The lines of the Fish and Keiskamma rivers passed through woods and ravines admirably fitted for the lurking-place of the savage, from which he could at any time with safety to himself spring on his prey, and with the greatest facility eventually secure it. If these lines had been continued, the feeling of insecurity was such on the frontier, that Albany and Somerset, after the recent severe blow, would have been abandoned by the inhabitants, and would have relapsed into their former desolation. The line of the Buffalo was little better: for the fastnesses of wood and mountain, at its upper part, covered many miles of country, the vicinity of which never would have been safe. His excellency was therefore obliged to go on to the Kye: the steep banks of which river, the few passes or drifts, and there being no dense bush about it, or for miles on either side of it, to conceal an enemy, fitted it by nature for defence;

required fewer troops and fortifications; and besides was fifty miles shorter than the other proposed lines of frontier, from the trending of the coast to the northward.

It would have been neither unduly harsh nor severe to have compelled the Gaikas and T'Slambies, after wantonly provoking a war and still refusing submission, to live on the eastern side of the Kye: for both towards the Stormberg and Natal, there are thousands of square miles of very fertile and well-watered country *without a single inhabitant.* Besides, it was intended that the Tambookies and Fingoes, who were far better neighbours than the Amakosas, should have taken the place of the latter: so that there would have been no crowding of the Gaikas and T'Slambies on the other tribes beyond the Kye. The declaration of expulsion was politic, in so far as it tended to humble the people against whom it was made; its effects will afterwards be shown.

Hintza had, after much urging, ostensibly fulfilled an article of the treaty when he was a perfectly free agent at the Izolo, by sending messengers as paramount chief to the borderers, still in arms, desiring them to submit, and to throw themselves on the mercy of the British. But it was now discovered that this message was deprived of all its power, by a private intimation of Hintza to Macomo, Tyalie, &c., "to take care of themselves, for that he was a prisoner:" which was a gross falsehood.

It has thus been seen that, during the whole course of the negotiations and transactions with this savage chief, he never acted otherwise than with the greatest duplicity and bad faith; and only in the single instance of his stopping the massacre of the Fingoes, when under the influence of fear for the consequences to himself, did he ever act otherwise: but the day of retribution was at hand.

On leaving the bed of the Kye we discovered, rather late, the dangerous situation in which we had been. There is a *blaauw tulp*, or pale blue *morœa*, which grows there in considerable abundance; and this, when other vegetation is scanty, the cattle devour, with fatal effect to themselves. As we ascended the heights, we passed ox after ox in the agonies of death; and we lost by the poison plant, which inflamed and swelled their insides, at least a hundred head of cattle. Some Fingoes also died from eating the tainted flesh. We passed a high and isolated knoll, overlooking the deep bed of the Kye, with its shrubby islets, and all the country round: this was selected as the site of a permanent work, to be called Smith's Tower. A large white bird on a pool of the river, recalled to my recollection these beautiful lines :

> "Low bend the bulrushes
> In the water bright;
> Up the swan comes sailing
> Plumy all and white:
> Like a ship at anchor,
> Now he lies at rest;
> And little waves seem daintily
> To play about his breast."

We then encamped on the banks of a small stream called the Impotshana, near to a long ravine three hundred feet deep, with precipitous sides which almost approached each other, throwing the bottom, filled with trees, into deep gloom. It became a "valley of death:" for into it were hurled seventy oxen and horses which died here. The Impotshana glen was soon a favourite haunt of the grey vulture. We were five or six miles from the Kye, and on a fine commanding site. His excellency accordingly selected this for the first military post of occupation, to secure possession of the new territory. Colonel Thompson, Major Michell, and myself, were desired to lay out the work: accordingly, a square redoubt of sixty yards each face, enclosing a circular cattle

CONSTRUCTION OF WARDEN'S POST. 159

kraal and stables for forty horses, with a ditch and abattis outside, and thorn fence fifty yards distant, out of assegai range, were all speedily traced; and with jackets off, and working parties of pick, shovel, and hatchet men, we set to vigorously to complete the work. Here, in a general order, the new territory was named "the province of Queen Adelaide." Three or four days had elapsed, and the redoubt was finished, with beehive huts for the men and officers who were to occupy "Warden's Post;" and two barbettes for guns to point into and command the kloofs around: when Colonel Smith's corps, with more Fingoes and cattle, joined us from Hintza's country, bringing the following singular intelligence.

On the morning of the 10th of May, after his excellency the commander-in-chief had with due ceremony proclaimed the future boundary of the colony, the chief of the staff, with his mixed force of five hundred men, marched from the eastern boundary of the Kye, accompanied by Hintza, his favourite counsellor Umteenee, and three or four other attendants; and directed their course towards the Bashee.

Hintza, still viewed in the light of a hostage, had been treated with every kindness and respect during his residence in his excellency's camp;

had been allowed to retain his arms and horses; and had now, at his own request, been taken with Colonel Smith's force, the better to enable him, as he said, to fulfil the principal articles of the treaty, and recover the colonial cattle and horses.

The great chief acknowledged the consideration with which he had been treated in camp; and, in order that there might be no misunderstanding as to his position on the present occasion, on the first day's march, as he rode along with the chief of the staff, at the head of the column, followed by the guides to whose charge he was expressly confided, Colonel Smith said to him, "I am responsible to my king and to the general for the safe custody of the great chief. You say you are sensible of our kindness towards you, and call yourself my son; you requested that the troops under my command should accompany you, to enable you to fulfil the treaty of peace into which you have entered with the governor; you voluntarily placed yourself in our hands as a hostage, therefore you are to look upon me as having full power over you; and if you should now attempt to deceive us, and *endeavour to make your escape, you will assuredly be shot.* My nation is at peace with your people, though still at war with the Gaikas and T'Slambies; and if your people behave peaceably, and will bring in the cattle, I will retain the bullocks, and return the cows and calves." Hintza expressed himself quite satisfied with all this; and said he came to fulfil the treaty, and not to make his escape, or else he would not have left his son in our hands. Having been again warned, Hintza rode on with the colonel; and they bivouacked on the Gona. A circumstance, however, which occurred at the first halt, rather awakened suspicion. Some Kaffirs, with a few head of cattle, approached to speak to the great chief; he sent out one of his people on horseback, on pretence of bringing them in; but the messenger and the others all disappeared and could no where be seen.

Next day, the march was continued to the Guaningee. Here Hintza became very communicative, saying, "We are not far from the cattle now: halt here a short time, and march again at midnight." They did so; and on the morning of the 12th, left a level and open country for one which was a succession of abrupt ridges, with steep and wooded ascents. At this spot the spoor of cattle was numerous and recent. The great chief became uneasy, and said, "What have the cattle done, that you want them; and why must I deprive my people of them?" The colonel answered, "Seven thousand of our people are now starving through the conduct of your people towards them; you know that perfectly well: we don't want your people's cattle; we want our own; and we are resolved to have them." The great chief now fell for a short time to the rear, and was seen to dismount and tie a small knot of "lucky grass" in his necklace; and rejoining the colonel he said, in high spirits, "See how my people treat me; they drive the cattle off in spite of me: but let me now send Umteenee forward, to tell my people not to drive them off; and that only the colonial cattle will be taken." This proposal appeared so reasonable, and seemed to afford such a good prospect of attaining the desired object, that the chief of the staff consented to Umteenee and an attendant leaving the escort, on promise of returning at night. They immediately went off at full gallop; and Hintza, with great delight, but with a lurking devil in his eye, exclaimed, "Now we need not go to the Bashee on the Gnabacka: you will get more cattle than you can drive."

The day was bright and clear; and the troops marched cheerfully on, and reached the Gnabacka about noon. Here it was seen that the great spoor of cattle divided into two branches: the one to the left crossing a high mountain; and the other leading over the river, and up a narrow cattle-path on the opposite steep and wooded bank. Hintza said, " There is no use in following the spoor up the mountain: let us cross the river and follow the other." The column accordingly forded the river, the banks of which were deep and rugged with precipice and bush; and commenced the ascent on the eastern side.

On this day's march it was remarked, that Hintza rode for the first time a very powerful bright bay horse: of which he seemed to be very careful, dismounting and leading him up and down inequalities in the road. Colonel Smith, his light and sinewy form in oil-skin chako and blue jacket, rode up the steep ascent at the head of the troops, followed by Hintza leading his horse; and after them the guides and the rest of the cavalry leading theirs. The colonel had nearly reached the open country at the summit, when he heard a cry of " Hintza!" behind him; and at the same moment the great chief passed him: he and two of his followers having suddenly thrown themselves on their sheep-skin saddles. The colonel called to Hintza to stop, and presented a pistol. The great chief, unable to penetrate the bush by the road side, returned to the only path, smiling;

which made the colonel, for a moment, ashamed of his suspicions. The chief of the staff then turned round to watch the troops ascending the defile, when he heard another cry; and looking for Hintza, he saw him galloping off across the plain at full speed, followed by the lieutenant of the guides, George Southey, an active, light-made, and good-looking young man, William Southey, and William Shaw. The colonel, spurring his horse violently, strove to overtake Hintza; and the fleet bay soon left the three guides far in the rear. Hintza urged on his long-tailed charger at full speed; whilst the colonel, unable to stop the great chief, drew a pistol and snapped it at him: it missed fire; his second pistol also failed him; and he then struck Hintza on the back of the head with the but. The great chief turned round, and grinned in derision. The colonel then threw his pistol after him, which struck him; and redoubling his efforts, after a hard gallop of a mile, succeeded in closing with the athletic chief, who retained his assegais. Twisting his hand into the collar of Hintza's leopard-skin mantle, and assisting the effort with the weight of his horse, the colonel dragged the Kaffir king with violence to the ground: he fell heavily, with a look of mingled rage and despair. Hintza quickly sprang to his feet; drew the *izaka*, or man-killer assegai with barbed neck, from the bundle of javelins; and launched it after the colonel. It fell short: the colonel's horse having run away with him for some distance towards a few huts. Hintza then continued his flight on foot, towards the bed of the river on the right.

During this time George Southey was gaining ground; and after Hintza fell, he sprang from his horse, and running toward the chief, called to him in the Kaffir language to stop, or he would shoot him. Hintza looked round as he ran, and took no farther notice. Southey then fired, and wounded him in the leg. Hintza fell on his hands, but got up again, and ran swiftly down the hill. By this time Colonel Smith had managed to stop his horse, and returned near to the spot where Southey was: who again called out to the great chief to stop, but he would not; and Colonel Smith then ordered Southey to fire a second time. He did so, when Hintza was two hundred yards from him. Hintza fell: but, strange to say, he got up again; kept on the same course down the hill; and disappeared in the bush skirting the river's bank. Lieutenant Balfour, the colonel's aide-de-camp, had galloped to intercept Hintza, but failed. Some of the cavalry, who had mounted quickly and come up with shouts of impatience, fired into the bush, but without effect. Southey, having speedily reloaded, scrambled with Lieutenant Balfour down a steep descent of the Gnabacka; Southey going up the stream, and Balfour down it, searching for Hintza: no one else was near. They had each proceeded some distance, when Southey heard an assegai touch the stone on which he stood: quickly looking about him, he saw a Kaffir head, and an assegai uplifted close beside him; he stepped back a pace for room, fired, and shot Hintza through the head. He fell into the water quite dead. Southey then took, as " spolia opima," the assegais and brass belt of the great chief, and returned to Colonel Smith, who gave Southey Hintza's horse.

The body of the Kaffir king was stripped of its ornaments, but not of the kaross; and left on the bank of the river. It was intended to have buried it: but time would not permit; and the bugle sounded the assembly and march. It was pretty evident that Hintza had expected the co-operation of an ambuscade, which was a little too late to assist him. Kaffirs were soon seen in the bush near his dead body. Umteenee, who had gone off in the morning, saw the whole transaction from a neighbouring rock out of reach: whilst, of the two who fled with Hintza, one was shot by two of the provisional Hottentots to the right of the column; and the other, " our friend with the turban," got clear off.

Thus fell the paramount chief of the Amakosa, a victim to the treachery and perfidy of his own character : having, instead of assisting Colonel Smith to recover the colonial cattle, as he had engaged to do, tried every means to mislead him, and to take him to districts where the cattle had been driven off by his own orders. His attempt at escape was a bold enterprise; and he showed considerable intrepidity and obstinacy on the occasion: but as it was made in defiance of a solemn warning of the consequences, he owed his end to himself alone, and met the reward he so richly deserved.

The march was continued in pursuit of the cattle, but without guides to direct the chief of the staff where to find it. The column soon reached the Bashee, and saw on the eastern banks of the beautiful and wide-flowing river, several herds belonging to the people of Hintza, whose authority extended along the coast to the Umtata. Colonel Smith crossed with the cavalry in the face of numerous bodies of the enemy; captured many head of fine cattle, some of which were colonial;

and encamped on the left bank. Fingoes came in for protection: one of whom, a great witch, was a good wagon-load, so enormous was her size. The troops had accomplished, in three days from the Kye, a journey of eighty miles, which is capital marching. Captain Ross, Cape mounted rifles, was left on the Bashee with a detachment, in charge of the jaded horses and captured cattle; Captain Bailie was ordered to sweep down with his company of Hottentots between the Kocha and Bashee, and then rejoin the camp; whilst at three o'clock A. M. on the 13th, Colonel Smith, with the rest of the force, pushed onwards in the direction of the Umtata.

They reached the Kocha, twenty miles distant; saw most beautiful pasture, from which the cattle were driven off in all directions; and there being no chance of securing any more, the colonel accordingly retraced his steps, after having seen the bed of the Umtata. Kaffirs then collected in great numbers, and made a demonstration to intercept the force; they were allowed to come very near before they were fired at; they then followed with war cries; and ambuscades were laid for them among the long grass by the way side: by which means Lieutenant Charles Bailie, with a party of the rear-guard, destroyed a number of them. Fourteen were tumbled over on the road in one heap, but scrambled off on their hands and knees. Then some Fingoes, who had been attached to the column, were marked out for the vengeance of the Kaffirs. Lieutenant Bailie again pushed to the rear with some of his Hottentots behind the Fingo shields: the Kaffirs boldly advanced, but were confounded and dispersed with an unexpected volley.

Captain Bailie, in the mean time, passed with his detachment through a most rich and fertile country; and as they approached the well-constructed kraals, they were saluted with the crowing of cocks. The deserted houses were full of corn and milk; and one old mad woman only was found. In riding through the corn, it was higher than man and horse. The detachment arrived within a mile of the sea, and was reluctantly obliged to return at two o'clock P. M., without looking into some valleys where there might have been cattle: Colonel Smith's instructions to Captain Bailie being positive that he should rejoin him on the same night. The Kaffirs followed the detachment, and called out from behind the bushes, " What do you seek here? There is none of your cattle among us: they were all sent over the Umtata, four days ago, by Hintza's orders. We won't let you back alive." The Kaffirs then endeavoured to surround and destroy the detachment on the banks of the Bashee. The Hottentots, "whose blood was up," pursued some of them to a kraal, and saw two men enter a hut, who refused to surrender. The hut was set on fire; one rushed out, and was shot getting over a fence; and the other, assegai in hand, died nobly at the door. Captain Bailie's detachment, after marching from three in the morning, returned safe at eleven o'clock P. M. Highlanders could not have done more than these active Hottentots.

It is now our painful duty to relate a great calamity which at this time befel the eastern province of the Cape of Good Hope, in the death of one of the most public-spirited and intelligent of the settlers,—Major T. C. White, assistant quarter-master-general of the burgher force. The abilities of Major White were of a high class: he was an excellent scholar and surveyor; his private character was most honourable and correct; and he was a very warm friend. He set a most excellent example to the community amongst which he had placed himself, as a practical sheep-farmer, agriculturist, and grower of vines. His garden and vineyard have been already described;

and he conferred great benefits on the colony generally, by introducing from abroad wheats of various kinds, to withstand rust. In every public improvement he took the lead; and above all, he was a most powerful advocate for his most shamefully abused fellow-colonists, who deeply felt and will long deplore their irreparable loss.

On the 13th of May, Major White, anxious to add to his carefully constructed map of the country through which the troops had passed since the commencement of the war, remained with Captain Ross's detachment on the banks of the Bashee. After breakfast, he said to Captain Ross, "As the Kaffirs seem to be collecting, it would perhaps be as well to get the men under arms. I am going to the top of this hill above the camp, for a short time, to sketch the country, and will be back soon." Captain Ross and Mr. Cæsar Andrews, Colonel Smith's secretary and interpreter, tried to dissuade him from running the risk; but his desire to add to his sketch was irresistible: besides, he had had several escapes before, and he despised the Kaffirs too much for his own safety. Accordingly Major White, who was a man of middle size, in the prime of life, and in the enjoyment of vigorous health, with an old Hottentot corporal and three men of the mounted rifles, rode up the hill and disappeared from the view of those in camp. Shortly afterwards shots were heard; and the three troopers were seen running down the hill towards the camp. They narrated as follows:—The major had placed them at different points of observation; and with the corporal beside him, and his surveying-table before him, he was looking down a *crantz*, or precipice; when a dozen Kaffirs crept on him from the bush and long grass, threw an assegai from behind through his back, and ran up and finished their work. They also stabbed the corporal through the heart; and then collected the horses. The three videttes, unable to render any assistance, fired off their pieces and retreated.

A party of the rifles was sent up to bring down the bodies. They found them stripped and bloody; and the double-barrelled guns, and the major's gold chronometer, surveying-instruments, and map carried off. Tying the bodies on horses, they brought them into camp. They were buried, wrapped in thatch, in graves dug with bayonets, under a retired bush on the banks of the Bashee; and grass was strewed over the remains to conceal them from Kaffir insult. Thus had Hintza's Kaffirs an opportunity of revenging themselves for the loss of their great chief, by cutting off one who could have been less spared than any colonist in South Africa.

"Thus yields the cedar to the axe's edge,
Whose arms gave shelter to the princely eagle,
And kept low shrubs from Winter's powerful wind."

In the face of thousands of armed Kaffirs on the neighbouring heights, who did not venture to attack him, Colonel Smith again crossed the Bashee, and rejoined his excellency: thus having given another proof of his skill and activity; and the troops of their determined spirit and powers of endurance. They marched two hundred and eighteen miles in seven days; and brought with them a thousand Fingoes, rescued from destruction, and three thousand head of cattle, the fruits of their bold inroad.

Besides the commander of the expedition, the following officers were thanked in general orders: Captains Murray and Lacy, 72nd regiment; Crause, Bailie, and Gilfillan, 1st provisional battalion; Ross, Cape mounted rifles; Lieut. Oliver, assistant quarter-master-general; Lieut. C. Bailie, 1st provisional battalion; Lieut. Balfour, aide-de-camp; Mr. Cæsar Andrews, secretary and interpreter; Assistant-surgeon Ford, 72nd regiment; Field-commandant Groepe, Kat River legion;

and Mr. Southey, of the corps of guides. His excellency also expressed how severely he felt the loss of Major White.

During the progress of the field-work at the Impotshana, the Kaffirs were continually hovering about and keeping us on the alert. Thus, one morning a wagon driver's son ran into camp with assegai wounds in his face; a Kaffir having thrust at him as he went to drive out a span of oxen to graze, within two hundred yards of the camp. When shots were fired by the sentries at night, Captain Beresford and myself had generally a race to see what was the occasion of them, and report to the general accordingly. Kaffirs used to steal up singly from the ravine to spy; or several together have been watched creeping up to horses and cutting their halters, before they were fired at. One, perhaps with worse intent, got within twenty yards of the general's tent; but a Hottentot sentry lying on the grass saw him between the sky and the ground, and shot him.

One night there was a volley from the picket of the 72nd regiment; and the bugle sounded "the turn out." I ran up to the picket to see what was the matter; and found the canny Scot, whose shot the rest had followed, lying beside a

ALERTS IN CAMP. 175

bush, and preparing to give the enemy another salute. "What did you fire at?" I asked. "I dinna weel ken what it was, sir; but it was either a coo, or a caaf, or a man on horseback!"

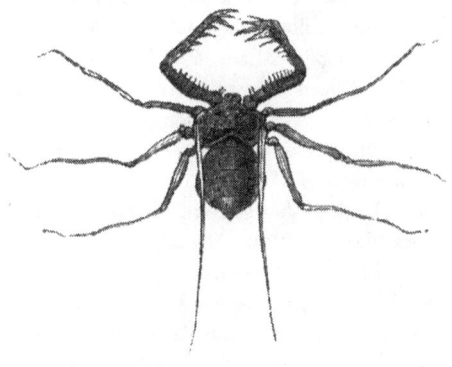

Spider of the Impotshana.

CHAPTER XXIV.

Treaty with Crieli—Bookoo and Kinki retained as Hostages—Kaffir Characteristic—The Second Division creditably concludes its Services—Colonel England—Gallantry of the Bowkers—Mr. Collett again Attacked—The Third and Fourth Divisions—The Queen Regent of the Gaikas—Mysterious Occurrence—Lieut. Granett's Mission to Macomo and Tyalie—They meet Major Cox—The General's Message—The War continues—Capture of Macomo's Horses and Recapture of Prize Cattle—Death of Jan Greyling—Head-Quarter Division marches from Warden's Post—Death's Doings—Canine Fidelity—The Heights of Wellington—Rapid Construction of Fort Wellington—The Adelaide Spice Tree—Glen Aberdeen and the Valley of Peel—King William's Town—Buffalo River—Captain Beresford sent to England with Despatches—Hostages attempt to Escape—Jock Maclaughlin "no sae saaft"—Honourable Conveyance of Prisoners—Lieut. Williams, R. E.—Construction of Forts Hill, Hardinge, Beresford, Murray, and White—Herbert Taylor's Hill—Botany of the Buffalo—The Lictor Insect—Expedition to clear the Country towards the Mouth of the Buffalo—The Surveyor-General—The Curiosity Hunter—Expedition to clear the Buffalo Mountains—Kaffirs harass the Fingoes—Expedition to clear the Banks of the Keiskamma.—Fatal Accident.

CRIELI, now the paramount chief of the Amakosa, and Bookoo his uncle, were still hostages in the hands of the British general for the fulfilment of Hintza's treaty. Deeming, however, the presence of Crieli absolutely necessary among his people, who, while without a leader, might be attacked and scattered by the neighbouring tribes; and being still anxious, notwithstanding their misdeeds, to spare them from destruction; the general determined on sending back Crieli to his country: first, in due ceremony, making with him a treaty to this effect:

Crieli engaged to fulfil the unexecuted treaty of his father Hintza, on which peace was declared to exist between the British and his people. He acknowledged the Kye to be the new boundary of the colony, and promised to respect it; as the British engaged to respect his territory. He expressed his willingness to give an asylum in his country to the Gaikas and T'Slambies; and he promised that he would endeavour to prevent their crossing the Kye westwards in future, for the purpose of plundering the colony. Crieli further solemnly engaged not to allow any hostilities to be carried on against the Tambookies of Vodana; and if they should wish to leave their present country, he bound himself to permit them to pass through his territory in safety, and to enter the colony.

This having been done, on the 19th of May, in presence of Crieli and his relatives, Bookoo and Fadana, and the counsellors, Suto, Nontso, and Kinki; and the treaty having been fully explained to, and been understood by Crieli, and having been ratified by him; he was dismissed with Fadana, Suto, and Nontso, and with handsome presents for himself and his mother Nomsa, consisting of a horse, cloth, cutlery, beads, &c. Captain Warden, with a guard of honour, conducted Crieli and his suite to the Kye: on which the young chief expressed his "great satisfaction at the arrangement just concluded; and at the kindness and attention with which he had been treated during his residence at head-quarters."

The commander-in-chief, however, in thus dismissing Crieli to take possession of his inheritance, and concluding with him the above treaty of peace, judged it necessary to detain Bookoo, with the counsellor of the latter, Kinki, as hostages for the fulfilment of the treaty of the 30th of April last, and according to one of its stipulations: on hearing which determination of his excellency, Bookoo's countenance fell. He said nothing, but seemed oppressed with grief and care. Poor old rogue!

A Kaffir characteristic may here be given.

Crieli's counsellor, Suto, was a well-made, intelligent, and even amiable man in appearance; had come into camp at the Izolo to arrange about Hintza's conference with the general; had been variously and actively employed by the late great chief; and had driven in sundry head of cattle lately, in part fulfilment of the treaty. He arrived in camp after Colonel Smith, but from an opposite direction; and his excellency sent for him to communicate to him the death of Hintza, in order that he might disclose it in a proper manner to Crieli and Bookoo.

Suto seated himself on the ground in the general's tent; and Mr. Shepstone, the interpreter, went over the whole of the circumstances attending the death of Hintza. Yet, though Suto heard the detail for the first time, he expressed no sort of surprise: but shortly after the narrative had commenced, feeling a thorn in his foot, he drew out a knife from his buck-skin bag; took his sole in his hand; and cut away at it for some time, giving a low "*uh!*" of assent occasionally. After he had extracted the thorn, and the interpreter had finished, the general dismissed Suto to communicate the manner of Hintza's death to his son and brother in a neighbouring tent: but his excellency, fearing from Suto's seeming inattention that it would not be properly conveyed, desired Mr. Shepstone to go with him and hear what he said. He did so; and Suto repeated, word for word, what had been told him: at which also neither Crieli nor Bookoo seemed much surprised. But so it is with Kaffirs generally: they will receive a long message; travel a couple of hundred miles; and deliver it correctly at the end of their journey; making neither mark nor symbol to assist their wonderful memories.

Colonel Somerset, with the second division, had succeeded in conveying in safety across the Keiskamma the missionaries and traders; also the Fingo nation; and likewise, though not without some skirmishing, the captured cattle, which were then distributed and disposed of according to his instructions. At the conclusion of this service, the commander-in-chief expressed his approbation and thanks for the manner in which Colonel Somerset had fulfilled this important duty. The general also thanked the officers and men of the second division, for the unwearied care with which they had complied with the commandant's orders; particularly Captain Forbes, who commanded the rear-guard during the whole march. Also Field-commandants Lindé, Rademayer, Van Rooyen, and Dreyer; deputy-assistant commissary-general Trotter; and Dr. Morgan.

The second division being now no longer required for the invasion of Kaffir-land, it was broken up: the officers employed in it resuming the duties which they had previously been fulfilling; and the burgher force of Swellendam, Albany, Uitenhage, and George,—with the exception of a small part,—returning for the present to their respective homes, with thanks for their zeal, gallantry, and good service. Colonel Somerset resumed the command of the troops in Albany and Somerset; and Colonel England, that of the 75th regiment. To Colonel England the commander-in-chief desired to express his thanks, for the great care and attention with which he had performed the duty of commanding the first line of defence, during the absence of the invading force.

Small parties of Kaffirs had stolen into the colony and had disturbed the farmers, who were now gradually returning to their lands: but no large body had ventured to cross the Fish River. Some white men and Hottentots were killed in Albany, in the month of May, by imprudently exposing themselves; and Mr. Bowker and his brave sons made a gallant defence at one of their farms on the

Kleinemond River. One evening, there burst into their cattle-kraal from twenty-five to thirty Kaffirs: one of whom had his thigh immediately broken with a spring-gun set in the kraal. This spring-gun did good service on two or three occasions, and was set opposite a false entrance to the kraal. It consisted of an old gun-barrel with a percussion cap, which could take no injury from exposure to all weathers; and the log of wood in which the barrel was fixed traversed on a swivel. The cap was acted upon by a bit of iron hoop, which was fastened by a string to one of the rails of the false entrance. The discharge of the gun gave the alarm; and the Bowkers and their Hottentot servants turned out and fought the Kaffirs. The latter threw many assegais, and wounded two of the Hottentots, before they ran off to the bush: but some of the defeated savages died of their wounds. The Kaffir with his thigh broken in the kraal, threw assegais to the last; and cheered on the others, like a certain wounded Highland piper.

Mr. Collett of the Koonap was now again attacked. Hearing a noise at his kraal, he ran out with his servants to save a few head of cattle which he had collected there; and on returning to the house, he found Kaffirs inside and out. They retreated by the back-door, and had a volley of heavy shot poured into them: but managed to get away, after killing a Mrs. Trollip, and wounding her child inside the house. The fatal assegai was not aimed at her, but at her husband who was sitting with her. The Kaffirs afterwards expressed their vexation at having killed this woman: but next night they carried off sixteen oxen and cows, the last of Mr. Collett's stock; whose determined resolution to defend his property was unfortunately on this, and on former occasions, unavailing.

The third and fourth divisions had been employed harassing the enemy in their fastnesses in the Amatola. The fourth was then broken up; two-fifths of it were attached to the third division; and the remaining three-fifths to the first or head-quarter division. Nothing extraordinary had occurred westwards, until, on the 11th of May, Hintza's message to the border-chiefs brought out Suta, the great widow of Gaika. At her request, she was conveyed in a wagon to Major Cox's camp, under T'Slambie's Kop, from her retreat in the mountains: with the wish, as she said, to have an interview regarding her "children," or the tribes subject to her late husband. Suta and eleven female attendants were accommodated with tents in camp, and received every attention from Major Cox. The Kaffir ladies said, that they would have come out before, but that a staff-officer had on one occasion in the mountains taken liberties with a " maid of honour ; " and that they were therefore afraid to leave the bush. We never could get at the truth of this story; and can only hope that the jesuits of the anti-colonial party will not make a handle of it at home, to the ruination of our characters.

The queen-mother, forty years of age, is a very fair Tambookie; has high cheek bones, and an agreeably plump person; and sometimes wears European clothes, with a striped silk handkerchief about her head. At other times she is arrayed in fine skins, with a splendid blue and white head-dress of buck-skins covered with beads. Suta is fond of a pipe of canaster; and cried when she saw her wagon driven by an old friend and favourite of hers, Jeffries, an Englishman.

On the 12th, Suta sent a message to Macomo and Tyalie, that they must come out and hear a message from the governor through Major Cox. Next day they sent to say that they were ready. Lieutenant Granett, 98th regiment, was accordingly despatched with two dragoons, one of whom was an interpreter, to the foot of T'Slambie's

Kop; and was there told by some Kaffirs in the bush, that the chiefs were at the top of the mountain. Although he was unarmed, Lieutenant Granett immediately passed up the hill, and through the bush, with the interpreter; and soon found himself in the midst of hundreds of armed Kaffirs. Macomo and Tyalie came up to him and saluted him; they talked of some officers whom they knew, of the war, and of their own condition; and added that they would not come out of the bush, until they had spoken to the great mother. Lieutenant Granett then handed Macomo his flask of liquor, from which he took a hearty draught, a *waaly waught:* although he had *subscribed* to a temperance society at the Kat River. Poor man! there was no one now faithful enough to warn him of his error.

The emissary returned to camp, and Suta to the bush. But Major Cox was determined to see the chiefs, and to try by negotiation, as he had been instructed, to finish the war. He accordingly, unarmed, left the camp with Lieutenant Granett and two dragoons; rode to the Intabakandoda Bush; and met the chiefs in conference. They formed a semicircle of warriors about him, and as an old friend, received him with every demonstration of respect. The governor's message was:—That the chiefs should come into Major Cox's camp on a solemn pledge of personal safety; that they should give up their arms, and be at his excellency's disposal; and that they should also give up Suta, and Sandilli, the young heir of the Amakosa between the Kye and the Keiskamma. Their cattle was not demanded. Peace would then be made with the Gaikas and T'Slambies.

The chiefs said that they would have agreed to these terms, if they had not received a private intimation from Hintza not to surrender; for that he had been made a prisoner at the Izolo: which was false, as formerly stated. But the truth is, that besides Hintza, the border-chiefs had secret advisers *within the colony*: white men, traitors, in short, who told them that there was a party in their favour on the western side of the Keiskamma, and who urged them to hold out.

The negotiation was therefore soon at an end; and hostilities recommenced. Patrols entered the bush, came up with the Kaffir rear-guard, and captured five of Macomo's horses; and among them his own charger, saddled and bridled, and in excellent condition. But Lieutenant Bissett, with thirty Hottentots, after securing eight hundred head of cattle, was attacked by some hundred Kaffirs; obliged to fight his way through them; and compelled to abandon the prize cattle. Field-cornet Jan Greyling, whose father had been killed by the Kaffirs; who himself had long suffered by their continued plunderings; and who had done excellent service in the war; was destroyed on his way home to the Tarka at some Kaffir huts. A single savage rushed out upon him and assegaied him; but Greyling's companion revenged his death, by instantly shooting the Kaffir.

On the 20th of May, the entrenched camp on the Impotshana, for the reception of the first post of occupation of the new province, having been completed, detachments of artillery, cavalry, and infantry were placed in it, under the command of Captain Warden, Cape mounted rifles; and the commander-in-chief moved westwards with the remainder of the head-quarter division. A hamlet of Fingoes was formed near Warden's Post, to be of assistance to the troops in various ways.

On the road, we saw traces of the removal of the Fingoes, in the shape of dead bodies of men and bullocks, torn karosses, mats, baskets, &c. Men who have been long familiar with death, and have seen his approach in many and various shapes, ought to be well hardened to the "fell destroyer:" but that heart must be very callous indeed, which, even after a long probation, can remain unmoved near the remains of those "who may have gloried in their strength, and whose bones were full of marrow," but have now been suddenly and violently cut off. We were wearied and distressed with seeing stretched on the field, in many strange attitudes of final agony, the naked corse from which the impure vulture would rise on heavy wing, and with jealous eye:—but lest we should provoke our readers' disgust toward ourselves by exciting the same pain in descriptions, we shall, as much as possible, spare such details for the future; and shall only here add that, on this march, we witnessed a painfully interesting example of fidelity even to the death!

The entire body of a Kaffir, who had been shot at least a week, probably when hanging on the rear of the retreating Fingoes, lay a little off the road, wrapped in its kaross; neither vulture nor hyena had touched this body; and we saw the cause of their forbearance on approaching it. A small yellowish dog, with a black muzzle, lank with famine, rose from its dead master's breast, where it kept watch, and angrily snarled defiance at every intruder. It was impossible to remove the dog for the purpose of saving it from starvation, until some Hottentots threw a noose of hide round its neck and dragged it off.

We reached the Gonubee Hill, now distinguished by the name of the "Heights of Wellington," after a seventeen miles' march; and immediately after a hasty repast, his excellency directed a post of communication to be traced out and constructed the same day, below the principal summit. Here we were again hard at work, and as busy as bees. As we stand on no ceremony about dirtying our fingers, and delight in the labours of our crest—the beaver, we were soon covered up to our knees and elbows with sand and dust. Nor is this mentioned boastfully, but only as a hint to younger officers, who may depend upon always getting their men to work vigorously if they set them an example, *and are sparing of abuse*. A circular work of an hundred feet in diameter, with a parapet of sods, six feet high, having six feet of base and three of crest, with a good ditch round it, was commenced in the morning and completed in the evening.

A detachment of böers, rather surprised at such rapid movements, was sent down in " double quick" time to the bush, and desired to cut boughs for abattis; and two strong fences were picketed down round the work, one on the counterscarp of the ditch, and the other out of assegai range. Next day, a little more time having been given, a raised sentry-box, or pulpit, was placed in the centre of the work to command the approaches to it; and was thus constructed. Four stout trees were cut to the length of twenty-one feet; let into the ground, eight feet apart; and left eighteen feet above ground. At the height of twelve feet, there was a platform of straight boughs bound to the four posts by thongs of leather; on which one or more sentries were to stand, defended from the weather by a light roof, and from bullets or assegais by hide or other side screens. The advantage of the raised sentry-box was afterwards proved here; and for cattle-kraals, placed either at the entrance or in the centre, it is a good defence.

Under the Gonubee Hill, Dr. Murray found the *fugara armata*, and named it "the Adelaide spice-tree." It is elegant, but not large; its branches are thorny, like those of almost every tree in Kaffir-land; its leaves lanceolate, and many paired; and its seeds, the size of allspice, enveloped in coriaceous orange-coloured capsules, hung in irregular racemes. The seed is aromatic; but the strong spicy pungency, and the delicious fragrance of the lemon-peel essence, reside chiefly in the seed capsules, which would yield an excellent perfume by distillation. The seeds have been sent to England; and the Adelaide spice-tree will ere long, we hope, be found there in many conservatories.

Fort Wellington, with some Fingo families, was left to the care of Lieutenant Leslie, 72nd regiment, and ten mounted and forty dismounted men, Highlanders and Hottentots. We reached the sources of the Cahoon on the cold morning of the 22d, after a thirteen miles' ride. The richly wooded and beautiful glen in which we breakfasted, is now named Glen Aberdeen: and here, among other plants, I found *grewia* sp. and *buddlea* sp. The fertile and extensive valley on the high road from the Buffalo to the Kye, where we encamped near the source of the Nameka, received the title of the Valley of Peel. Next day, after a short march, we reached the Buffalo River, and encamped on a fine plain on its banks. Hills of two or three hundred feet elevation were round us, lightly covered with bush; and looking up the stream beyond the walls and garden of the burnt mission-station, we saw, at the distance of nine or ten miles, the very picturesque mountain ranges at and beyond the sources of the river. We were on the interesting ground from which this general order of the 24th of May was dated:—

" The river Buffalo, from its source in the mountains of its name to the sea, is established as the central line of occupation of the province of Queen Adelaide; and the ground on both banks of this clear, rapid, and beautiful river, along an arc crossed by four fords, to which corresponding roads from all parts of the country converge,—near the former mission-house destroyed by the savages,—is hereby appropriated and set apart to such an extent as may hereafter be judged expedient, as well up as down the stream, as on each of its banks respectively, to the purpose of building a town, which with the site now selected for it, is named King William's Town."

The commander-in-chief now determined on sending Captain Beresford, aide-de-camp, to England with despatches for the secretary of state; and with orders, on his way to Cape Town, to take charge, with a suitable escort, of the hostages Bookoo and Kinki, as far as Graham's Town. Captain Beresford's clear intelligence and ready activity in the field, had often attracted his excellency's notice. The night before the aide-de-camp left us with his charge, the hostages, or *ostriches*,—as a certain Scotch officer used to miscal them, made a desperate attempt to escape. It was nine o'clock; and three shots were fired in quick succession by the picket at the tent occupied by Bookoo and Kinki. On our running up to see the occasion of this, the Highland sergeant and his men were found cursing in broad Scotch, and tying firmly with hide riems the wrists and ankles of the hostages. " What is the meaning of all this?"—" Thae scoondrels," answered the sergeant, " tried to disgrace us, sir, and get clean aff:—tak anither turn wi the strap, Maclaughlin:—but I'm thinkin' we've fixed them noo, at ony rate."—" What was the firing at?"—" I'll tell ye aboot that, sir.—Hegh! I'm oot o' breath. You mind Jan, their servant that was?"—" Yes: but where is he?"—" I hope he's gotten a lead peel, sir, for he had three shots. He jist asket leave to gang to the front o' the tent for a minute; and after he was oot, he gaed a great rax, and a gant, to pit oor lads aff their gerd. Then in a moment he jumpet, like a mawkin, through that hole in the hedge; spread oot his kaross behint him for the shot he expecket; and then took a sherp turn to the left, doon by the water there. The lads fired after the soople thief; but were no sae saaft as to rin efter him: no, no; but turned roond wi' fixed begnets on them twa that are lyin' there so quate.—Ay! ye may blink ye'r een. Bookoo pretended to waaken oot o' his sleep; held up his head; and speer'd what the noise was aboot. The twa thought to get oot by the back o' the tent, when oor lads were aff efter Jan; but they're ta'en in for ance, the Kaffir loons!"

Jan did *not* get his quietus: for the cry of a jackal was, shortly after this, heard in various directions; the preconcerted signal for the three to collect after effecting their escape. How to get the hostages to Graham's Town in safety (seventy-five miles) was now the question, determined, as they seemed, to attempt their escape, under the impression, I believe, that at Graham's Town they were to be put to death. I remembered the way in which we used to secure prisoners in India; and it was practised on the present occasion. Bookoo and Kinki were mounted, and their ankles tied together below their horses' bellies; their hands were left quite free, but they were saved the trouble of guiding their steeds, which were led for them; and thus, in two days and a half, they reached their destination in safety, and were well lodged and carefully attended to in the Tronk.

Great assistance was now afforded by the arrival of that excellent officer Lieutenant Williams,

BOTANY OF THE BUFFALO. 195

royal engineers, in the new province; and a principal work was laid out and commenced under the title of Fort Hill, at King William's Town, to contain a thousand men, of two hundred feet face, with redans in the centre of the faces. Opposite to this, and on an eminence commanding the fords of the Buffalo, was Fort Hardinge, a smaller work. Nine miles distant, between the spruits of the Buffalo, was Fort Beresford; and Fort Murray was placed at the same distance down the river, near Mr. Boyce's old mission-station, and on the very beautiful site of Mount Coke. To keep up the communication between King William's Town and Fort Willshire, there was also Fort White, named after the late assistant quarter-master-general, and situated near T'Slambie's Kop, which is now called Herbert Taylor's Hill, in honour of his majesty's private secretary and principal aide-de-camp.

Among the plants about King William's Town are the following: acacia caffra, olea capensis, celastrus sp., buddlea sp., tecoma capensis, kiggelaria sp., asparagus sp., (hanging on the) azima tetracantha, (near them) cassia tomentosa, sida sonneratiana, hibiscus sp., aizoon sarmentosum; and the splendid estreliza regina, with its golden crest and red and green neck, darted its pointed sheath, like the beak of a magnificent bird, among the vegetation by the river's bank.

That strange insect, the lictor, or bundle of sticks, occurs here; and, with its caterpillar-like tunic, on which are stuck the ends of little sticks, all raking aft like the quills of a porcupine, it may be seen walking along by projecting its head and six legs from its case. In some of these insects the sticks are irregular, the longest being near the tail. In others again there are three sets of regular fasces connected by a "diarthrodial articulation," which makes the ingenuity of this insect the more remarkable. All the fasces are about the same length: but the set about the head are thick; the middle are less so; and the tail fasces taper nearly to a point. This variety is found suspended to dried rhenaster bushes. A third species, more delicate than the other two, feeds on yellow everlasting flowers; and has one set of regular fasces about its body. This everlasting, by the by, the leaves of which are silky and adhesive, has very remarkable properties; an infusion of it curing female complaints when other medicines fail.

Kaffir spies were continually prying about us; a couple of whom were shot by the sentries at night, and three made prisoners. They came, they said, to look for their wives, and gave themselves out to be either of the friendly Nonubés, or of Pato's people. The general was actively employed, as usual, either writing or riding about the country and closely examining it; and though I was now the only aide-de-camp left with his excellency, he gave me three days' leave to go on an expedition with Colonel Smith, to clear the country near the sea, and examine the mouth of the Buffalo.

The expedition consisted of six hundred men, as the T'Slambies were said to be collected in force. We had with us Highlanders, provisional Hottentots, and three hundred mounted burghers under Piet Erasmus, and his field-adjutant Rennie, of Glen Lynden. We left the head-quarter camp on the 28th of May; and at Mount Coke we saw traces of a large and recent Kaffir bivouack: plenty of spoor of men and horses; the remains of slaughtered cattle; and fires still burning. We passed rapidly with the cavalry along the ridge between the Buffalo and Chalumma rivers in pursuit; and saw the white walls of the Reverend W. Shawe's celebrated mission-station of Wesleyville on our right, and before us the sea. At half-past four in the afternoon, the three rifles in advance suddenly dropped on the necks of their horses, wheeled round, and pointing with their carbines said, "*Daar's de Kaffirs.*" And surely enough, on reaching the top of a rise in the road, we saw a large body of plumed warriors, with horsemen and musqueteers, in the plain below us.

Every firelock was out of its cover in a moment; and we galloped impetuously onwards to get within musquet range. We were just pulling up to endeavour to scatter the enemy with a volley; when one, out of the clump of horsemen, advanced towards us waving his hand: but it was some time before we recognised the well-known bush-ranger, Lieutenant Moultrie, 75th regiment, in his little blue bonnet, and dusty and torn garments. He told us that, after Colonel England had lately made a sweep through the Fish River bush, Pato had been persuaded to turn out, with Kama and Umkye, and a thousand warriors, to co-operate with Captain Halifax with a hundred provisional Hottentots from Fort Willshire, and five hundred Fingoes with shields and assegais under Hermanus; and that this was the force we saw before us. For this time, then, we saved our lead; and, like Matthews, we might have exclaimed, "Nobody to be shot to-day? oh dear! oh dear! we are losing *all* our amusements."

We bivouacked on the right bank of the Buffalo in two bodies; and the enemy in strong force came down at nightfall to the left bank opposite Captain Halifax's mixed force, and dared them to attack them. But as it would have been impossible to have distinguished friend from foe in the dark, Colonel Smith thought it advisable to wait till dawn. On the morning of the 29th, the colonel taking with him the mounted men crossed the Buffalo, and passed down between it and the Cahoon; whilst the infantry, Pato's Kaffirs, and the Fingoes were disposed so as to scour down towards the sea on both banks of the Buffalo.

We soon came on "warm" spoor; and as we passed the huts and kraals, applied the firebrand. We then pursued hotly for several hours, took some cattle, and saw a few Kaffirs: some of whom were shot; and the Fingoes also sustained loss. We passed deep dells full of trees, over very rich pasture, and across several streams; crossed the Cahoon; passed a waterfall; saw calves, overdriven, lying on the road; and thought we were sure of a large body of the enemy. But after a hard ride of six hours, we were "brought up" by heavy rain, muddy and slippery roads, and tired horses, at the deep glen of the Kameka, or Eland's River; and saw below us two tired Kaffirs under a tree, at whom Colonel Smith would not allow our men to fire. From our position we also observed Hermanus and his Fingoes, burning and ravaging in the direction of the Gonubee.

We halted and refreshed for a little; recrossed the Cahoon; and, after a severe and wet day's work of thirty-six or forty miles, we bivouacked near the mouth of the Buffalo among Kaffir gardens. Next morning, Kaffirs and cattle were found among the strange sand hills by the sea shore; but by swimming the kine over a creek, they got them clear off. We galloped to the mouth of the Buffalo; and within it found a flat of sand, on which was much spoor of hippopotami, and the river running deep and full under the steep right bank. Upwards it opens out into a fine lake, and is quite unfordable for four miles, to the junction of the fresh and salt water. There is twelve feet water on the bar at high water, and six at ebb; and with beacons on the sand hills at the mouth, the Buffalo promises to be a good port for the new province: but there are besides, the Kye and Fish rivers with excellent mouths, practicable at all times, at least for steam-vessels.

There were three lines of moderate surf along shore, and an amazing quantity of drift wood on the beach. Many of the böers had never seen the sea before, and were much delighted and surprised; as, indeed, we all were, with the amazing beauty and promise of this part of the new province.

We left Captain Halifax's force, and marched northwards again; bivouacked at the Guansa; crossed the Nameka; and firing all the kraals, returned to head-quarters, after accomplishing about a hundred miles in three days.

The surveyor-general was now busy finishing his map of the route during the war, drawing a plan of King William's Town, and taking the levels of the river: whilst I returned to my occupation of fort building. The men, white and black, worked amazingly with encouragement, and a good *zoopje* of rum. A few of the officers in camp were collectors of Kaffir curiosities; and one in particular was most indefatigable: absorbing, like the great whirlpool "Maelstrom," whatever could be termed a curiosity; and having emissaries every where to pick up assegais, karosses, plumes, necklaces, rings, 'newas, 'nais, or bits of scented wood. Cunning fellows of course turned this mania to account: thus, one of the Scotch soldiers was seen one day cutting and carving at a bone. "What are ye doin wi that, Jock?" asked a comrade. "Doin! what should I be doin wi't, but makin a Kaffir snuff spune to sell for a dram."

The circumstance of the friendly chiefs having taken the field, seemed to promise that the war would now be brought to a speedy conclusion; and advantage was made of this circumstance to despatch Colonel Smith with another expedition, still more to humble the proud enemy, by bringing against him those who best knew his haunts. A force similar to the last mentioned, with twelve hundred Congo Kaffirs, and three hundred Fingoes, marched on the 1st of June from King William's Town, and joined the third division at the Deba Flats. Captain Jervis, 72nd regiment, had been previously sent with a corps behind the Buffalo mountains. On the 2nd, Major Cox, with a corps of the third division and the Fingoes, ascended T'Slambie's Kop; whilst Lieutenant C. Bailie, with a hundred Hottentots, and the Kaffir warriors under Pato, Kama, and Umkye, advanced up a kloof, to the east of Herbert Taylor's Hill, to sweep round and descend one of the spruits of the Buffalo. Colonel Smith, with the rest of the force of the first division, at the same time marched below the Buffalo range eastwards, to attract the enemy's attention, then occupying the heights in considerable force; sent Captains Murray and Gilfillan into the bush with their men; and making a detour with the cavalry, drove the enemy towards Captain Jarvis.

The result of these combined operations was very fortunate. Eno had a brother killed, and many other Kaffirs shared the same fate, with small loss to our people; thirty horses, thirteen hundred head of cattle, and flocks of goats were captured; and the smoke of many kraals obscured the heavens. The officers and men endured their fatigues with cheerfulness; the zeal and activity of Lieut. Granett principally contributed to the success of the day; and the friendly Kaffirs were not backward in meeting their brethren in combat.

The Fingoes now had frequent skirmishes with the enemy, who used to slay and rob them at their new location opposite the Line Drift of the Keiskamma. Of a party of Fingoes coming to camp, four were killed and five wounded by a large body of the enemy, who had concentrated on both sides of the Line Drift road; and it was therefore necessary to beat up their quarters. Colonel Smith again left the head-quarter camp on the 4th, with a mixed force and a six-pounder gun; and arrived at the Line Drift: where, into the wooded ravines, running down to the Keiskamma, he immediately sent infantry to sweep them to the river, and rendezvous below; whilst the colonel scoured the ridges above, fell in with the enemy, took his cattle and goats, and occasioned him some loss.

Next day the Chalumma was swept by the cavalry from Wesleyville to its source; and more of the ravines were scoured about the Keiskamma: the troops intrepidly driving the Kaffirs from their strong ground of rocks, precipices, and woods. By the third day's operations, the wooded range called the Ilikye, to the north of the Line Drift road, was cleared of the enemy. The Kaffirs had fled so rapidly that only two hundred and fifteen head of cattle, some horses, and two thousand goats were captured, besides several scores of their women and children. These last were fed with beef and biscuit, and recommended to seek a new country beyond the Kye. Several hundred huts were burnt; and the Kaffirs now felt that the day of retribution had arrived, and that they were at length reaping the fruits of their atrocities on the colonists.

As seed time had come round, it was necessary to provide for the ensuing harvest, by sending the remainder of the böers to their homes. A selection was therefore made of their horses, of which they usually had two each; and after getting a check for a reasonable price for one of them, they were dismissed, with thanks for their services, to their respective districts. On leaving the camp at night, they commenced and continued such a fire by way of saluting us, or of rejoicing

FATAL ACCIDENT. 205

for themselves, that it was imagined we were attacked by all the border-chiefs at once; and a fatal accident was occasioned by this unmilitary proceeding of the böers. Volunteer Okes having ran to a wagon for his gun, in pulling it out by the muzzle from under some forage, it unfortunately went off; and the ball, after passing through one of his own legs, and severely injuring the bone, wounded a man beside him in the face, entered the breast of a fine young Hottentot, and stretched him lifeless on the spot.

Adelaide Spice Tree.

CHAPTER XXV.

The New Province left in Charge of Colonel Smith—The Troops are thanked—First and Third Divisions discontinued—The General arrives at Fort Willshire—Conference with Suta, the Great-wife of Gaika—Arrival at Graham's Town—Employment there—Panics—Successful Patrols in the New Province —Valley of the Cowie — Anecdotes of Settlers —Bathurst— Forbes's Redoubts—Schemes of the Philanthropists to defend the Frontier—Kaffir Drift—Hortus Siccus—Fredericksburg— An Ostrich Hunt—The Gualana—Py the Counsellor—Line Drift—Fingoes on the Iquora—The Queen Nonubé—Escape of a Prisoner—Conference with the Fingo Chiefs—A Beauty —The Age of Cant—March to Forts Willshire and Beaufort —Block Drift—Fingo Location—Ride up the Kat River— A Lion Hunt—The Beaufort Stot—The Kat River Settlement —Camp Adelaide—Abominable Plot—Andries Stoffel, *Esquire* —Balfour—The Vagrant Act—A New System—Ride towards the Chumie—Magnificent Prospects—Fort Beaufort—Return to Graham's Town.

THE province of Queen Adelaide being so far secured by military works as we have just described, though the border Kaffirs still continued obstinately to hold out in the Amatola; it became necessary for his excellency the commander-in-chief to proceed to Graham's Town, to make further arrangements for the suffering colonists of the eastern province; and also to inspect and secure the old border line, and to locate the Fingo nation. Besides which his presence *within* the old colonial boundary had become indispensable for the due order of the civil government.

The impartial reader, who has accompanied us thus far in our narrative, will it is believed allow, that there had been little "folding of the arms of indolence, or slumbering on a carpet of repose," during the operations in the field: characterized, as they undoubtedly were, by excellence in their arrangement, and energy in their execution. Every exertion had been made to chastise the enemy, and bring him to submission, in a manner worthy of civilized soldiers: abhorring cruelty, and using the weapons of offence only in a war most literally undertaken " pro aris et focis." It will further be admitted, that the duty of avenging the cause for which the war was commenced, had been discharged in accordance with the principles of mercy; that, besides, no pains had been spared to finish the war by negotiation; and that, his excellency's terms having been rejected, it was evident the proud Gaikas and T'Slambies were not yet sufficiently humbled.

On their own heads, then, was their further punishment.

The commander-in-chief now, in a general order, stated that his presence having become indispensable at Graham's Town for the due ordering of his majesty's service, he was compelled, however reluctantly, to separate for a time from the troops in the new province: whose conduct, since they had been under his personal command, had given him unqualified satisfaction; and of whom he took leave with every sentiment of approbation and regard. His excellency said that he had little to add to his former acknowledgments during the late successful campaign, beyond this record of his deliberate opinion—as an old soldier who had seen some service—that they had admirably upheld the character of British soldiers, and had faithfully done their duty to their king and country: an opinion which, they might rest assured, he would not fail to place at the feet of his majesty, our most gracious king.

It diminished withal the regret of the commander-in chief, on quitting the personal command of the troops in the province of Queen Adelaide, that he left them in charge of Colonel Smith: an officer in whom they must all have the fullest confidence, as well on account of those high military qualities which they had witnessed, and which had rendered him a main cause of the recent successes, as because they knew from experience that he was the soldier's friend, and would always have a watchful care of all that could contribute to their health, comfort, and convenience.

The commander-in-chief again thanked Colonel Smith, and the officers of the colonel's personal, as well as of the general staff; Colonel Peddie and the officers and soldiers of the first division; Major Cox and those of the third division; and Captain Southey and the corps of guides, which deserved high commendation. His excellency further duly acknowledged Dr. Murray's very valuable services, and those of the medical staff generally. Indeed, through the excellent arrangements of the general himself for the campaign, assisted by the old experienced "Peninsular" heads of the medical and commissariat departments, and the great salubrity of the climate, the army had kept very healthy throughout, and we had scarcely any sick. Colonel Thompson, royal engineers, was thanked for his suggestions and assistance: as also Lieut. Williams, royal engineers; and Messrs. Sandford and Spencer, and the officers of the commissariat and ordnance departments generally, both in the field and in the colony, were praised for the able manner in which they had performed their duties.

Thanks were also, in the same public manner, conveyed to the officers of the general's personal staff: including his military secretary, aides-de-camp, and commandant of the escort. The valuable services which the surveyor-general had rendered in the topographical department, were duly acknowledged. Besides, then, the satisfaction of having endeavoured to do their duty, commendation coming from so high a quarter was very gratifying to all these officers.

Colonel Smith, C. B., was now therefore appointed to the command of the province of Queen Adelaide, and all the troops therein, until his majesty's pleasure should be known. Lieutenant Oliver, 72nd regiment, became his brigade-major; and from the 16th of June the establishment of the first and third divisions was discontinued: the officers employed in them respectively returning to the duties which they had previously fulfilled.

At six o'clock in the morning of the 11th of June, the general, with his personal staff and escort, mounted to quit King William's Town, and passed between the infantry at extended order: whilst the cavalry, under the fine old veteran Lowen, were drawn up on the heights, and the artillery thundered a salute from Fort Hill. We breakfasted at the Umdezine bush, which we afterwards heard was full of Kaffirs at the time; fixed on the site of Fort White; and in the evening, after a thirty-five miles' ride, reached Fort Willshire. Here we found Suta, the Kaffir queen, "the great wife of Gaika," waiting to have a conference with his excellency; and here we were well entertained by the commandant, Captain Halifax, 75th regiment, and his Lieutenant, Mr. Bingham of the same corps. By Captain Halifax's able arrangements at Fort Willshire, the convoys for the force in the field had been effectually expedited. His excellency, and several of us, not having slept out of our clothes since the month of March, we felt rather awkward on hospital stretchers; and not having been in a bed for a long time, I rolled off mine, and got a contusion on the shoulder, besides having had an ankle badly bruised in Kaffir-land.

On the morning of the 12th, Suta acknowledged to the general that, though Macomo and Tyalie still refused to submit, their people had suffered greatly, and were tired of the war. She herself wished to live in peace, and under British protection, with her son Sandilli: but that young chief was kept in close custody by his brothers,

Tyalie and Macomo, who were older though inferior in rank. Suta farther promised to use her influence to bring the border-chiefs to comply with his excellency's terms, or to separate herself from them, and leave them to their fate.

We mounted again; left the banks of the Keiskamma; and, descending the long hill of Double Drift, crossed the Great Fish River by a new punt. In a star fort, just completed, we found Captain John Van Der Reit, of Uitenhage, with a party of burghers. Continuing our route westwards, we discovered that, having left behind us in Kaffir-land good roads, abundant pasturage, wood and water, we were now to expect in exchange only bad roads and sterility in this part of the colony. We found the post of Hermanus' kraal in good order, under the command of a very zealous officer, Lieutenant Brown, 75th regiment; and after a ride of forty miles, arrived in Graham's Town: which was illuminated, as a public expression of respect for his excellency, and of cordial approval of his late measures.

I again took up my old quarters in the comfortable house of Mr. W. R. Thompson; and was constantly employed for three weeks in writing for his excellency, whose labours as usual were unceasing. It was impossible for those who had the good fortune to serve under the general to be remiss in their duty; since it was seen how little he spared himself, living as he did " non sibi sed patriæ."

His excellency's services were now duly appreciated by those who enjoyed the benefit of them, and who, therefore, best knew their extent; and meetings were held of the inhabitants in all parts of the colony, and addresses of thanks and of congratulation were presented to him. The language used was expressive of sincere gratitude for the governor's measures to alleviate the great distress of a large portion of the colonists, and of entire confidence in the result of his plans for their future safety.

About this time, his excellency instituted certain inquiries, and made arrangements for organizing a militia for the defence of the frontier: for, strange though it may appear, this essential point seemed to have been altogether overlooked by former governments. At spare moments, I collected information for assisting to defend the frontier by other means: such as an annual mission to maintain friendly relations with the chiefs Crieli, Vodana, Faku, and perhaps Dingan; the establishment of telegraphic communications along the old frontier, and from thence to the first post on the Kye; the selection, at particular points, of defensible villages and defensible farm-houses, &c. On the last subject, a paper with diagrams, in English and Dutch, was circulated among the farmers, by order of his excellency; showing how by fire-proof roofs, porches to give a raking fire, loop-holed walls, towers or look-out houses, hand grenades, prickly-pear hedges, district kraals, and fortified churches, as places of rendezvous, the enterprising farmers of the frontier might labour in peace, sleep in security, and with the assistance of the regular force, defend their property against all hostile inroads.

There were some panics about this time, as before, in and around Graham's Town. Among such incidents, was the fact of a civilian on sentry firing at a star one night, thinking it was a Kaffir approaching him with a pipe in his mouth. A lady also ran home one evening in great alarm, on seeing a soldier carried to his quarters by two of his comrades, wounded, as she thought, by Kaffirs, but only "kilt by brandy." Farther, an old cow with the belly-ache, grunting outside a barrier, received a volley in the dark, being mistaken for " the enemy at the gates:" but there was nothing serious to speak of within the old colony. In the new province there was always something stirring,

SUCCESSFUL PATROLS. 215

as the commandant was not a likely person to allow the enemy much repose.

The patrols were most active and successful against the enemy. After the late expeditions of Colonel Smith, and the manner in which the country had been scoured by him, from the Upper Keiskamma and Buffalo to the ocean; patrols, under Lieutenants Bailie and Biddulph, swept through the ravines on the banks of the Keiskamma; and Captain Heddle pursued a body of the enemy from Fort Beresford towards the Kye, and took from them about a couple of hundred head of cattle.

Captain Warden, from his post Fort Warden, made an able and spirited movement towards the mouth of the Kye; took the enemy by surprise; killed and wounded a number of them, his Fingo warriors being particularly forward on the occasion; and captured seven horses and three hundred and five head of cattle. Ensign Campbell, with a patrol of the Cape corps, wounded some Kaffirs, and captured horses, cattle, and goats on the Cahoon; whilst Captain Lacey, 72nd regiment, from his post Fort Murray,—so named after the colonel of the 42nd royal Highlanders,—patrolled the country about him, and prevented the Kaffirs from assembling. One capture by

Ensign Nourse, of this post, consisted of thirty women; who were loaded with beef and biscuit, and conducted over the Buffalo.

On the 8th of July the general, with Colonels Somerset and Thompson, Dr. Murray, Major Dutton, Lieutenants Williams and Wade, Mr. Alfred Thompson, and myself, mounted to ride round the old frontier; place it in a state of defence; and arrange the Fingo settlements. Tents and provisions were carried on horses led by the rifle escort. We rode down the valley of the Cowie, accompanied by Commissary-general Petrie, from the Cape, and his assistant, Mr. Trotter, who were going to inspect the mouth of the Cowie. The commissary-general had been most indefatigable since the commencement of the war in keeping the troops and inhabitants, who must otherwise have starved, well and abundantly supplied; and it was also fortunate that he had a most invaluable assistant at Graham's Town, in Mr. Palmer, one of the most zealous and faithful servants of the public that I ever saw. Mr. Petrie was now desirous of saving the public money and long land carriage, by seeing if the Cowie, Fish, or Buffalo rivers, would be practicable for the landing of stores and provisions. Suffice it here to say, that the bar of shifting sand at the mouth

ANECDOTES OF SETTLERS. 217

of the Cowie, precluded all hope of its ever being a port for Albany; though large sums had been expended there by Lord Charles Somerset in public buildings; and a town had also been laid out. At the mouths of the Great Fish and Buffalo rivers, there is every prospect of establishing ports; and they will probably soon be turned to good account.

We were surprised to see in the Cowie Valley some of the poor farmers ploughing again, singly, in their fields, and driving wagons along the road. All this was very hazardous: but, as they said, they must run some risk, or where should they get bread next year? Their locations all down the valley were very beautiful; and the soil was rich, yielding in particular very heavy crops of Indian corn. We take leave here to ridicule the strong prejudice of our emigrant countrymen in favour of wheat; and we pity no one who has plenty of maize to eat. It is exceedingly nutritive for man or stock, and not liable to rust; and we have a lively recollection of the agreeable messes of *mush* and *hominy*, and other preparations of Indian corn, on which we feasted in the back woods of America. Some of the settlers of the Cowie committed strange mistakes when they first " set up their staff here." One planted Indian corn by dibbling the ground, and then setting an entire cob or head; and another was advised to cultivate water-melons. Accordingly, he "inspanned" his wagon; went to a Dutch farmer; purchased all the melons which he had; returned to his own location; made large holes in his field; and in each buried a huge melon: thinking, perhaps, to have a very abundant increase on the new principle of planting whole potatoes.

We were met by Captain Forbes, 75th regiment, commanding the southern sub-district of Albany and Somerset; were conducted by him to his head-quarters in the very pleasant village of Bathurst; and were well entertained by my countryman and his excellent lady. Next morning we were up at an early hour; and, proceeding to the long hill above the village, laid out two redoubts (Forbes's) for the defence of Bathurst, and broke ground. We were also directed to enclose the handsome stone church with a parapet and ditch. Confidence was thus immediately restored to the inhabitants, and property rose in value. In looking from the hill, the country declined with undulations to the sea, distant eight or nine miles, and was clothed with fine grasses; whilst on the right was the Cowie bush, extending from the deep bed of the river on to the plains. Strange to say, among this bush were scattered the white houses of Bathurst, with as little means of defence as if they had been placed in the centre of England.

Formerly there used to be a gun above Bathurst, and another at Kaffir Drift post; and when the Kaffirs made a foray about the former, the gun being fired and answered, turned out the patrol, and the marauders were intercepted: but, of late years, even this simple precaution had been discontinued. According to the pseudo-philanthropists, themselves *living at a safe distance*, the frontier required, for its defence, nothing but infant schools among the Kaffirs, plenty of missionaries, and no soldiers! Can our savage neighbours acquire the angelic nature in a day? Certainly we live in an age of humbug and delusion!

On the 10th, we rode towards Kaffir Drift, descended to the Fish River, and forded it without difficulty. Toucans and jays are frequent here; and we saw the spoor of buffaloes and hippopotami. Bringing up our right shoulders we pushed on, and bivouacked under some bushes at the head of the Gualana River. Among the plants which I gathered at Kaffir Drift were the following:—fagara sp., arctotis sp., mesembryanthemum aureum, senecio sp., volkameria sp., polygala myrtifolia, plumbago capensis, conyza sp., senecio venusta, adelia acitodon, scabiosa sp., teucrium sp., helichrysum ericoides, and tarconanthus camphoratus.

We were now near the abandoned military settlement of Fredericksburg, wisely placed here by Sir Rufane Donkin for the defence of this part of the frontier, and composed of half-pay officers and old soldiers. Unfortunately, owing to a disagreement between this very superior officer and Lord Charles Somerset, when the latter resumed the reins of government he reversed all the arrangements which General Donkin had made whilst acting governor. The establishment of Fredericksburg, among others, fell to the ground; the consequence of which was, that the Kaffirs, who had been quiet for eighteen months, immediately recommenced murdering and plundering the colonists.

We were visited here by a nice little Kaffir girl, Conkey, the daughter of the chief Cobus Congo. She spoke English very well, having been brought up at Wesleyville; like Eve, on her expulsion from paradise, was clothed in skins; and had a child hanging behind her in the folds of her kaross. About the Gualana River there are sometimes scenes of high interest in the occurrence of ostrich hunts. The Kaffirs nimbly pursue that fleet and powerful bird, and enclose him: when he makes a rush at a part of the circle, kicking out furiously, and clearing all before him, if not mortally and speedily assegaied.

Next morning we rode northwards, in a drizzling rain and mist, and came suddenly upon three or four black men driving a few cattle with guns on their shoulders, and dressed in jackets and leather trousers. They gave us a rough "*daag!*" and attempted to pass: but on Colonel Somerset recognising one of them as Py, the chief counsellor of Eno, going as he pretended with cattle to supply us, but really as a spy, the whole were secured. We diverged to the right; inspected the Line Drift of the Keiskamma; and the general selected the site of a post there. Again travelling north-west, we pitched our tents among the Fingoes, who had been placed in the meantime on the Iquora, under the care of Mr. Bowker, J. P., and Ensign Pierce Lowen, with a detachment of Hottentots.

The Kaffirs seemed determined not to let these new subjects of the British crown rest in peace. Thus, they had lately swept off a thousand head of cattle from them: but the Fingoes collected and pursued them to the Line Drift; and though some of them were there shot, they rushed on with stabbing assegais, and retook the cattle at the Deba, killing several of the enemy. The Kaffirs then tried a more secure plan. Three of them came to the Fingo camp, and pretending that they were of the friendly Congoes, smoked with the Fingoes and exchanged assegais: but watching their opportunity, they stole away; slew a Fingo herdsman; and with impunity carried off a herd of cattle. What valuable assistants such fellows would have been to Donald of the Cave in Waverley!

The Kaffir queen Nonubé, the mother of the young Siwana of the T'Slambies, came here to visit his excellency; also Pato, Kama, and Umkye. Nonubé is the great widow of Dushani, who with the prophet Makanna attacked Graham's Town in 1819. As I before noticed, Nonubé has European blood in her veins, being of the tribe of Depa by the Umtata. She is about forty years of age; is pleasantly stout, and light brown; and wears a smile on her countenance, which is agreeable, though her eyes do not roll in unison. She wore a blue and white striped dress, with a silk handkerchief round her head;

and by some accident was in the family way. The general thanked Nonubé for her kind feeling towards the English; for her endeavours to prevent the war; and for her successful efforts in saving the lives and property of some missionaries and traders. He promised to give her, with her son and people, an ample settlement in the new province. Siwana was now under the care of a worthy missionary, Mr. Dugmore.

At night, there was a shot and a cry that Py was off. It appeared that the wagon-driver with whose reins the counsellor had been secured, having occasion for them in the morning, took them off. Py waited very contentedly all day, sleeping and eating under a tree, and in charge of a sentry. At dusk he requested leave to go a few yards off; and a young Hottentot sentry accompanied him, but with his gun cased. Py noting this, made a sudden snatch at the gun, and a dash at the sentry's legs; then sprung down the slope like a deer; and doubled and disappeared. A tardy shot was fired after him. The carelessness with regard to Py was very provoking: for being known to have been one of the chief promoters of the war, if threatened with death he might have made very important disclosures.

Next morning, there was a grand assemblage of the Fingo chiefs and warriors to meet the general, and have a new country given to them. They were all in full dress, feathered with cocks' tails; girt with those of foxes and jackals; and bearing a cow's tail pendant below the knee. With their strange decorations, and with their assegais and variously coloured hide shields, they made a gallant display. The principal chief, Umhlambisu, was a little old man, distinguished by a band round his head of red and white beads in a vandyke pattern. He thanked the general in the name of the rest, for rescuing them from Kaffir bondage; for protecting them on their way here; for giving them corn, and promising them a new and a good tract of country for their locations; and for assigning them a missionary whom they knew and respected, the Reverend Mr. Ayliffe, to live among them. In conclusion, they faithfully promised to conduct themselves as good subjects of the king.

The Fingoes then testified their determined spirit, and their joy, by sham fights and war dances. A party of young warriors rushed forward, leaping through and over the scattered bushes; extended, and threw with shouts their assegais and keeries; retreated, covering themselves with their shields; rallied, again advanced rapidly, recovered their arms, and brought in one as a prisoner; formed a ring, sang, danced round him, and thrust at him on the ground with their assegais.

Attention was withdrawn from the war dance, by the appearance of one of the young women who were looking on. Tall and well made, and wrapped in an ample kaross of white sheep-skin, she had one of the most regular and pleasing countenances I ever saw. Her complexion was light brown; her nose, lips, and teeth beautiful; her eyes "globes of fire;" and her dark hair "ensnaring the hearts of lovers." On inquiry who this African beauty was, I found that she had come from the far Umzimfoobo; was supposed to be of Malay descent; and was now the wife of Mr. Ayliffe's bastard wagoner. Lucky bastard! I was annoyed with the narrow-minded prejudices of a missionary here. He objected to some Hottentot soldiers playing the Jew's-harp in a tent one day, and told them it was improper. He likewise condemned the war dance of the poor Fingoes: for *that* also, according to this man, in his ignorance of human nature, led to sin. Shall we never have done with this canting nonsense of the conventicle?

The general now rode round the country to fix on a location for part of the Fingoes; decided on its being on the Clusie, from Mount Somerset towards the Fish River; and directed that, at the same place also, a military work, Fort Peddie, should be constructed for their defence. Lieut. Moultrie, now located at Commatty's Drift as ranger of the Great Fish River, was left at the Clusie, joint commissioner with Mr. Mitford Bowker, Captain Halifax, and Mr. Ayliffe, for the location and settlement of the Fingoes; and we then marched off towards Fort Willshire, distant eighteen miles.

A son of old Tzatzoe, the petty Kaffir chief over one hundred and fifty men, whose other son Jan had been brought up at Bethelsdorp, met the general, and said that his father and followers were close at hand. The general said, "Did your father get the cloak I sent him for his fidelity to the colony?"—"No, he got no cloak." "Come! as it is not far out of our way, we'll ride past the kraals and see the old gentleman." We did so; and the first thing that we observed was the cloak on old Tzatzoe's shoulders. His son, detected in a lie, merely laughed, and said to a companion, "I see I can't get another cloak from the governor."

On the 16th, we saddled up at Fort Willshire, and rode towards Fort Beaufort, which we reached after a pleasant ride of thirty miles over a fine country, with the view bounded by the snowy peaks of the Winterberg. We were hospitably entertained by Captain Armstrong, commanding the northern sub-district of Albany and Somerset, and by Major Blakeway commanding the Beaufort levy. We found Fort Beaufort without a fort: that is, it was only a military cantonment, consisting of a square of barracks and store-houses. These, with a line of stables, and huts, and scattered officers' quarters, occupied a low, flat-topped hill, in the midst of a magnificent grassy plain, through which the Kat River meandered. The horizon was bounded by a picturesque amphitheatre of mountains. A fort was here soon laid out and traced in the centre of the plateau; and its construction was entrusted to a hard-working officer, Captain Boyce, of the 75th regiment, whose name it now bears. A village was also destined to rise here, in the centre of one of the most promising districts in the colony. We then rode to the Block Drift of the Chumie, where the general fixed on the site of another post, Fort Thomson, for the defence of that pass, and for the protection of the other Fingo location, under the commissioners, Captains Armstrong and Bain, the Reverend Mr. Thompson, and Dr. Minto. About the same period Fort Cox, in Adelaide, had been traced out, and the ground occupied on the Upper Keiskamma near Burnshill; to correspond with Fort Thomson; to connect it with King William's Town; and to overlook and command the passes of the Amatola.

The temperature of the eastern provinces may be estimated by this register of the thermometer at Fort Beaufort for one year.

Date.	Maximum.	Medium.	Minimum.
20th January	90°	86°	78°
,, February	110	90	80
,, March	95	80	75
,, April	94	80	70
,, May	90	70	59
,, June	78	65	50
,, July	63	57	46
,, August	75	64	55
,, September	78	66	57
,, October	79	70	60
,, November	80	74	64
,, December	84	76	65

Our next march was up the Kat River; whither we were conducted by Captain Armstrong and Captain Bovey, of Devonshire: the latter, late of the commissariat and now of the Beaufort levy, being famed as "the crack-shot of the colony." With his bush-boy Donald, he is well known to all lion hunters in South Africa: as he, Major Cox, Captains Aitchison, Warden, Eyre, &c., first showed how lions could be killed on the open plain. Until they set a better example, the Dutch hunters followed the old precaution of tying twenty or thirty horses together, backing them towards the king of beasts, and firing long shots from behind the animal breast-work; so that if the lion charged, the sportsmen escaped.

Not in such wise did Bovey and his bold brother huntsmen attack their noble game on the Bontebok Flats, over the hills, at no great distance from the spot where we now were, and where we hoped one day to enjoy the same grand sport. It was their custom to trot off from Fort Beaufort, with a tent, bag of biscuit, and a cup of comfort, on led horses; pitch their marquee near water; and then, with their *achter rijders* to hold their horses, wander up and down the shallow kloofs of the flats, looking for their prey. Suddenly, at the distance of fifty or a hundred yards, on a slope among rocks, where he had been lying in wait for a fat buck, would rise the lord of this splendid wilderness: with shaggy mane erect; lashing his sides and the ground with his tail; and his eyes glaring with rage and wonder at the invaders of his kingdom. For the lion, unlike other hunted animals, always shows himself; stands up and looks around, whether he be among stones or long grass; and seems to dare his enemies to the combat. Enjoining silence, the huntsmen would dismount, and the Hottentots run up and take the horses, snorting and terrified, to the rear. Three or four then with cocked pieces, and led by Bovey the oldest sportsman, would walk towards the lion. He would usually receive them with a deep growl; and hardly believing he was to be attacked in this open manner, would make a short rush, and squat within twenty-five yards. Then was the moment to fire. The sportsmen, in line, poured in a volley, and generally with fatal effect; or else the lion, with a terrific roar, would make a death-bound toward them; and on one occasion, in particular, mangled an officer so dreadfully, before he was finally destroyed, that he was revenged by the death of one of his assailants.

If the extreme of excitement and danger affords the best sport, a lion hunt after the English fashion on the Bontebok Flats, would satisfy the cravings of the most determined chasseur. What are clearing hurdles and swimming brooks after reynard, to bearding a lion in the above fashion?

Or, on nimble arab, and spear in hand, whilst the Polygar dogs hang on his flanks, pursuing and bringing to bay the fiery wild boar of India, who charges desperately, and in a moment overthrows horse and rider, both of whom perhaps are ripped up by his tusks?

A gun such as Bovey's, which had brought down thirty lions, was not suffered to stand in a corner on the occasion of the Kaffir invasion; but in the hands of its burly master did execution against wild beasts, no less ferocious, in the shape of ravening Kaffirs. Thus, a flock of sheep having been carried off from Beaufort, Bovey and some burghers pursued; and the Kaffirs fled to the bush. Bovey called to his companions to follow; dashed in singly; had an assegai thrown at him from below a ledge of rock; and fired and brought down two Kaffirs, mortally wounded, by the same ball.

To help on the narrative, I may here notice a ridiculous panic which took place at Beaufort, when the border-chiefs threatened to carry the place. It was seven o'clock P. M., and some of the junior officers were sitting together in the evening, after dining with a friend; when bang! went a great gun; and a second, and a third report, quickly followed. A corporal then ran in breathless, and said that the major commanding ordered them to turn out instantly. " What's the matter?" asked the jolly host. " The matter, sir! there are hundreds of Kaffirs all about; we shall be attacked to-night, and eaten up before morning." Crack! went a musquet near our friend, after he had crossed the threshold, and a ball whistled close past his ear. " What are ye firing at?" cried he to an Irish soldier, who took his piece from his shoulder. " Firing at, sir! I saw him as plain as I see you."—" Saw what?"—" A Kaffir thief of the world, to be sure, sir!" The troops stood to their arms all night, and volleys of musquetry, shot, and shells were expended; and Lieutenant Moultrie, being ordered out to patrol a short distance, was struck on the leg by a rocket, his party being mistaken for the enemy! The gallant defenders of the post expected to see the plain strewed with bodies in the morning: but not a broken assegai was found. What then had been the occasion of the great expenditure of ammunition? An old bullock! It appears that a shoemaker had gone out before dusk, to look for a horse which had strayed; and in returning to the post he saw an old black ox, which had been out all day in the sun, bobbing its head up and down, and groaning among the long grass and bushes, in a vain attempt to rise. The ox and the bushes, in Crispin's fancy, were immediately converted into Kaffirs; he rushed through the river up to his neck; gained the post; and reported that he had seen a large body of the enemy close at hand. Hence the absurd alarm.

We breakfasted near the Blink-water, a most charming part of the country for beauty of scenery and richness of pasture; and heard some heavy firing near us. On the alert for a skirmish, two men were sent off to reconnoitre, and came back with a report that it was only some böers with wagons, practising and lavishly expending the king's powder. We rode up the Kat River, and were soon in the midst of a glorious valley, with mountains and wooded kloofs around. Here was the favoured Kat River Hottentot settlement; at which his excellency arrived at a critical juncture.

Looking from a height, we saw a high and rocky peninsula below us, round which, except at a narrow neck, ran the Kat River: a bell rang on the peninsula of Camp Adelaide; and five thousand human beings, crowded thereon in huts of mud and reeds, with their cattle kraals on the river's bank, turned out to receive the general. The Rev. Mr. Thompson, Mr. Christian Groepe, the field-commandant, and some of the field-cornets, rode out to meet his excellency. They conducted him across the river, up the hill, and past the Hottentots and some Fingoes of all ages: collected by Captain Armstrong on this strong position, from which the Kaffirs had in vain attempted to drive them. But the principal danger now was not from the Kaffirs, but from traitors in Camp Adelaide itself.

In noticing the Kat River settlement in another chapter, I said that there were unfortunately two pastors here, whose flocks were at variance. A former governor, and the ex-commissioner-general of the frontier, had committed the oversight of allowing the Independent or London Missionary Society to establish one of their body here; who immediately set to work to collect a large congregation, in opposition to that of the regular clergyman, the excellent Mr. Thompson. The flock of this latter gentleman were the industrious, well-conducted, and loyal bastards; the other congregation was the refuge for all the destitute vagrants and desperate scoundrels of colour of the colony. Mr. Reid, the missionary, had been removed from the Kat River on the commencement of the war, as it was found that he was not a proper person to have the charge which had been assigned to him; and his congregation, being pent up with the others at Camp Adelaide, planned all sorts of mischief against the bastards, and even laid a plot, which the presence of the general frustrated, to cut the throats of Mr. Thompson and all his people, and then go over to the enemy. All this, too, after the fertile lands of the Kat River Valley had been given to them; and after they had been supported by government rations since the commencement of the war! A field-cornet, Andries Stoffel, *Esquire*, as a certain party used to address him, a Gona Hottentot—that is, half Kaffir and half Hottentot—was one of the ringleaders of the above infernal plot; and Dr. Philip, the superintendent of the London Society's mission here, has now taken home this man, as a specimen of the aborigines, with Jan Tzatzoe, and Mr. Reid's son by a Hottentot woman. Truly we live in strange times!

The site of a post was fixed on for the Kat River: Fort Armstrong, on the peninsula which the captain had so judiciously selected, and so well defended. Like the other works, this was erected at little or no expense, except that of some spirits: for there was, unfortunately, no other way of paying the labourers at the time. The materials for these numerous and indispensable works were every where at hand; and they can easily be converted into permanent defences with a trifling outlay of money; if the well-matured plans of the general for the safety of the colony are approved of and supported at home. We passed on to Balfour, a collection of three or four houses, in one of which we spread our sheep-skin karosses. In front of Mr. Thompson's house, the general received the heads of families of the Kat River, all respectably dressed in jackets and trousers, and with powder-horn swinging at their hip; and addressed them to the following effect:—

" I have come among you as soon as I possibly could, and am now ready to hear what you have to say: I thank you for your services during the war, particularly those men in the field under Field-commandant Groepe; and I hope that all of you will conduct yourselves like good subjects in peace, as you did like good soldiers in war. I know that you have suffered much loss by the Kaffirs; but not more, and in fact less, than the other colonists. It is my earnest wish to alleviate your distress; and, by means of rations and cattle, I have done as much as I was able to do for you. I now desire that an account of the losses sustained by each individual be sent in to me, in order that I may see what further assistance can be given you. Finally, I wish it to be clearly understood that, as the English laws, under which you live, make no distinction of persons, any one who takes the law into his own hands, to the injury of his neighbour, will assuredly be most severely punished; and in seeking to obtain indulgences, the claims of those of good character only can be taken into consideration by me, and they only can hope to obtain reward."

Andries Stoffel and his party were evidently taken by surprise at the general's decided tone, and were for some time silent. At length Stoffel, —an orator, as *some* said, who would do honour to the British senate,—mustered courage, though under considerable trepidation, to say, that he thanked the governor for coming to see them, and for the ground on which they now stood, which they had received from government; that if it had not been for the government rations, they must have starved; but that the Kat River was now too small for their numbers; and that they were already tearing the ground to pieces to make a living out of it. Field-cornet Andries Botha, one of the same party, then stood forth and said, " When we came here, we were told that we were all Hottentots, and all equal: but we are not so. There are bastards among us; and we think that they wish to rule over us, and make us slaves. Some time ago they signed a petition for a vagabond law, a vagrant act, that every one might be taken up who had no visible means of subsistence; and we now wish to hear from the governor's own lips, that that law is not to pass."

His excellency said that they ought to know perfectly, that many months ago he had opposed the vagrant act, and prevented its becoming law; but he now assured them that, as far as he was concerned, the vagrant act should not pass. After hearing some other spokesmen in the same strain as the above, he wished them good night. The truth is, that if the vagrant act had passed, at the time it was under discussion, immediately before the Kaffir invasion, and if a power of taking up and confining coloured men who had no master, had been placed in the hands of the authorities, it would have opened a door to much tyranny and oppression; and would have caused serious abuses, tending to produce rebellion on the part of the Hottentots: who instead of being, as they were, of great use to the colony during the war, would probably all have been in the enemy's ranks. The bastards of Kat River, like many other people, had been advised to sign a petition for a vagrant act, which would have applied equally to them as to the others. They thought at the time they signed this, that they were complying with the wishes of the governor, whose sentiments were not known on the subject, until he put his *veto* to the act. The Independent faction of Kat River knew all this perfectly, and merely used the signing of the petition as a pretext for venting their spleen on the loyal and honest bastards: of whose industry and good conduct they were exceedingly jealous, as these qualities were contrasted with their own idleness and bad habits.

It was the pious congregation of Mr. Thompson which made the Kat River settlement look like a smiling garden: the others were refractory, lazy, and filthy; were taught no habits of industry; and could only boast of an infant school and hymn singing. But this state of things will not be allowed to continue; the moral thraldom under which a large and valuable portion of the coloured race have been kept, will now cease; and they will receive additional locations, with title-deeds: which essential charters of freedom were always withheld by the Independent pastors, that their power over the liberties of their flocks might not be diminished.

In the evening, we had a good deal of amusement. seven of us being stowed very close on the floor of a small room, through the window of which an old horse thrust his head to see what was the cause of the merriment; and next morning we mounted and rode farther up the settlement, passing under the peninsula of Camp Adelaide. Here the infant and an upper school were drawn up before his excellency. They had no books, so that there was no opportunity of examining them; but the young people sang hymns. In the upper school we witnessed a disgusting instance of Independent disrespect to his majesty's representative: the sulky Hottentot master, standing in the midst of his scholars, neither lifted his cap from his head, nor took his hands from his pockets, when the governor approached and addressed him.

After a ride of sixteen miles, over very beautiful ground, whilst the air was dry and elastic, we reached an old post on a hill side: which had been placed there for the defence of the settlement against the Kaffirs; but which showed now how little defensible it was, by its burnt remains. It was, in fact, only a "wattle and daub" unenclosed post, of an officer's quarter, barracks, and stable; it adjoined a wooded kloof; and it was quite overlooked. But such a prospect as from this post I have seldom seen; or one more calculated to absorb the senses in admiration of the magnificence of the Creator's works.

In the distance was seen the lofty mountain of the Chumie; its double head crowned with a skeleton ridge of rocks, and its sides furrowed with ravines of rich sienna colour. Before us, and on the opposite side of the valley, was the broad face of the Eland's Berg; whose masses of dark green forest were contrasted with the light brown of the pasture. Clear skies were above, and clear streams were around; and a noble yellow wood tree, "in pride of place," waved above us in the fore-ground. It seemed as if the beauty and variety of the primitive creation was here exhibited as a type of the heavenly paradise.

After our morning's repast, we ascended the hill behind us; and then diverging to the left through *proteas* and *gladioli*, looked down on a calm retreat,—the missionary institution of the Chumie,—a thousand feet below us, the walls of which were built, and the gardens laid out, by those worthy men, Messrs. Thompson and Weir. We noticed the dark figures of Kaffirs about the buildings. Our view now took in a grand panorama from the Winterberg to the ocean, and from thence to the Bushman's River's mouth; a few white points on the broad landscape below, showed where were the tents of Major Cox's force on the Upper Keiskamma; whilst the most conspicuous object in the scene was the lofty conical mountain called Gaika's, or 'Quira, "the doctor," the head-quarters of lions, and now named, after our physician, "John Murray's Hill." A high compliment to the chief of our medical staff.

We passed across a face of a mountain, and descended by a path cut by Captain Warden to the lower ground. I collected here specimens of the guidia imberbus, rhus viminalis var., Watsonia iridiflora, muraltia sp., relhania sp., sebea aurea, Watsonia meriana, athanasia sp., buddlea sp., pelargonium sp., Weinmannia sp., and hellaria lucida. The side of the mountain was an elysium of wild flowers. In the South African spring month of October, the splendour of these and their diversity of colours, with the myriads of strange insects among them, would delight a common observer, and fascinate a naturalist. A clump of forty or fifty Kaffirs seemed waiting for us on a hill under which we had to pass; and we were on the *qui vive*, expecting a skirmish: but they merely watched our progress as we descended at nightfall into the dark glen, where

Lieutenant Sutton was attacked and worsted at the beginning of the war. We reached Fort Beaufort in safety; and returned, after a three weeks' absence, by Hermanus' kraal, now an entrenched post and named Fort Brown, to Graham's Town.

CHAPTER XXVI.

Concluding Events of the War—The Health of the Troops—Patrols harass the Enemy—The New Town—Kaffir Revenge and Cunning—Their Women take a part in the War—Captain Stretch's Success—Bloody John Bull—Fate of Lieutenant Bailie's Party—Fingo Bravery—Bookoo released—Death of Captain Lingard—The Kaffirs in Despair, resolve to pour again into the Colony—Successful Result of Operations under Major Cox—Captain W. Alexander brings the Chiefs to bay—They submit and sue for Peace—Hostilities cease—Brigade-Major Warden and the Author sent on a Mission to the Amatola—Meet the Chiefs at a Grand Conference—Kaffir Superstition—Plaatché, the Kaffir Adjutant-General—Renewed Conference—The Governor's Message—Interesting Debate on the Terms of Peace—The Result of the Conference—The Governor meets the Chiefs at Fort Willshire—Negotiations unexpectedly broken off—More Fighting—Treaties of Peace and Settlement finally made with the Gaikas, T'Slambies, and Congoes—Importance of the Arrangements now concluded.

One of the most remarkable features in the Kaffir war, was the general good health of the troops, considering the great exertions and hardships to which they were exposed. According to the testimony of Dr. Murray, the only diseases of importance that occurred were amongst the

HEALTH OF THE TROOPS. 245

burghers and newly levied men; and these mostly owing to their not having been inured to a military life. For, during the campaign, up to the 1st of July, not a single officer or soldier of the regular force had died, or required to leave the field on account of sickness. This healthy condition of the troops was ascribable, as I have before noticed, partly to the judicious and perfect manner in which the army was organized and equipped in the first instance, and partly to the salubrity of the climate: in which latter respect, it was thought that this country is not surpassed, if it be equalled, by any other in the world.

Mounted and foot patrols, from thirty to a hundred strong, were now pushed continually from the different posts in the new province, and had constant skirmishes and adventures with the enemy. To enumerate all these would be tiresome: suffice it to give a few of the most important. Lieutenants Granet and Sutton killed Kaffirs, and took cattle and goats, towards the Keiskamma. Tzatzoe, the friendly Kaffir chief, engaged in a successful encounter with some of Eno's Kaffirs. Colonel England, in returning from King William's Town, had one of his escort wounded by the enemy. Captain Ross, with Ensigns Campbell and Thompson, of the Cape mounted rifles, fought a skirmish on the Cahoon with some Kaffir horsemen armed with guns: of whom they killed and wounded several; and took nearly five hundred head of cattle and many goats from them. Whilst Lieutenant Leslie, 72nd regiment, and Lieutenant Bowker, with their Highlanders, Hottentots, and Fingoes from Fort Wellington, had two or three sharp skirmishes with the enemy on the Gonubee: killing eleven in one day, and taking two hundred and thirty head of cattle, eight horses, and many goats.

The Kaffirs afterwards made a desperate effort to carry Fort Wellington. They watched one morning when the horses of the post were turned out to graze; made a rush upon them; and carried them off, assegaing a soldier of the 72nd regiment. They then attacked the post, firing furiously from behind the abattis. Their bullets passed through the raised sentry-box in the centre of the post; and some of them were shot in attempting to clear the outer fence: but after vainly striving for some hours to penetrate into the work, they retired.

Lieutenants Bailie and Biddulph found the Kaffirs in such strength in the Umdezine bush, that they were compelled to send for assistance to Colonel Smith: who detached Captains Craven and Rawstorne to their assistance; whilst Lieutenants Sutton and Granet were directed to the Deba Flats. Some sharp skirmishes took place, in which a lieutenant of the provisional Hottentots and some Fingoes were wounded; whilst the enemy lost many men and horses in retiring over the flats. Eno's white son, a huge albino, with red hair and reddish eyes, was seen in one of these affairs. Captains Murray, Jervis, and Lacey of the 72nd regiment; Ross and Warden, of the Cape mounted rifles; Crause, Gilfillan, Cowderoy, and Bailie, of the first provisional battalion; Rawstorne, Stretch, and Crowe, of the second provisional battalion; and Field-commandant Groepe, with their subalterns, killed, in the course of ten days, above a hundred of the enemy in various affairs, and took a hundred horses and four thousand head of cattle.

Agriculture and horticulture were now rapidly advancing at King William's Town; two ploughs of the Caywoods had turned up much ground; and barley and oats were sown for forage: gardens also were dressed and planted; roads were formed; and houses of stone were built.

It is not to be understood that the enemy fled from the patrols like timid deer. On the contrary, they often made desperate onsets, particularly to retake cattle, and were sometimes successful. Thus, Captain Ross, on the lower Gonubee, had some of his men wounded, as well as his own horse, in three places; he was obliged to retire from the bush to an open spot, with the loss of his pack-horse and twelve troop-horses; and he there kept the Kaffirs at bay with his double-barrelled carbines until assistance came up, and the enemy were driven back with loss, and six horses recaptured.

Lieutenants Bailie and Biddulph, each with thirty picked Hottentots, had been again clearing the dangerous Umdezine bush; and the latter, not finding Lieutenant Bailie at the rendezvous under T"Slambie's Kop, returned to King William's Town. Heavy firing was once heard behind the Intabakandoda range: but Lieutenant Bailie's party never returned to camp; and patrols sent out in search of it were quite unsuccessful. The fate of that gallant officer was therefore, for some time, wrapped in painful mystery.

The Kaffirs, irritated to the highest degree by the losses which they had sustained, and the little repose which they now enjoyed, still did not forget their native cunning; and left nothing untried to be revenged. Thus, fifteen men of the first provisional battalion went from King William's

Town to collect corn at the yellow wood trees, on the Nameka River; women came in their way; and they were thrown off their guard. A large body of warriors then attacked them; they retired into the bed of the river to fire over the bank; but were all assegaied, save two, who fled under the bushes to camp. When a patrol went to the spot, the bodies were found stark naked in the water; and one of the slain, who had formerly lived in Kaffir-land, had his bowels taken out and hung upon the stump of a tree above him. Major Cox, posted on the Upper Keiskamma to construct a fort there, Fort Cox, lost seven of his men within sight of his encampment, in a similar manner to the above: whilst a party from Kat River, enticed by women into the gardens about the Chumie, were also set upon and destroyed. Thirty of Macomo's mounted Kaffirs, clothed and armed like Hottentots, next took some Fingoes by surprise near Fort Willshire; slew some of them; and carried off their herds in a clever manner.

Captain Stretch, half-pay, and now of the second provisional battalion,—a very valuable officer, who had been engaged in the previous Kaffir war, —was conducting a patrol of Major Cox's force back to camp, along a neck of land under the Amatola, when the Kaffirs assembled round him in great numbers, shouted, leaped into the air quivering their javelins, and showing how they would destroy their enemies. Captain Stretch took no notice of them for some time, but at dusk cooked the evening-meal; after which, making a great fire, he left it: when, in a short time, a volley was poured into the fire from the bush, and the disappointed Kaffirs were then seen round it. Still they followed him; drew up across the neck of land; and dared him to advance. He immediately charged them with twenty-four Irish bayonets of the 75th regiment, followed by his Hottentots; and the enemy fled in dismay.

We know that in England contests are reckoned of no account, unless they are accompanied with a considerable return of killed and wounded *on both sides*. The greatest generals, indeed, are those who inflict the heaviest blows on their enemies with the least loss to themselves. But our countrymen at home are not satisfied, unless they hear that a conquered foe was a worthy antagonist. John Bull likes blood. There is no denying this; and our men know it so perfectly, that on one occasion, in the Peninsula, when the British army had suffered severely, a soldier was overheard to say to his comrade, " I think the people in England will be pleased with us to-day,

FATE OF LIEUTENANT BAILIE. 251

at any rate, when they see our loss." Our Kaffir war was not a bloody one for either party: but we now record a loss which we all much felt.

No traces of Lieutenant Charles Bailie and his detachment were found for weeks. At last old Ganya, a counsellor of Gaika's, and who wished to see an end of the war, said in a parley, " A white officer and thirty Hottentots came after our people, and got as far as the Gaaga River. We watched them closely; counted their numbers; and determined to follow them and cut them off. We began fighting them early in the morning, when they were marching back to your big kraal, (King William's Town); by the time they had arrived at the hill above the old mission-station of Perie, they had lost eight men; and we also had lost a grandson of T'Slambie's, and other brave warriors. Some Amakosa were then sent to wait for our enemies in the bush near the drift; we rushed on from before and behind; some of our people were killed; and the white officer and his men fought desperately: but we closed upon them, and destroyed them all. They fell in one heap; and in a ravine you will find their bones." Captain Bailie, the father of the gallant and too-adventurous lieutenant, accordingly went with a patrol; and found in a wooded hollow and near the banks of a stream, over which there was a natural arch of fallen trees, the remains of his favourite son, lying beside the skeletons of two Kaffirs, whom he had slain. The bodies of the Hottentots lay around. Thus perished Lieutenant Bailie and his detachment.

The commander-in-chief, whilst he lamented the loss of this amiable and excellent young officer, who from the commencement of the war until his death had never ceased to merit approbation and thanks, recalled to the recollection of the troops a lesson which he had used every effort to inculcate from the opening of the contest:—never to adventure with small detachments, and especially in a country of thicket, mountain, and ravines, out of the reach of corresponding and sufficient support. For, in neglecting this precaution, if the troops should gain an advantage, they would be unequal to pursue it; and if they should meet with a check, it might end in a fatal disaster.

The Kaffirs had rather the best of it one week, in which we lost an officer and fifty Hottentots killed, besides thirty Fingoes and cattle, on the Clusie. But these losses were amply compensated afterward; and without any reinforcements or supplies of men or money from England, the commander-in-chief and his lieutenant in the new province vigorously pushed on the contest. The Fingoes on the right bank of the Buffalo, and opposite King William's Town, neglecting to set a watch as they had been directed, were attacked at twelve o'clock one night, by two hundred Kaffirs, under Mannel, a son of Dushani. Two Fingoes were killed, and a third wounded, whilst asleep in their huts. The alarm spread; the Fingoes were roused, and with shouts attacked the Kaffirs: Colonel Smith heard the cries of the furious contest; fired off a nine-pounder; and turned out Captain Bailie with a detachment to assist. The Fingoes, who had six men wounded, drove the enemy into the bed of the Buffalo River, and slew there Mannel and twelve of his men, whilst he was rallying his people; a few distant shots from Captain Bailie caused the Kaffirs to flee; and the Fingoes pursued them for three miles, and returned in triumph to their kraals. One day after this, the Fingoes killed fifteen Kaffirs at the sources of the Kabousie, where they had gone for corn.

His excellency, who had now reason to be satisfied with the conduct of Crieli with respect to his engagement,—for he had sent into Fort Warden a white ox in token of friendship, and several hundred head of cattle,—released the hostages

Bookoo and Kinki from durance in Graham's Town, and sent them back to their own country: where Bookoo's great influence might be of service to his people in enforcing a compliance with his orders, and those of the great chief, his nephew, for the fulfilment of the treaty. Bookoo was well satisfied with the treatment which he had received; and at one of the posts his arms were restored to him. This also raised our people in his estimation. He was surprised, too, at the strength of the field-work; and on a nine-pounder being fired for his edification, it was reported that "he was petrified with astonishment" at its effects. And no wonder: for a poor troop-horse, grazing quietly at the distance of a mile, was accidentally knocked on the head with the ball.

About this time, Captain Lingard, of the schooner *James*, on a trading voyage from the Cape to Mozambique, and with whom I had some years before sailed on the coast of Arabia, touched at the Cowie; and he again most imprudently visited the coast in the seat of war at the mouth of the Chalumma, *as it was said*, for wood and water. When a party from the vessel were proceeding some distance along the beach, fifty Kaffirs, headed by a white-haired chief, came out of the bush and appeared very friendly, shaking hands with Lingard and his boat's crew. The Kaffirs went to the boat, saw arms in it, and immediately plundered it: they then drew their assegais; and the captain calling out, "They are going to kill us!" attempted with his men to escape by swimming the river. But Lingard and his steward were stretched dead on the beach; and the rest swam into the sea and escaped, the Kaffirs throwing assegais after them. The schooner returned to Cape Town in charge of the mate, and resumed her voyage, but has not been heard of since.

The commander-in-chief had now the satisfaction to announce to the troops the progress and results of a series of successful movements against the enemy, under the conduct of Major Cox, in the mountains of the Chumie, Amatola, and Keiskamma. The judgment with which these operations were carried on, and the merciful forbearance shown to the vanquished foe, were alike deserving of high praise. To explain the circumstances which led to those events, it is necessary to revert to the situation of the savage enemy. Emboldened by their late partial successes, and encouraged to a prolonged resistance by the dangerous doctrines industriously disseminated in the colony in their favour—one of the advantages of a free, and most unnatural, colonial press, the border Kaffirs had assembled in considerable force; and from their bold attacks on the Fingo and Kat River people and their cattle, it was evident that more mischief was meditated. Their system of signals seemed to be good; for the moment a patrol moved, a long column of smoke rose from the neighbouring wooded hill side, and was answered from a distance.

Colonel Smith had accordingly reinforced Major Cox on the Upper Keiskamma, giving him at the same time the outlines for a general movement, and leaving the details to his own well-proved soldiership; while Captain Armstrong detached Captain W. Alexander from Fort Armstrong, to co-operate with part of the Beaufort levy and Kat River legion. Captain Alexander marched on the night of the 9th of August, and reached the Chumie, where he was joined by some Fingo warriors sent to reinforce him from Captain Baine's post at Block Drift. Seeing many fires of the enemy in the direction of the sources of the Chumie, and on the Amatola, the captain, on the 10th, with two patrols,—one under Field-cornet Piet Camphor, a bastard,—pursued the enemy, who assegaied eighty head of their own cattle, and burnt their huts.

On the 11th, the Kaffirs were seen in large bodies on the wooded acclivities, but out of musquet shot. Captain Alexander concentrated his force, which he concealed; and he then sent out a few of the Kat River legion with the Fingoes as a decoy, who on being attacked were directed to make a precipitate retreat over an open plain. They did as they were directed; Macomo on a white horse immediately rushed from the bush with his warriors; and one hundred and fifty of them, armed with musquets, fired upon the Fingoes, and pursued them rapidly. Captain Alexander having now the enemy on the plain, suddenly displayed his whole force; pushed on towards the deceived Kaffirs; and killed twenty of them on the spot: whilst many wounded fled with the rest in alarm to the cover of the woods. There, next mornng, riound an expiring fire, were found the bodies of eight Kaffirs, who, having been wounded, had crawled so far to die.

On the 12th, Captain Alexander joined Major Cox. On the 13th, the major moved with three columns: the centre one, under his own command, marched over the eastern heights of the Amatola; the right, under Major Maclean, 72nd Highlanders, moved by Burnshill up the Temaka; and the left, under Captain Alexander, by the head of the Amatola down the Temaka. These combined operations were so far successful, that nineteen of the enemy were killed before they could escape from the troops, this loss being again principally inflicted by the Fort Armstrong force:—a circumstance at which every true son of the old clan Alister, or Alexander, may be permitted to rejoice. On the 14th, the captain hemmed in a large body of the enemy under a precipitous rocky ledge; when the chiefs seeing further resistance impossible, sent out a counsellor to parley and to sue for peace.

Foreseeing what must probably soon occur, as the Kaffirs, besides their severe losses, every day felt the power of the posts of occupation to coerce and restrain them, were suffering from want of food, and were without the power of cultivating their gardens for the ensuing season, the commander-in-chief had sent instructions, that when the enemy evinced a disposition to submit, forbearance should be shown towards them; that hostilities should then cease; and that their overtures should be listened to. Captain Alexander accordingly, on this occasion, and in conformity with the general's humane intentions towards an enemy who little deserved mercy, did not pursue his advantage, but rejoined Major Cox with the messenger of peace, old Ganya. Major Cox and Brigade-major Warden, with an interpreter and two orderlies, now met the chiefs Macomo and Tyalie, with their counsellors, in conference;* and, in token of submission to his excellency's will, they sent two assegais which I had the honour of presenting to the general. I was then despatched with Brigade-major Warden, and Mr. Shepstone the interpreter, carrying a message and terms of peace to the chiefs. I need not describe how much gratified we felt, on being thus employed; and in thus assisting at the conclusion of a contest prolonged for a period of eight months. There was now of course a provisional cessation of hostilities.

We slept at Hermanus' kraal, and Fort Willshire, and early on the third day reached Mount Cox. There we found Major Cox in command of a detachment of the 75th regiment, and Hottentots of the provisional force: their tents surrounded with abattis and pitched on a hill, which is partly encompassed by the Keiskamma, and between three and four hundred feet above the level of a plain. The great Amatola mountain and other heights of inferior elevation rose above this scene; and around were beautifully wooded

* See Appendix.

slopes, and romantic glens. This position is the key of the fastnesses of the Amatola, and is admirably situated to keep the Kaffirs in check.

We found Ganya, the respectable old counsellor, smoking his pipe, with a red cap on his head, and his body wrapped in a leopard's skin mantle. He immediately despatched a clever and confidential old messenger, Plaatché, to tell Macomo and Tyalie, that a mission from the governor had arrived, and that they must hear it to-morrow, with a few followers, on an open spot under the Amatola, and about a mile and a half from our camp. We assisted the major to lay the foundation of "Fort Cox," with due ceremony; and beside a fire in the evening, I got into conversation with old Ganya about the war. "Macomo and Tyalie will tell you the causes of the war," he said: "in which, though we succeeded at first, we lost our best men. *You* know how many you have lost; *we* cannot count our slain: the kloofs are full of them. The Fingoes, protected by you, have taken away our corn and cattle; our people are starving; we had therefore become very angry (desperate) of late; and if this truce had not taken place, we would have been in the Addo bush again."

Next forenoon, at 11 o'clock, on the 24th of

August, we went unarmed, and with an escort of eight tirailleurs of the 75th regiment, across the Keiskamma, to the place of conference. The day was clear, and the temperature delightful; and the grand features of the Amatola towered above us. Looking up the valley of the Keiskamma, the bush on which waved with a light breeze, the grave of Gaika was pointed out at a deserted kraal; whilst on the river's bank below us were the two white buildings of the missionary station of Burnshill. We waited three hours under the bushes, and lying on the grass, for the chiefs; and then Ganya despatched a young Kaffir to see why they delayed. He asked permission to pass by the grave of Gaika, which was granted; and rolling his kaross round his loins, staff in hand, he ran off towards the sources of the Keiskamma.

At four o'clock P. M., a body of Kaffir horsemen was seen coming down the valley; whilst pushing vigorously after them were long black lines of footmen, staves in hand, and karosses flapping behind them, nimbly overleaping the bushes and other obstacles with their brawny limbs. "What active troops these would make," I thought; "and, if properly handled, how useful as defenders of the British possessions in this beautiful part of our mighty empire! We may compel them for a time to leave this country; but with their habits and their knowledge of the mountain paths, it will be impossible, without a larger force than will be likely to be given from home, to keep them from continually returning and plundering the colonists."

Horse and foot collected in two large bodies below the eminence on which we stood; and the whole then ascended it, and drew up three hundred yards from us in a mass, on a neck of land connecting our position with the Amatola. We were not prepared for this demonstration of strength, as it was contrary to agreement: however, we said nothing, and ran all risks. A dark body of an hundred separated themselves from the rest, and advanced towards us. In the centre, supported under the arms by two counsellors, was a short thick-set and very black Kaffir, wearing a blue cloth surcoat and leather trousers. Round his waist was strapped a brown ball-pouch, recognised as Lieutenant Bailie's, whose bones were lying on the side of a hill in sight. The eye of the chief was very keen, restless, and intelligent; his nose was depressed; and his lips were thick, with lines of debauchery about the mouth and chin. This was Macomo, the great warrior of all the Kaffir chiefs, the most active and daring in the

CONFERENCE WITH KAFFIR CHIEFS.

field, and cunning in council. Beside him walked a tall, handsome, and rakish-looking Kaffir, with a red cap set on one side of his head, and a leopard-skin mantle on his shoulders. His complexion was dark brown, and his features were regular, with an insidious smile on his countenance. This was Tyalie, chiefest of Kaffir *roués*. In the party were some of the other sons of Gaika, of inferior note: such as Cloo Cloo, a Kaffir of gloomy aspect, slightly wounded by Sutton at the commencement of the war; and Jan his brother, who threatened to squeeze the breath out of Sutton's body, without being at the trouble of assegaing him. The rest were counsellors and warriors, all bare-headed, some with torn karosses, and having a rough and desperate air about them, as that of men hunted in the woods, and ready to give or receive death at short notice.

We shook hands with the chiefs; sat down on the grass with them; and observed,—but too far off to be of any assistance,—the troops drawn out on Mount Cox. A single assegai was held up behind the chiefs, and all the staves. The governor's message was then produced, and the paper shown to the chiefs: who were told that it would take up much time to discuss all the points in it; and that, as the sun was now declining towards the west, the reading of the message must be deferred till next day. To this the chiefs acquiesced and said, " Tell us, then, any other news; our ears are impatient to hear news of any kind to sleep on." They were told that more red soldiers had arrived from England, and were now in ships on the coast—for the 27th regiment had arrived to relieve the 98th; that the böers who had been sent to their homes for the sowing season, would be again called out if required; and that the governor's hands were now stronger than ever.

All this they heard with attention, and expressive glances passed from one to the other. " We shall die of hunger, if we stay here all night," said Tyalie. " You shall have a couple of oxen to kill," said Major Cox; " and now we must wish you good night, and on the firing of the gun from the hill we will meet you to-morrow." We got up, took leave, and returned to Mount Cox; from which the oxen were sent to the Kaffirs, whose fires were soon observed among the dark bush on the mountain side. But those who had been sent from the camp with the oxen, saw also ten head of cattle driven from the bush towards the Kaffir bivouack. So much for starving warriors, and a badly supplied commissariat!

KAFFIR SUPERSTITION.

We now discovered that some time before this period, whilst Major Cox's force was encamped on lower ground, and their tents surrounded with a simple kraal of thorn bushes, they were saved by a strange circumstance from a desperate attack which the Kaffirs meditated upon them. The enemy were collecting in the kloofs around, and preparing for a deadly rush on the weak post: when one day some of the soldiers of the 75th regiment having caught a crow, at night in an idle frolic tied a burning stick to its feet and let it go. Away it flew over the camp and over the kloofs, cawing and flapping its wings in alarm, ascending and descending, whilst sparks fell from it like from a fiery meteor. The Kaffirs, waiting for midnight and the signal to attack the post, saw this omen of evil in the air, and immediately fled in affright from the neighbourhood of the demon! Our men were alert enough on their posts; but the Kaffirs, if determined to do it, could have penetrated the abattis. A sentry one night passed the word *drowsily*, " No. 13, and all's well;" the next, " No. 14, and all's well; No. 13 not alert:" on which No. 13, in rich brogue, awoke the camp with " You're a big liar!"

At night, at the fire, we asked Plaatché, the Kaffir adjutant-general, " Why the chiefs had come so well attended to the place of conference, contrary to agreement."—" The Amakosa never hurt any one at a *praat plaats*," (place of conference,) said Plaatché. " Were not the Landrost Stockenstrom and his people massacred at a conference on the Zuurberg?"—" That's true," was the answer: " but T'Slambie was very angry when he heard of it." In such a way did a lawyer answer a client, who told him, " Such a one threatens to shoot me."—" Only let him do it," said the legal adviser; " and you'll see how we'll work him for it."

A red soldier, who had been found napping on his post, was flogged in the morning out of sight of the Kaffirs in camp: but Plaatché soon found it out; and came back much astonished: imitating the punishment, shaking his head, and saying "*no joko*." He afterwards went to a howitzer, examined it and the shells, and said, " That is a very bad way to kill men; God will be very angry at this."—" It is very well for you to talk about God being angry," cried Piet Camphor, the bastard: "what do you think he will say to your tearing up and destroying his word at Burnshill?" Plaatché had nothing to offer.

On Mount Cox there grows a most remarkable tree, (similar to that noticed in chapter ii., vol. i.)

from the leaves of which, from eleven to four daily, water drops. Dr. Murray gave me a shoot from it, which I planted in government gardens, Cape Town. It may be called the Adelaide Fountain-tree.

At eleven o'clock on the 25th of August, the signal-gun fired; and, with the same escort as before, we proceeded to meet the chiefs. We had not waited long in company with old Ganya and Plaatché, when suddenly the country below us became black with Kaffirs. Horse and foot, they appeared from brake and bush, with shining musquets and bristling assegais, recalling forcibly to mind the effect of the shrill whistle of Roderick Dhu.

> "Instant from copse and heath arose,
> Bonnets and spears and bended bows;
> On right, on left, above, below,
> Sprung up at once the lurking foe:
> From shingles gray their lances start,
> The bracken bush sends forth the dart,
> As if the yawning hill to heaven
> A subterranean host had given."

The Amakosa collected silently on the slope, three or four hundred yards from us, in three dark columns. Three hundred horsemen and two hundred footmen were armed with guns: the rest with bundles of javelins. The whole might have amounted to four thousand warriors, and presented a very fine and imposing sight; and such was the intention of the chiefs. The scene too was suitable to this martial display: for the great Amatola reared its crest in the background; and trees and bushes, scattered about, increased the apparent numbers of the Amakosa behind them.

Old Ganya, looking towards the sons of Kahabe with evident satisfaction in his eye, and taking his pipe from his mouth, thus soliloquized: "These men appear very strong: but hunger is stronger than they; and if they wanted food for three days, where would they be? We have lost as many as are here in the war." Plaatché then ran towards the host like a deer, and came back to us with this message: "The chiefs hope you will not be alarmed at seeing so many warriors assembled; they have brought them together merely to show you how many of the Amakosa are dying of hunger." The answer returned was, "Though faith has been broken with us, and we have come unarmed and with a very small escort, expecting the chiefs to have done the same: yet we feel no sort of apprehension on seeing so many warriors, and are only anxious, as envoys, to deliver the general's message."

THE GOVERNOR'S MESSAGE. 269

Major Cox, as an old acquaintance, now said he would go forward and salute the chiefs. He did so: when the columns became a line, extending right across the neck of land, with the horsemen and musqueteers in front. He took off his hat, and was received with a strange whistle, now low, now loud, like the chirping of thousands of birds. A war song followed from many deep voices, the notes of which rose and fell wildly, like those of a mighty Æolian harp; and then savage yells were uttered by some as they sprung in the air with joy at the prospect of peace. " A clump of spears " broke from the main body and advanced towards us: these were the chiefs and their suite. We sat down as before; and were soon encircled and completely in the power of two hundred armed Kaffirs. The governor's message was read :—

His excellency stated that he had heard the earnest supplication of the Amakosa for peace; their contrition expressed for their conduct towards the colony; and their utter helplessness to continue the war. That though he had now increased power to chastise them, he would refrain from doing so: provided they placed themselves entirely at his disposal; gave up Suta and Sandilli; and surrendered their fire-arms, ammunition, and the colonial Hottentots still among them. He pledged himself to give them a country *on this side of the Kye*, though not the Amatola, and to uphold the authority of their chiefs, as long as they conducted themselves peaceably towards the colony.

Tyalie then said, "We have heard the governor's word, and are happy to receive his envoys. But why does he ask us to give up our fire-arms; and who is to defend us from our enemies if we do this?" Answer: "The governor with his troops will defend you, if you are friends with the colonists." Macomo: "These are the terms of peace we have just heard: is peace made in this way between other nations at war? We hear of conditions: we thought we should have obtained peace without these; and that the governor would only have said,—there is no more war between the English and the Amakosa." Answer: "It is usual in making peace between two nations who have been at war, to draw up certain terms; and you have now heard those granted by the governor: if you comply with them now, perhaps he may give you greater indulgence hereafter."

Macomo, when not speaking, sat reclining on the breast of Plaatché, and occasionally smoked a curious double-headed pipe, which was passed round; when he spoke, he leant forward and delivered himself with energy. Tyalie sat with his arms on his knees and wrapped in his kaross. The rest were silent and orderly, and paying the deepest attention.

Macomo continued: "We wished to make peace long ago."—"Why then did you not do it?"—"We did not like the terms, which were, to come into your camp below the Intabakandoda and give ourselves up. Hintza told us not to do this: besides, we know that when two great men came to you, one was killed; and the other was made a prisoner." Answer: "You allude to Hintza and Bookoo. Hintza was treated by us with great distinction: but he deceived us, and broke the peace; his blood, as you know, was unintentionally shed; it was by his own treachery and by his attempt to escape, after due warning of the consequences, that his death was occasioned. Bookoo was kept for a time as a hostage; and has now gone back to his people, to make them fulfil Crieli's treaty." Macomo: "What will be done with Suta and Sandilli?" Answer: "They will be taken to Fort Willshire; and the governor will give them a country: to Suta for her good deeds, and to Sandilli as the principal chief of your tribe." Tyalie: "What will the governor do with the Hottentots who have been with us: will he kill them? We don't refuse to give them up, we only ask the question."—"He will send them back to the colony; we don't believe he will kill them." Macomo: "If these conditions are all fulfilled, what advantages will the Amakosa derive from the governor?" Answer: "He will protect them, and try to make them happy and comfortable."

The chiefs being in the midst of their warriors, and we being completely in their power, they naturally, at the time, forgot their real circumstances, felt uplifted, and did not now speak in that low submissive tone which they had used when they first implored for peace and mercy. Still they were not in the least insolent.

Macomo: "There were three great things in the world: Hintza, Gaika, and cattle. Hintza we don't see any more; Gaika died of sickness; and our cattle are all gone. Who is to make up to us for our great losses?" Answer: "Though you plundered the colony, the governor does not ask you for any cattle now: he looks to Crieli for cattle. As to Hintza and Gaika, we could not help their deaths." Ganya: "What pledge have we that we shall be protected, if we agree to the terms of peace?" Answer: "The governor's word; and it now rests with yourselves, whether peace is made or not." Tyalie: "What is that about our leaving the Amatola?" Answer: "You will get the country between the Gonubee, the Kabousie, and the Kye."—"What will be in the Amatola?"—"Military posts: but to save a long discussion, the chiefs had better now see the governor, and speak to him themselves."

Here I offered to remain as a hostage with the tribe, for the safety of the chiefs; and Captain Stretch said, if two were required, he would also stay. Macomo: "We wish to send a message to the governor about the terms of peace, before we see him: all we now wish is, to stay peaceably in our kraals, hunt bucks, and cultivate the ground." Answer: "That is just what the governor would like to see." Macomo: "When God made the world, he told the nations to live at peace with each other."—"Why, then, did you go to war with us?" Macomo: "Hei! hei! No, no; we did not begin the war."—"Did you not invade the colony and lay it waste?"—"If you ask at Fort Willshire and Kat River, you will hear there how the war began: some people there, are not in the dark about it." Answer: "We heard that at these places there were some bad Hottentots, who agreed to help you, when you proposed to them go to war." These were men, discontented when the vagrant act was agitated. "But not to talk of old things at present, let us discuss the terms of peace. You have conducted yourselves and talked to-day like men; let us now hear what you wish." Macomo: "We wish to be allowed to live in our own country, and to be the governor's children:"—British subjects, in short. Tyalie: "What is to be done with the T'Slambies?" Answer: "They have not sent in their submission yet: they will be dealt with afterwards." Tyalie: "If we give up your Hottentots, you ought to give us up our Fingoes: they have turned against us, and plundered us terribly. Macomo has lost his own cattle by them." Answer: "All that was lost in war; and in a war which you have brought on yourselves."

Here a short Kaffir, with a very intelligent look, and who was recognised to be Elias, formerly a trooper in the Cape corps, stood up and said, "We are thankful that there is now a prospect of peace between us and the English; we wished a peace such as Lord Charles formerly made, and without any terms; we cannot bear to leave the grave of Gaika and the Amatola." Answer: "Peace cannot be now granted without

THE TERMS OF PEACE. 275

terms, after the destructive sweep which you made into the colony, without any declaration of war. Our king has heard of the war. The governor is now stronger than ever; he has more red soldiers; and the böers will all be called out again if necessary."

Macomo, with great energy, and striking the ground with his hand, said, " Don't talk to us of the böers: the böers are your enemies. We have been supplied with powder by some of them; and they have told us to continue the war: others also have told us not to submit." Macomo here alluded to certain böers who had fled with their slaves when the emancipation took place; and who were now beyond the boundary. As to the last clause, that referred to some villainy hatched in Cape Town, and communicated through certain Kat River Hottentots:

"Some treason, masters, yet stand close!"

The conference had lasted five hours, and the day was drawing to a close: for what I have related is merely a specimen of the Kaffir style, and I took a note of every thing that was discussed on the spot. We therefore now desired to finish the conference, and obtain the ultimatum of the chiefs. Macomo, touching Tyalie, then said, " We are Gaikas: he was a friend of the English;

we now wish to be so also. When Gaika died, he gave us in charge to Hintza: he is gone, and the governor will be our father. We will tell you of your bad people whenever we find them out; for we wish the government to be strong. In the name of the children of Gaika, we thank you for the trouble you have taken this day; we hope the governor will also thank you; and that you will not tire of assisting us. You, Cox, and Warden, are our old friends, and never did us any injustice or wrong: plead for us, and speak in our favour. We are now reduced very low, and are under the foot of the governor: but say to him, we do not wish to leave the Amatola. Our cattle would all die in new pasture. We will become his children in our own country."

We promised to report all that passed at this great conference to his excellency the governor, whom the chiefs must be prepared to meet before long. We then took leave of them; the Kaffir host soon disappeared; and the splendid wilderness was silent and solitary as before. We rode rapidly back by Willshire to Graham's Town, distant about sixty miles; and submitted the report of the proceedings under the Amatola to his excellency. He then sent a message to the chiefs to meet him at Fort Willshire; Colonel

Smith and Captain Warden had another conference with the chiefs at Fort Cox;* and on the 8th of September we were again in the saddle, and on our way to the Keiskamma. Colonel Smith came to Willshire to meet the general; and Colonel England was also there, with twelve other officers and several hundred red jackets of the garrison and of the out-post reliefs. The young officers sported on the hills; rowed about in a boat in a long pool of the beautiful river; and had social meetings in the evenings. Captain and Mrs. Halifax had the charge of entertaining the general's party; and their kindness and hospitality were very great.

On the 11th, the chiefs were announced to be approaching; Colonel Smith rode out to meet them; and conducted them into the fort. The dark horsemen drew near; rain fell as they entered the gate; and then a rainbow spanned the green and rocky banks of the Keiskamma,—an emblem of hope and of future good for Kaffir-land. Macomo and Tyalie were now accompanied by Umhala, the regent and chief warrior of the T'Slambies, a stout and dark Kaffir, and of an open and frank address; and with them also was Eno, a shrivelled and exceedingly cunning-look-

* See Appendix.

ing old man. Kusia, Ganya's son, and Fadani, Botma's son, were here too. But Botma himself, having had charge of the Amakahabee cattle on the other side of the Kye during the war, had not yet given them up.

The general met the chiefs under a tree in the square, with all the officers in attendance; said that he was happy to see them, and listen to their prayers for mercy, and to be received as British subjects; and that he had now come to Fort Willshire to conclude a peace with them. That then the friends of the king of England would be their friends, and his enemies would be their enemies also; and that now, during the discussion of the terms of peace, they would be supplied with every thing of which they stood in need. At their own desire, the chiefs occupied tents outside the fort, and every thing betokened a speedy arrangement of the important measure for which they had at last met his excellency: when the negotiations were most unexpectedly interrupted.

The commander-in-chief now received reports, that several bands of Kaffirs, in breach of the truce, were making inroads within the old border line; plundering cattle, and having, in one or two instances, murdered the herds. He therefore called the chiefs before him, and told them that the treaties must now be broken off, and the war renewed, unless a stop was promptly put to these atrocities; that for this purpose he would now dismiss them to return to their tribes; that he recommended them, if they wished for peace and mercy, to take the most energetic and effectual measures for recalling their people from those inroads; and that for this object he would allow them three days. If they faithfully fulfilled it, he would then proceed to confirm the treaties, now broken off; but in failure of it, he would instantly attack them, and carry on the war to the last extremity, and until they should be utterly rooted out of the country. The chiefs immediately proceeded to their respective tribes for the purpose enjoined.

The cause of these extraordinary proceedings among their people was, that those among them who had lost every thing in the war, seeing a prospect of peace, were determined to collect a stock of cattle to begin the world with again. Accordingly, they had banded together and committed the forays to which we have alluded. But many of them suffered severely for their temerity. Lieutenants Moultrie and Bingham, and that fine specimen of a British veteran, old Sheffield, of Commatty's Drift, and others, lying in wait for them in the bush, shot several of their number as they were returning with cattle from the colony. Field-cornet Piet Uys, the very gallant Dutchman upon whom Hintza had vainly endeavoured to impose, as before related in these pages, pursued, with some burghers and Jan Tzatzoe, a considerable body of Kaffirs, who were plundering the Fingoes of the Clusie; hemmed them in at a kloof; and summoned them to lay down their arms. They assegaied his messenger; a desperate conflict then ensued; the Kaffirs broke their assegais for stabbing; and some of the burghers were wounded: but Piet Uys brought down eighteen karosses; and the rest then fled. Field-cornet Rontenbach, at this time, killed also fourteen in a similar manner near Bathurst; and Field-cornet Dreyer, seven at New Year's River.

The foraying ceased, and human blood, with which the frontier-land had been so long drenched, now no longer ebbed out in death. Long may it cease to flow! The chiefs returned to Fort Willshire on the morning of the 17th: when the governor, having reason to be satisfied that they had done their utmost to recal their straggling people, and to stop the marauding for which they had been sent away, concluded with them a treaty of peace, of which the substance is now given :

The tribe of Gaika, represented by Sandilli, the young and principal chief, Suta his mother, Macomo and Tyalie, his elder brothers, Eno and Botma, his relatives, having prayed for peace, and to be admitted as British subjects to live under British laws; the governor, in the name of the king his master, granted their prayer.

The above representatives of the tribe, solemnly promising and engaging for themselves and their people, to bear true and faithful allegiance to his majesty the king of England; to be friends to his friends, and enemies to his enemies; to obey the commands of his majesty's governor and the duly constituted colonial authorities; and to live in submission to the general laws of the colony: the governor and the laws would, at the same time, extend to them the same protection and security, as to the other subjects of his majesty.

The chiefs and representatives were made aware, that the British laws inflict severe punishments, and even death itself, on those who commit treason or rebellion, or take up arms against the king or the government of the colony. That these laws also punished with death, murder, rape, setting houses and property on fire, theft, whether of horses, cattle, sheep, goats, or other property; and that such penalties would be equally incurred, if they were committed by any member of the above tribes against each other, as if committed against other inhabitants of the colony. The Fingo nation, having also become subjects of the king of England, any molestation of them would be most severely visited upon the offenders.

Proceedings against any one for the pretended crime of *witchcraft* were expressly forbidden, and would be severely punished. At the same time the chiefs and representatives were to understand, that the English laws would not interfere with their domestic regulations, nor their customs, in so far as they did not involve a breach of the above-cited laws.

The chiefs and representatives engaged to prevent now, and for the time to come, all predatory incursions on the colony; and also to deliver up the musquets in their possession: the governor at the same time promising them perfect protection of their property, and the maintenance of their rights.

The governor, yielding to the earnest supplication of the aforesaid chiefs, and under the promise of their keeping peace and good order, would

FINAL TREATIES OF PEACE. 283

not turn them out of their native districts; but continued them in the Amatola and country included between the mountains, the Chumie, Keiskamma, Deba, Kabousie, and Kye, as was more minutely described in the treaty: reserving places and lines for churches, schools, magistracies, military stations, outspans, and roads. Suta and Sandilli had land assigned to them at Burnshill; and to Matwa and Tinta, the two sons of Gaika, who had come out from their people at the commencement of the war, were lands appropriated about the Chumie.

In token of fealty to the king of England, and in acknowledgment of holding the land under his majesty's sovereignty, each of the chiefs engaged annually to deliver, to a proper authority, *a fat ox*, or else forfeit his lands, until re-granted.

English resident magistrates, ministers of the gospel, and schoolmasters, would be appointed to the above tribe; and the chiefs were also to act as magistrates over their people, and to give up any one of their own or other native tribe, or any English, Dutch, or Hottentots, guilty of crimes against the colony. They promised also, at all times, to communicate information of danger threatening the colony. The chiefs were farther held responsible for giving up stolen property found among their people. Commissioners,—officers and ministers of the gospel,—were appointed to carry the treaty into effect, and to locate the tribe: Colonel the Hon. H. G. Smith, C.B., being chief commissioner. When the above treaty was fulfilled and ratified, and all the above arrangements completed, the commission would be dissolved, and a resident agent appointed for the tribe.

Finally, none of the tribe of Gaika were to be allowed to come into the old colony without a pass, signed by the commissioner or resident agent; and then they must be unarmed.

The tribe of T'Slambie, represented by the young and principal chief Siwana, his mother Nonubé, his uncle the regent Umhala, and his relatives Tzyolo and Gazelli, had a treaty similar to the above made with them: whilst the land assigned to them was the tract of country bounded by the high road between King William's Town and the principal ford over the Kye, by the Lower Kye, by the sea-coast, and by the Cahoon. The tribe of Congo, represented by Pato, Kama, and Cobus, had also a separate treaty; and were located from the Buffalo westwards to nearly the Great Fish River. Tzatzoe had land allotted to him on the Buffalo.

" Now, therefore," as his excellency remarked, " these people being placed as his majesty's subjects, under the power of the British laws, and upon lands granted to them by his majesty, there will be tried, and upon the only basis which could ever have offered the most distant prospect of success, the great experiment of gradually introducing among them the habits and obligations of civilized life, and a sense of the sacred duties of religion."

The importance of all these arrangements will be best estimated by reflecting that the war had now been brought to a favourable conclusion; that the security of the old colonial border was thus apparently most effectually secured; that between six and seven thousand square miles of territory had been annexed to his majesty's dominions by conquest; that nearly a hundred thousand souls, Amakosa and Fingoes, were added to the former population of the colony, previously estimated at one hundred and forty thousand; and that all this had evidently been effected to the great benefit of the new subjects of our most gracious king.

His excellency again visited the Fingo location on the Clusie; and, on the 25th of September, returned to Graham's Town.

CHAPTER XXVII.

Results of Peace—Board of Relief—A Contusion—The Governor leaves Graham's Town for Cape Town—Unpleasant Adventure—Salem—Uitenhage—Our future Policy—A Word in Favour of Cape Town—Uitenhage Water and Widows—Bethelsdorp—A Word on the Missionary Schools—Port Elizabeth—Good out of Evil—The Christening of the D'Urban Lighthouse Rock—Steam Navigation—Captain Gardiner arrives from Natal—The British Territory there—Dingan and the Zoolahs—Uitenhage—Vanstaden's River—Human's Farm—Moolman's—Needy Hottentots—Meeding's—Rademayer's—Goose Kraal—Cradock Pass—George—Pakelsdorp—The Cayman's Hole—The Zitzikamma Forest—Mossel Bay—Muller's—Lombard's—Swellendam—A Comparison—The Patriarch Lindé—Caledon—De Kock's—Monuments to the Surveyor-General—Character of the Böers—Somerset—Sandfleet—Arrival in Cape Town.

THE Kaffir war was now, therefore, brought to a very satisfactory conclusion; though we were still, and for months afterwards, kept in perfect ignorance here how the war was viewed at home. For the governor had received neither answers to his reports, instructions for his guidance, nor assistance in men or money. This silence was to be attributed, I believe, to the secret and false intelligence conveyed to government by the London mission, and anti-colonial and radical party.

We now began to think of our return to Cape Town: but before I quit the frontier, it may be well to notice the proceedings of a board appointed by his excellency for the relief of the sufferers left in a state of destitution by the invasion of the colony. According to the very clear report of the chairman of the board, the Rev. Mr. Heaviside, acting government-chaplain at Graham's Town, who bore testimony to the becoming temper with which the colonists of all classes had endured their most undeserved misfortunes, the numbers relieved by the board, which distributed charity in the shape of rations of food, clothing, medicines, &c., amounted to twelve thousand individuals, English, Dutch, and Hottentots. But, besides these, there were many sufferers who, having saved a wreck of their property, did not apply to the board. The claimants for compensation for losses sustained by the invasion, amounted to three thousand; and the value of their property in horses, cattle, sheep and goats, houses and wagons, was estimated at about three hundred thousand pounds.

In the colony, in India, in the Mauritius, &c.,

handsome subscriptions had been made for the sufferers, and the amount administered through the board of relief. But in the mother-country, the barefaced and malicious falsehoods published by the radical press* in Cape Town, and also privately conveyed to England, seemed effectually to have prevented any sympathy for the suffering colonists, and to have stopped up the principal channel through which relief was anxiously expected. Among these gross fabrications were such statements as, that the colonists had brought the war upon themselves; and that the impoverished Kaffirs had been driven to desperation by bad treatment: though the fact was, that they had never before been so rich in horses and cattle, as they were when they burst into the colony. It was also falsely and audaciously asserted that the irruption was insignificant; and that the war was carried on with undue severity, and needlessly protracted: as if the war could have been closed consistently with British honour, or a peace have been made, till the enemy sued for mercy. But it is not too late yet to grant assistance from England. Thousands of British colonists have been reduced to beggary by a savage enemy,

---

* This was under the chief of the London mission; and the communications were made to Mr. Buxton in England.

and shamefully insulted by an unnatural faction; and will the British public, ready at all times to succour distressed foreigners, withhold compensation and relief from their ruined fellow-subjects in South Africa? Sincerely we hope not: if this, and other narratives which like this speak facts, obtain the belief which is due to the plain unvarnished truth.

The governor was detained in Graham's Town nearly six weeks, in September and October, by pressing frontier business; and I was therefore enabled to lay up, as I ought to have done before, for a contusion on the ankle. In other parts of the world I have seen bruises and wounds, in sound constitutions, heal rapidly. But not so in South Africa: for though the climate is most healthy, it is necessary to beware of having the skin ruffled, or allowing inflammation, as I did, to get into a joint. In such cases, weeks, months, and even years may elapse before the is cured.

Having been mercifully permitted to enjoy almost uninterrupted good health in all situations hitherto, I now felt severely my long and tedious confinement to the sofa, and to the shade of a blossoming pear-tree in the garden of my hospitable entertainer, Mr. W. R. Thompson. I set myself down as incurable, and fancied there was now an end to all future enterprise in my country's service: but I was consoled by the opening and daily increasing beauties of the South African spring. The rustling foliage, the verdant and flower-enamelled slopes, the murmur of waters, the voice of birds, and the accents of kind friends, were altogether sufficient to beguile me of every dispiriting thought; and eventually I was most particularly indebted to the skill and attention of Dr. Murray for a perfect recovery.

It was the end of October before we left Graham's Town for the Cape, from which the governor had now been absent nine months. Sir Benjamin D'Urban had spent on the colonial border a much longer period than any former governor; and he now quitted it, carrying with him the high esteem and sincere affection of the community in general. They felt that their gratitude was due both for his public acts as a military commander and civil governor; and for his great efforts to alleviate the distresses, and to ensure the future safety of so many sufferers by every practicable means, and often from his own private resources. Such were the sentiments expressed in the frontier journal, and in the addresses from all parts of the colony.

We bade farewell to our kind friends, with every feeling of regard, and with heartfelt wishes for their prosperity; and mounting on a very stormy and rainy day, we took the direction of the Cape. His excellency, Dr. Murray, and the reduced escort, made a detour by Bathurst; slept there; and next day were lost for nine hours in rain and mist between the Cowie bush and Salem: which last place, they did not reach until ten o'clock, P. M. Major Dutton and myself went direct to Salem by the romantic pass called Howison's Poort. At Salem we were entertained by the excellent missionaries Messrs. Palmer and Davis; an additional grant of commonage was given to the village; and other arrangements were made for its benefit. The Wesleyan church, and Mr. White's well-conducted school, which have been long established there, seem to give it every prospect of thriving.

Accompanied part of the way by the heads of families, we next rode towards Assegai Bush, and slept at Mrs. Pollard's inn at Bushman's River, famous for spitch-cock and Devonshire cream. On the following day, we reached Webber's comfortable hostel on Sunday River: crossing the stream by an indifferent punt, out of which some of our horses rolled into the swollen current. Then passing by the grazing-ground of the Gora, we dismounted at the drostdy-house of Uitenhage, the residence of the civil commissioner, Mr. Van Der Reit: from whom, and from whose excellent family, we experienced great hospitality for many days. The town was illuminated and salutes fired in the evening, in honour of his excellency.

Uitenhage, with its wide streets and garden houses, is situated on a slope, and in the midst of a noble valley of the Zwartkop's River: up which, and in the distance, are the grand features of the Winter Hoek mountains. Uitenhage is the heart of the Cape colony, and its natural capital; it is close to Port Elizabeth; and stands in the centre of the most thriving districts.

One of two things must be done before long. Either the seat of government must be removed from Cape Town hither; or additional expense must be incurred for a lieutenant-governor for the frontier. After which, by watching well our boundaries on the north and east; by occupying and fortifying Natal on our eastern flank; by securing both the respect and fear of our neighbours; by maintaining friendly relations with them; and by increasing our influence through constant intercourse—by all this, and by additional capital and additional hands for the colony, and by good government, the Cape of Good Hope, from its situation, capabilities, and climate, must become a most splendid possession of Great Britain.*

Amidst all these objects, however, we must not overlook Cape Town and Table Bay. " Some of the old croakers," said a most intelligent naval resident to me, one day in conversation, "used very often to be telling me of the good old times, when Table Bay, thronged with shipping, gave life and spirit to the community; and all was hilarity and happiness. Being somewhat bored by repetitions of such relations, I determined to satisfy myself on the subject, by examining the records of the port-captain's office from the earliest periods, and I found none previous to 1808. An extract from this record will now show you what reliance we should place upon the memory and garrulity of old gentlemen who amuse themselves by lamenting the degeneracy of the present, and by pitying the rising generation."

Abstract of the number and tonnage of British

* Here let me pay a tribute of admiration to that very great and valuable achievement of Mr. Montgomery Martin,—his *History of the British Colonies.*

merchant ships, men of war, transports, and foreign ships of war, which entered Table Bay since 1808 : coasters not included.

Date.	Tonnage of Merchant Ships.	Number of Merchant Ships.	British Ships of War.	British Transports.	Foreign Ships of War.
1808	28,373	83	26	10	A prize.
1812	15,426	67	17	13	A prize.
1816	56,913	131	32	11	—
1820	67,563	180	4	8	2
1824	50,637	135	—	2	3
1828	73,331	192	5	—	4
1832	77,719	238	2	—	2
1835	104,259	328	4	—	3

Note.—If the port were secured by a jetty, almost all the vessels which now touch at St. Helena would touch here for supplies, where they are so much more abundant and cheap.

"This is a very flattering account of the increasing prosperity of the Cape," I said: "but at St. Helena, I saw by the returns that three hundred ships had put in there for refreshments in 1829, and six hundred in 1834."

"You will also observe," continued my friend, "that in the short space of ten years, the tonnage and number of vessels at the Cape is doubled. The expenditure, by disbursements for the crews of ships, for provisions and stores, together with the outlay of passengers, cannot be less than fifty thousand pounds per annum. And, in 1833, when I made the calculation on the best data which I could procure, the expenditure of visitors from India and other places to the eastward, residing at the Cape for the recovery of health, could not be estimated at less than another fifty thousand pounds. So that, without including the extensive refitting of dismasted vessels, or repairs to their hulls, a sum of one hundred thousand pounds a-year is put into circulation by the shipping and visitors, and is widely diffused amongst almost all classes of society in Cape Town and the vicinity."

" Have not the dangers of Table Bay been much exaggerated?"

" Undoubtedly; and by people interested in describing its dangers. From Table Bay there is egress at all times and seasons, save only during a northerly gale, which seldom blows more than twenty-four hours, and does not occur in a series of years. Thus, from July 1831 to January 1836, nearly six years, there has not been a severe gale from the northward; *and consequently no wreck:* although more than twelve hundred ships have entered the bay in that period; and there have never been less than ten, and sometimes twenty vessels at anchor, through the several winter months. If vessels were well supplied with ground tackle, and properly looked after, a wreck in Table Bay would be a rare occurrence."

"Why then was the dock-yard removed to Simon's Bay?"

"It is provoking to think of this. Every one acquainted with the Cape knows how south-east winds prevail, and how long they continue. In the event of a war, then, how could the navy in Simon's Bay protect the trade in Table Bay? I have known a fine frigate attempt for days together to get out of False Bay, but in vain. If the money laid out in the dock-yard at Simon's Bay had been expended on a break-water at Table Bay, the benefits to Cape Town, and *to the navy*, would have been very great. Additional protection would have been afforded to the town and shipping, besides an immense increase of trade. At Cape Town a squadron or fleet can be provisioned and watered in a few hours. Mr. Maclear, our indefatigable astronomer, gives the vessels the mean time, now, every day at a fixed hour; and this also is a great inducement to enter the bay when chronometers get adrift. But if a southeaster is blowing strong, and a vessel is beating in, do not let her anchor at Robben Island to leeward, and have to beat up again against the current and swell: rather let her keep under easy sail to the southward, between Robben Island and Green Point, until the gale subsides. She will then get easily into the anchorage, though in a manner quite contrary to Horsburgh's directions. I do not despair yet of seeing Cape Town one of the most thriving in the world, and I pray for its prosperity."

The Kaffirs had been all around Uitenhage, though checked by that determined old soldier, the late landrost, Colonel Cuyler; and it was necessary to provide for its future defence. Two redoubts were accordingly marked out; and, with Schlimmers, the active German miller, and a party of banditti, as the Dutch call convicts,

"Making sweet music with their feet,"

the bush was soon cleared away for these works, to be named the Ladies' and Cuyler's redoubts.

Uitenhage is famous for water and for widows. A new and a better course was assigned to the former for the supply of the town; but sorry were we that we had not leisure or opportunity to alter the condition of the latter: though one with a good house and garden of her own, good-naturedly said, she was willing to take as her second spouse either "*a predikant, an offisher, or a shentleman.*" She had broken the heart-strings of a poor fiddler, who had aspired to share her possessions. But she was not the only " character " of the place: there was also a heaven-taught midwife, and a *ci-devant* lieutenant; who, on the anniversary of any great battle in which he had been present, paraded through the streets in ancient regimentals, and helmet with flowing red mane, to the surprise and delight of the children.

Van Royen's farm being exchanged for the government land at Gora, three thousand morgen of additional pasturage was now assigned for free Hottentot locations, and for the use of this delightful village, which doubtless will be a considerable city before many years. Having a canny anticipation of this probable grandeur of Uitenhage, I purchased sundry morgen of land there, and introduced the emblem of peace, the olive, in the hope that it may ultimately be beneficial for the eastern province. The schools were examined here; and Mrs. Collins's young ladies' seminary, and Mr. Highman's coloured school, were found to be very creditable to the teachers.

After a fortnight's sojourn at Uitenhage, Dr. Fairbridge, a gentleman and scholar of extensive acquirements, accompanied Dr. Murray and myself to the London missionary institution of Bethelsdorp. Low hills were on the right; looking down on a bare country, some white-washed houses were seen built in a square, near the bed of a small stream; and round them were scattered decayed mud and reed huts. Such was this "oasis in the desert." Mr. Kitcherman, the superintendent, told us that on the books of the institution there were about fifteen hundred names of Hottentots, all admitted without any certificate of character; and that of these, four hundred were men,—a number of whom were still in the field, enrolled in the provisional battalions. Before the war some of them had occasionally employed themselves as wagon-drivers and leaders, between Graham's Town and Port Elizabeth: but we heard from the neighbouring farmers, that they experienced the greatest difficulty in procuring any hired servants from the institution. The sect of Independents (London mission) does not encourage the Hottentots to enter into service: neither could we discover that, among the Bethelsdorp flock, either marriage or agriculture was promoted; or that title-deeds were given to the Hottentots for allotments of missionary land. They were therefore kept for ever in a state of pupilage, immorality, and concubinage; and completely subjected to the jesuitical influence of the missionaries. But this we heard here:—that the children of the infant school had, the week before our visit, been enrolled as members of the temperance society; and that a white-headed Hottentot or two, eighty years old, might be seen learning the alphabet, spectacles on nose. What a wonder-working system it is!

The reader will not require spectacles to see that we do not think highly of some of these institutions, as they are now conducted. Schools of idleness they are, instead of schools of industry as they ought to be. The original institution of them was excellent: for wandering Hottentots, and vagabonds of all kinds plundering on the borders, were collected at these institutions, and in part reclaimed. There is also no doubt that, as regarded the coloured races, former governments neglected their duty, and allowed other people to do that which should have been their own peculiar care. But these days are gone by; and, we hope, for ever. A circular has lately been addressed to the civil commissioners by Sir Benjamin D'Urban, calling upon them to send in immediately an account of all ungranted lands in their districts, in order that allotments may be assigned to the Hottentots of good character in all parts of the colony, with means of moral and religious instruction. The missionaries will thus be relieved from the trouble of congregating them in large and dangerous masses at the schools.

From Uitenhage we rode on to Port Elizabeth: where his excellency for three weeks occupied a suite of rooms at that good house of entertainment Scorey's hotel. On the arrival of the governor, there was a grand illumination of the town; salutes were fired; and a round of dinners and balls were given by the hospitable and spirited inhabitants of this thriving sea-port. The tail of a Mauritius hurricane had just visited Algoa Bay with irresistible force; and, notwithstanding the excellent holding-ground, had driven on shore and totally wrecked three merchant vessels, whose anchors and cables were too light. No accident of any kind had happened here throughout the whole war; and a misfortune like the above, had been of very rare occurrence during the last twenty years.

But good often comes out of evil; "the tree of pain may yield the fruit of plenty;" and in order to obviate the necessity for the present surf-boats, the governor had now surveys made for a break-water or pier, for laying down moorings, south-east and north-west,—the direction of the prevailing winds. His excellency also projected the erection of a light-house on Point Recife, which the inhabitants petitioned might be called after him; and a beacon there was named after that active officer of the royal engineers, Captain Selwyn, who erected it.

The inhabitants made a grand party for his excellency at Point Recife, at the naming of the light-house rock. They went out there on horseback and in wagons, the distance being nine miles: though a party of young ladies and gentlemen made it a good deal more; having been lost for several hours in the bush and among the parallel ridges of sand hills. But at last they appeared, and among them " the Lady of the Rock," Miss Heugh: with whom we all proceeded to the site of the light-house; and, after witnessing " the breaking of the bottle," heard an impressive address, for the occasion, by the Rev. Mr. M'Cleland. The day was clear and fine; flags were displayed; a piece of artillery was fired; tents were pitched on the beach; and a handsome *déjeuné* was laid out. The sea-fowl, in amazement, careered round us in large white flocks; and a combat took place between a whale and a thrasher, all in honour of the occasion. If, indeed, the crowd of people had been seen from a vessel, clustering on the rock and moving on the sands, we must have been taken for cast-aways, or fugitives from the Kaffirs, and not for folks met, as we were, on such a joyous occasion.

At Port Elizabeth, I experienced great satisfaction in bathing every morning in a hole of the rocks near the mouth of the Baken's River; and all the party felt strong and healthful: though the good people tried all they could to kill us with kindness, which was "a chain about our feet."

From some inquiries which I made regarding the establishment of steam navigation from Cape Town to Port Elizabeth and the Fish River, it appeared to be very practicable and easy. A steamer of three hundred tons would be sufficient for the billows of Lagullas, and for entering the South African rivers. The fuel from the Cape would be coal: but as westerly winds prevail all the year round, the sails would be mostly used to stem the easterly current; whilst from the Fish River and Knysna, wood in any quantity can be procured. The expense, therefore, of fuel would be very trifling; and the advantage to the frontiers and to speculators must be great. Besides the D'Urban light-house on Point Recife, two others are required: one on Cape Point; the other at Lagullas. Let the South African land company, of which we hear, with a capital of five hundred thousand pounds, think of these things; and the shareholders will exceedingly benefit the colony, themselves, and commerce in general.

An important event now took place in the arrival of Captain Gardiner, royal navy, from Natal by land, full of information regarding that part of the eastern coast. Inspired by a noble and most disinterested enthusiasm to do good to his species, he had selected the untried field of the Zoolah country for the scene of his labours. Without fanaticism, and actuated by a pure philanthropy and with ample private means, he had come from England, a year before this, with a Polish gentleman, Mr. Berken; and they had passed through Kaffir-land, just previous to the indiscriminate massacre of the whites in the colony, and on the borders. Arrived at Natal, Captain Gardiner was surprised at the extreme beauty and fertility of the country; the salubrity of the climate; the abundance of water and grass; the great herds of elephants and buffaloes in the woods, affording in ivory and hides much wealth to the huntsman; the luxuriant wild growth of indigo and coffee; and an excellent harbour, with twelve or fourteen feet water on the bar at spring tides.

About thirty Englishmen were found at Natal:

wild and hardy rovers; traders and hunters; living in the woods and in Kaffir huts; shooting wild beasts; and cohabiting with native women. There was no head among them, no law, and no restraint; and though three thousand armed Fingoes lived under their protection, the white men were quite at the mercy of their neighbours, the warlike Zoolahs. For many years has this very promising possession of England been entirely overlooked: its history is told in few words. In 1688, M. P. Chavonne, the Dutch governor of the Cape, despatched the galliot *Noord* to Natal, to rescue the survivors of the wrecked crew of the *Slaverins*, and to purchase the port and adjacent country from Ingesé, the chief: which last object was accomplished for twenty-nine thousand guilders in merchandise. But more attention was subsequently paid to Delagoa than to Natal, both of which were undoubtedly Dutch possessions. By the articles of capitulation of 1806, the Cape and all its dependencies, of which Natal was one, fell to the English; and though American vessels, much to the danger of the Cape colony, have occasionally put into Natal to barter arms and ammunition with the natives, for their country produce, yet Englishmen only have been settled there since 1824.

It will hardly be believed, but such is the case, that the superintendent at the Cape of the London Society's missions belonging to the Independent connexion, instead of applying to his own countrymen for assistance, invited American missionaries over, to be placed with the two Zoolah chiefs of the coast and of the interior, Dingan and Umsuligas, *Masulicatsi*. Thus would be established a chain of American posts, as it were, behind his majesty's colony of the Cape of Good Hope, with, probably, very fatal effect on British interests. The Americans arrived in 1835, and went in two sections, two preachers and a surgeon in each, to their destinations. I saw one party at Bethelsdorp: good men, I dare say, but uncommonly reserved! How they will succeed remains to be proved: but it is to be hoped that we shall not go to sleep in the mean time; or, adieu to our eastern trade, and to our enjoying the high honour of introducing civilization and religion into South Africa.

Previous to the arrival of the republican missionaries at Natal, Captain Gardiner had visited Dingan, living at a distance of one hundred and eighty miles from the port on the Volosi River. "The great black one" refused for some time to see the captain: but at last he consented;

suddenly showed his head and shoulders over a fence; and "tried to kill him with a look." The gallant captain, however, undauntedly faced the great despot; who was then pleased with his boldness, and said, " You are come to establish teachers of your religion among us: I cannot allow that here; but I give up all claim to the country between the Tutugal and Umzimcoolu rivers, and the Quathlamba mountains:—there you may teach. I wish to be friendly with the white king, but some of your people at Natal are unruly. They have enticed away my people, taken Zoolah women, and traded where I did not want them. My counsellors asked me to kill them: but I did not do it. They must have a chief over them, to whom I can speak."

Dingan is a stout man, and wears a kaross. He is a great dancer, and prides himself on this accomplishment: but his hands are steeped in blood to the wrists. To become the great chief of the Zoolahs, he murdered his own brother, Chaka, who was also a monster of cruelty. Dingan is assisted by two great counsellors called *idona*, and the government is thus, in fact, carried on by a triumvirate. If any particular odium is attached to the acts of Dingan, he lays the blame on the idona. About the time of Captain

Gardiner's visit to him, he had just committed another atrocity. Having long been anxious to get rid of a younger brother, a clever man, but whom he suspected of intriguing against him, some pretext was made to destroy him; and with him all his people,—the population of three large villages. "The great black one," with all this, is a facetious fellow, and fond of a joke: but his jokes are quite in keeping with his general character. Thus, a certain sea captain had presented him with a powerful burning-glass; and he was in the habit of calling one of his courtiers to him, and making him submit his arm to the influence of the lens till it smoked again.

To see Dingan reviewing his legions, each warrior armed with one short lance, "the terror of South Africa," and each battalion distinguished by the colour of its shield and commissariat oxen, white, black, red, &c., must be a fine sight. Also to hear his guard shout the praises of the great father, of the great elephant, must remind one of Horace Smith's Timbuctoo Anthology.

> "Buffalo of buffaloes! and bull of bulls!
> He sits on a throne of his enemies' skulls;
> And if he wants more for to play at foot-ball,
> Ours are at his service, all, all, all!
> Huggaboo jaw, huggaboo jew,
> Hail to the royal Quasheeboo,
> Emperor and lord of Timbuctoo!"

I could fill a chapter with stories of Dingan and his Zoolahs: but I now refrain from doing so, as it has been proposed that I should go to him, and tarry near him for some time. On a future occasion, therefore, if I am spared "the scissors of the fatal sisters," I may be able to give more information regarding the land of Issibubulunga, and other portions of Eastern Africa; and not at second-hand, as I am now compelled to do: though my present authority is unexceptionable.

The result of the Kaffir war, and the death of Hintza,—which, though we are told "that the bloody and deceitful man lives but half his days," we thought, at one time, a misfortune,—have had a very salutary effect on the people beyond our borders. This was well ascertained by Captain Gardiner; as well as by the expedition under that enthusiastic and able naturalist, Dr. A. Smith; and also by the mission to Crieli, Vadana, and Faku, so perfectly conducted by Captain De Lancey, 75th regiment; and we must now take care that so desirable an influence does not subside.

Having fully acquired the confidence and good opinion of Dingan; and obtained the cession of no less than fourteen thousand square miles of territory, one hundred and twenty miles each face, to the third range of mountains from the coast, with ten thousand inhabitants in different large villages, including what was formerly purchased from the natives by the Dutch about Natal, and which therefore is a British possession; Captain Gardiner returned to the port. There, the white residents were highly delighted at their better prospects; gave the name of Victoria to the new colony; and proceeded to lay out a town, which is named D'Urban. They also petitioned Sir Benjamin to use his influence towards obtaining a full recognition of the new possessions by the home government; and they further requested to have a lieutenant-governor appointed over them, with some military force for their protection; and a clergyman of *the Established Church*, and government schools placed among them. For, as they represented, it was desirable to prevent fanatics from gaining a footing, or establishing a rival influence in this quarter; and thus promoting confusion among the colonists, and danger from without. Captain Gardiner now returned to England, (in the beginning of 1836,) carrying with him the strong recommendations of his excellency the governor for the completion of the above arrangements.

Leaving Port Elizabeth, we retraced our steps to Uitenhage, where we tarried a short time; and with the worthy and spirited German apothecary and sheriff, Mr. Brehm, we visited the remarkable hot sulphur spring of the Coëga: which will doubtless become famous for the cure of rheumatism and cutaneous disorders. We also saw the great salt-pan, or lake, which supplies the district with that valuable condiment; and after more frontier business had been transacted in the quiet village, and the governor's system for Kaffir-land seemed to be working perfectly, we left Uitenhage for the Cape.

On our first march, we looked back on a most charming picture of groves, pasture, and hills "raked with clouds;" and arrived in the evening at Mrs. Nieuwkerk's, on Vanstaden's River, in a beautiful glen, where lived some of the finest young women I have ever seen, daughters of the kind Dutch widow; very amiable, tall, with fresh complexions, and regular features. Travellers' hearts ought to be of nether millstone; or else, as Homer says, " they will sometimes pass anxious nights after burning days!"

Our next journey was over a sandy road, and through rich pastures, where the herds seemed too fat and lazy to eat. We crossed the Camtoos

River by a punt; and passed the night at Heuman's Farm. The farms were at long intervals; and our journeys, commencing at four o'clock, A. M., were commonly forty miles a-day. We had next a tedious and a hot ride to Moolman's: where the hardy Dutchman had no servants, but his own hands and those of his wife and young children. "*Verdoem de Hottentots!*" he said: "though you may give them good wages, they do nothing but eat sheep's flesh and sleep all day. These missionary schools have been the ruin of us."

I have already touched on the subject of missionary institutions or schools; and here I must beg to discriminate between them. Some are very well conducted: such as the Moravian school of Gnadenthal, where the Hottentots are taught carpentry, gardening, and other trades; and also the London school of Hankey. Others again are worse than useless; for, as Moolman and others complained, the farmers can now get no servants to help them in the vicinity of some missionary schools: where the Hottentots are collected to spend their time in idleness; and frequently plunder the neighbouring farmers. Thus, if any pseudo-philanthropist should ask with impatience, "the story" of a hapless Hottentot, near these last, whose hat and breeches were out of order, he would probably answer, like Canning's needy knife-grinder,—

"Story, myn lieve baas,* I have none to give you;
Only last week, a passing by a sheep kraal,
I was plenty hungry ; I tink I like to taste
    Small bit of mutton.
De constapples come to bring me fore de magistraa t,
Dey give me little bit of floggy in de tronk, sir :
But give me plenty eat; I eat not so good
    Since I last left him."

Moolman, not intending any disrespect, sat down to dinner with us in his shirt-sleeves ; whilst the children climbed on the backs of our chairs, and looked out for fat pieces. The farmers on our road had from nine to fourteen children each, all stout and healthy; one man, Uÿs of the Cromme River, had twenty four by the same vrouw ; and many of them had a good stock of cattle, sheep, and horses, and countless flocks of geese and other poultry, "all that these poor farmers have to live on!" The mode of conveying the post bags, through a considerable part of this road, was in a very light cart, or curricle, with two high wheels; the horses being attached by a breast strap, and unencumbered with collars.

    * My dear master.

We saw at a post house a tame zebra *tip*, which readily used its heels on the approach of strangers, but followed its acquaintances for bread. At the pleasantly situated house of Mr. Potgeiter, Essenbosch, we found a young woman on the eve of marriage, having her ears "punctured for pendants." A wagon with a new white tilt was at the door; and the bridegroom in his Sunday's best, with flowers in his hat, was about to mount a horse with a new bridle and saddle. When a young böer goes a courting, he is thus equipped; and if accepted, he presents his future vrouw with a *spiegel doosjé*, or little enamelled box with a looking-glass inside the lid: cooing doves, and flaming hearts outside!

A fine range of hills was now on our left: among which rose conspicuous the Zitzikamma-berg, looking down on the noble forests of that name, and beyond them on the sea. We rode along a quiet and beautiful valley; and slept at Mr. Meeding's at the Cromme River, where we were well entertained with excellent fare, and with the hearty good humour of Mrs. Meeding.

Major Michell, during his surveying operations in the districts of Uitenhage and George, was shown in several places the drawings executed by the former occupiers of the country upon the faces of overhanging rocks in the most sequestered spots: the access to most of which is now difficult, being overgrown with tough underwood. Some blackened parts of the rocks, and a few scattered remains of rude earthenware vessels, bear testimony to the fact of the natives having made these their places of abode. At present they afford shelter to the rock rabbit, (*hyrax capensis*,) heaps of whose traces clog the entrances.

Major Michell made faithful copies of all of these drawings, such as still remain uninjured by time and the weather, by which great numbers have been almost entirely effaced. The intelligent reader will readily perceive that these rude attempts of uncivilized artists are not utterly devoid of merit; and that although defective in proportions, there is more resemblance in them to the human figure, than is ever seen imparted by persons, however educated, who have a total negation of graphic talent. This, indeed, is rendered most evident on the spot, by sundry miserable attempts at figures, made beside them by some civilized bungler.

The colour of these drawings is precisely that represented in the engravings; and seems to have been produced by a preparation in which the rust of iron forms a principal ingredient.

The figures contained in the annexed plates, are only a few selected from the number found at each place; and we regret that we are compelled to confine ourselves to these.

The subjects of Plate No. I, are found in a ravine on the mountain side to the northward of the Cromme River, and near the estate of Mr. Field-cornet Meeding, called Jager's Bosch. The use of the bow, as here shown, may afford matter of speculation to South African antiquaries: as Kaffirs are never known to employ that arm.

The group in Plate II, appears on the face of a rock near the waterfall on the northern extremity of the estate of Misgund, in the Lang Kloof, the property of Jacobus Rademayer, Esq., field-commandant. It seems to represent an embassy of females suing for peace; or what may also be a dance of females, for it is thus that they range themselves in either case. No one can deny that their reception is a gracious one, to judge by the polite attitudes of the male figures, perhaps chiefs.

The subject of Plate III, was found in the defile through which the Braek River runs from the Lang Kloof into the Kamnassie country, near the farm of Messrs. Campher and Van Kooyen, sub-district of George.

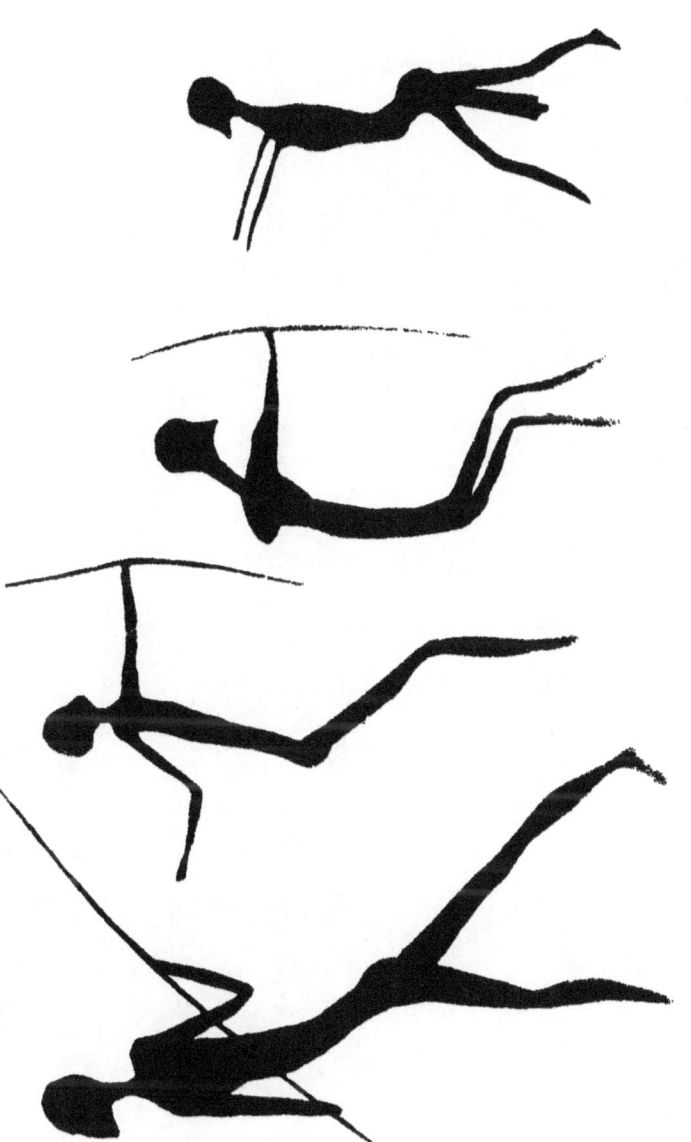

Drawings of the Aborigines of Southern Africa

Drawn by C.C.Michell

Published by Henry Colburn 13 G.t Marlborough Street 1837

Drawings of the Aborigines of Southern Africa

Drawn by C.C. Michell

Published by Henry Colburn 13 Gt Marlborough Street 1837

Drawings of the Aborigines of Southern Africa.
Published by Henry Colburn 13 Gt Marlborough Street 1837

We are unable to assist the reader, even by a conjecture, in elucidating the meaning of that which he here sees represented: but it may, perhaps, have allusion to the amphibious nature attributed to the whites by the natives in the olden day.

Our next breakfasting place, after quitting the hospitable roof of Mrs. Meeding, was at the house of a farmer of Portuguese descent, Mr. Ferreira. His grand-daughter, who made our tea, reminded us of the dark-haired and black-eyed maids of the Douro. Old Ferreira's coffin, as is usual among the Dutch, lay across the beams in the stable. After mounting our horses, three farmers, riding to meet us dismounted, fired off their *roërs*, as a salute, then rode up and shook hands. One of these was Rademayer, who fought so gallantly in the Fish River bush.

We were now in the Lang Kloof: a valley of varying breadth, and dotted with white houses at intervals of some miles. The best of these had the favourite centre gable with ogee or wavy lines. Two or three brothers, with their families, sometimes lived together on one farm of five or six thousand acres; and as we approached their places, they turned out, saluted the governor, and escorted him on horseback. We had often three generations with us. First,—the grandfather, in huge hat and coarse long-backed jacket, jogging silently on, Dutch-like, after a gruff "*daag, mynheer;*" then the next generation discoursed on the Kaffir commando, the rust in the wheat, and the horse sickness; and, lastly, we had the young böer, speaking a little English and with a smart jacket of fine cloth, prancing about on a long-tailed half-bred horse.

Rademayer, in the evening at his house, talked of the Kaffir incursions, murders, and plunderings in the Lang Kloof in 1804; of the hot pursuit after the forayed cattle; and of the dangers of an unprotected frontier, now no more to be experienced: unless, indeed, the fanatics and radicals should succeed in ruining the colony, and make Albany and Somerset a desert.

Suggested by our conversation with Rademayer, I have one word more,—and then I have done,—on the real character of the Kaffirs. Among others, Macomo has been held up, by a certain party, as a pattern of honour and noble feelings, in order to lower the character of us, the whites, by comparison with him. We will now give a trait or two of this paragon, to set, if we can, this matter at rest for ever. I confess, that it was an enigma to me, and I was unable to comprehend for some time, why the border Kaffirs should ask of themselves, of their own accord, and without any prompting, *to be admitted as British subjects.* However, immediately after the peace was concluded at Fort Willshire, "the cloven foot was betrayed," the mystery was solved. Macomo then, to the surprise and indignation of the general, said, " Now that we are British subjects, I wish the protection of British troops; so that I may take my people, and go and attack and plunder some of the neighbouring tribes." This was Macomo's notion of the advantage of being a British subject. Again, this "high-minded Kaffir prince," as the "clique" call him, on the same occasion was asked to give evidence about a horse which he knew, and the property of which was disputed between our interpreter and a sergeant. When Macomo came out from giving his evidence, the interpreter said, " Your evidence was of no use to me." " Well," said Macomo: " why did you not tell me before-hand what I was to say? But I'll go in again, if you like, and contradict all I have just stated." So much for the Kaffir demi-god.

After talking over the events of the war, our worthy host, Rademayer, took down his violin, and accompanied two nice young women playing on an ancient spinet. They also sang a favourite song among the böers, *Home, sweet home,* with Dutch words. After quitting this agreeable abode, our next breakfast was at the house of a burly old fellow, with a voice and back like a miller, Matty Sondag by name: whose *voerkamer* was ornamented with stiff oil paintings of the emperors, kings, and great men of Europe of the last fifty years, many of them apparently in the act of cutting off the heads of their own chargers. Napoleon was in a dark corner behind the bed: but Blucher was conspicuously facing the light; and pointing to him with great satisfaction, Matty roared out, "*Dat is de oud carle!*"

We descended the Commanatie Pass; and the general then desired me to note two necks of land, connecting the parallel range of hills, which are admirably formed by nature for military lines to stop an invading enemy, whether marching east or west, by this the only direct road between Cape Town and Port Elizabeth. We refreshed at Muller's, and passed on to Ganzé (or Goose) Kraal, Van Royen's: where, while wading over the saddle-flaps in a pool, and almost swimming, —a frequent occurrence,—a salute, fired in our faces though with no evil intent, occasioned our horses sorely to wet both our persons and our small wardrobe in our saddle-bags. "It was too much honour this entirely."

On our next day's journey we ascended the Cradock Mountain, and looked down on the broad plains of George. In descending the zig-zag and stony pass, we saw a wagon which had been five days stuck in mid air, as it were. Such a road for wheeled carriages I never saw: for it was as bad as the kootuls of Persia, which are hardly fit for hack mules. It was, in fact, every where strewed with broken yokes, and sprinkled with the blood of miserable bullocks. On the mountain side we had the great satisfaction of meeting again the surveyor-general, who had resumed his employment on the Zitzikamma, and who now pointed out a new direction, to the west, for the mountain road, "the wet blanket" of the Lang Kloof.

On the banks of the Keurboom River, the general was met by all the male inhabitants of George on horseback. The elders conducted us through a street of young men, who fired a salute, and then galloped on to repeat, three times, the same compliment: thus covering us all over with glory in the shape of dust and smoke, after the manner of an oriental *Istakbal*. But it was very gratifying to see, wherever we had passed, the good feeling of the people, and their perfect confidence in the government under which they lived. Some horses, unused to such rejoicings, parted company with their riders, sorely to the discomfort of the bones of the latter: " but they were bruised in a good cause."

George, on its flat, its houses shaded with trees and backed by a glorious mountain, was gay with flags; and as the general entered the drostdy-house, now the property of a worthy old Captain (of the merchant service,) Hollett, nicely dressed children strewed flowers in his path. On apologizing to the old sailor for the inconvenience to which he was now put, the governor was answered, "Don't mention it, your excellency: this is the happiest day of my life, except that on which I beat off two d—d French privateers." The Kaffirs had been expected at George; and Captain Hollett, unable to take the field from rheumatism, had made his house the citadel of the place, by barricading it, and mounting two ship guns on the roof. He also had collected all the tin in the village; and prepared *snuff* for the Kaffirs, by filling his canisters with musquet balls.

Major Michell and myself experienced every attention from the kind family of Mr. Kuys, the clerk of the peace; and there was a round of grand dinners given by Mr. Bergh, assistant civil commissioner, Dr. Paule, and Captain Hollett, to his excellency, who was here for some days fully employed, as usual, on district business.

One afternoon, a few of us rode out to Pakelsdorp, distant eight miles,—a London missionary institution, under the charge of the old teacher of the heathen, Mr. Anderson. But neither from this, nor from several other schools, were the Hottentots *encouraged* to go and assist the farmers for hire; nor had allotments of ground in the missionary lands been given over to them, in full possession, to make a living on their own grounds. "How did they live, then, at Pakelsdorp?" Some of them were wagoners; others cut down trees unlawfully in the government forests of the Zitzikamma; whilst many of their women, by the power of their sable charms, induced the slaves of the people of George to rob their masters. Ought such a state of things to continue? and whose report on the subject is to be believed? That of a witness who professes to be impartial, and who is unconnected with the schools? or the statements of those *who live by a continuance* of the system of delusive benefit to the coloured classes, and by the existence of these institutions?

Another day I rode through part of the forest of George, with an old schoolfellow and much esteemed friend, Mr. T. Duthie, late of the 72nd Highlanders, and now a considerable proprietor of land on the banks of that most picturesque river-lake, the Knysna. We visited Cayman's Gat, or Alligator's Hole, a black creek among steep precipices, where Le Vaillant said that he had encountered many perils.

The forests of Uitenhage and George occupy an extent of three hundred square miles, between the village of George, the mountains, the Zitzikamma River, and the ocean. The forest is not continuous; but there are open patches of pasture here and there, in some of which we saw certain squatters in log huts, who felled and sold the timber without a license. Elephants, leopards, buffaloes, and other wild animals, are found in this beautiful forest, which is composed of stink wood, yellow wood, white els, assegai, and other valuable trees. It is supposed that eighteen hundred loads of timber, each valued at four pounds ten shillings, were removed, in 1834, surreptitiously from the forest!

The surveyor-general has exposed these nefarious transactions; and also the wanton destruction of timber by felling the trees without regard to age or situation: for, as the branches were not removed, twenty other and younger trees were commonly destroyed by the fall of one. Besides which, the white and coloured hunters, to satisfy their gluttony by getting at the wild honey at the top, would, without hesitation, cut down a tree of five feet diameter. In 1812, Sir John Cradock appointed an overseer for the Zitzikamma forest; licenses were then taken out; and the abuses were fewer. The office of overseer has since, however, been abolished; and the forest has gradually melted away: but it will not now be suffered to be laid waste, as it has lately been. This forest is so valuable to the colony, that there is scarcely a house, mill, wagon, or agricultural implement, which is not made of the wood of it. It is now proposed that seven shillings and sixpence be paid on each load of timber that is removed; and that one or two gentlemen be appointed as overseers or rangers of the forest.

We left George to visit the excellent and central, but neglected port of the colony, Mossel Bay. We forded and swam the horses over some dangerous rivers, and reached Mr. Acker's house, very pleasantly situated on a verdant slope, backed by hills, enjoying a noble sea view, and with, perhaps, the finest climate in the world. In a creek sheltered by rocks, boats can land cargoes from ships at all times here; whilst Attaquas Pass improved, would bring the produce of the Lang Kloof, of the Congo, and of the rich valley of Oliphant's River, to an excellent port, and avoid the Cradock Pass and George, surrounded with dangerous rivers. Allotments were laid out for a new village here, to which the people of George will probably, from choice, all remove before long.

We next slept at an old farmer's, M. Muller; and then swimming the horses over the Goritz, and passing the excellent garden and vineyard of Mr. Van Wyk at the Crombeck's River, we tarried a night at the Juffrouw Lombards. The site of the widow's house was admirable: it was elevated; mountains, woods, and plains were seen from it; and a beautiful river rushed past it.

> " River, river, swelling river!
> On you rush o'er rough and smooth!
> Louder, faster, roaring, leaping
> Over rocks, by flow'r-beds sweeping,
>   Like impetuous youth.
>
> River, river, headlong river!
> Down you dash into the sea;
> Sea, that line hath never sounded,
> Sea, that voyage hath never bounded,
>   Like Eternity."

On the 24th of December, we rode into the most pleasant village of Swellendam, in company with the civil-commissioner, Mr. Harry Rivers, and a numerous company. Here we heard an excellent sermon from Mr. Robertson on Christmas-day; ate an excellent Christmas-dinner with Mr. Rivers; and were of opinion that the situation of civil-commissioner here, with five hundred pounds a-year, a wife and family, an excellent house, a large garden of many acres, abounding in shady walks, and with clear streams rushing through it, and a majestic face of mountain to back the landscape, was more desirable than the office of governor of the colony, with five thousand pounds per annum and all its expenses and heavy responsibility. In this estimate of happiness, it is true, we regarded only individual comfort; without considering the superior power of benefiting society, with which the governor of such a great colony is invested.

Strange to say, both at Swellendam, George, Uitenhage, and Graham's Town, the government schools were very indifferently conducted: but this will be amended.

Our next stage was to Field-commandant Linde's, on the Zonder-end River. We saw the old gentleman (born in 1760) sitting, after six

Kaffir commandos, by a vine at his door, hale and active, and silently looking towards the serrated summits of the dry and bare mountains opposite. It was the picture of a South African patriarch. Unfortunate as usual with horses, I had now left four on the road, quite knocked up with the hot and long marches. Here I hired and bought others. At Caledon we saw the hot baths resorted to by Indian visitors and others for rheumatic complaints; had a "turn out" of all the people of the district, to do honour to his excellency; and slept at De Kock's, on the Bot River. Then we benefited by the labours of the surveyor-general at Houw, Hoek, and Sir Lowry Cole's passes, where we rode over admirable mountain paths, constructed with great scientific skill. These improved passes, with gentle ascents and descents, now connect important parts of the colony by a few hours' journey, which it formerly took days to accomplish, accompanied with serious injury, and often entire destruction to the oxen and wagons. "If the mountain-cleaving Furhad were alive, from beholding the performance of this wonderful art, he would fall into the whirlpool of astonishment and confusion."

And now, with regard to the Dutch farmers, of whom we had seen so much on this journey, I am bound to observe, that we found them every where sober, moral, religious, civil, and worthy people. Instead of his excellency being met every where with memorials for additional grants of land, remission of taxes, complaints of the authorities, of want of servants, and other grievances, there was little or nothing of the sort occurred on the road. Many of the farmers were very poor; and some seldom touched meat: but they seemed to bear with what could not be helped, and trusted to their own exertions, and to an over-ruling Providence, for better times. However, we must not forget, that on the high road, between the frontier and Cape Town, where the farmers see more strangers, and get a constant sale for their forage, they must naturally be superior in manners, and more comfortable in their circumstances, than those living at a distance from this road. But, considering the great intervals between the farms generally in South Africa, the difficulty of procuring education for the children, and religious ordinances for the parents, and the white people also having been subject to the contamination of a slave system: considering all this, I say, the character and conduct of the Dutch böers, generally, are very creditable to them; and if approached in a proper manner, they will almost invariably be found to be very hospitable and obliging.

We had a distant view of Cape Town, Table Mountain, Table and False Bay, from the top of Sir Lowry Cole's Pass; and then descending in furious gusts of wind, we left Hottentot's Holland behind us, and cantered over the sands to the village of Somerset. Here there was a congratulatory address delivered to his excellency; a *déjeuné* laid out; much firing, cheering, and galloping to and fro of horsemen; and then we went off to sleep at Mr. Cloete's, of Zandvliet.

On the 30th of December it rained heavily; and for the first time in South Africa, his excellency travelled in a horse-wagon for ten miles to Manenberg. We then mounted our horses; were met by the Baron Lorentz, judge and superintendent of police; the chief justice, Sir John Wylde, and Mr. Justice Kekewich, the Honourable Mr. and Mrs. Pillans, and many hundred more; and finally we reached the foot of Table Mountain, glorious with clouded summits, bare ribs of granite, and wooded slopes. Riding between the white garden-houses of Rondesbosch in gleams of sun-shine, and through crowds of well-dressed people, in carriages, on horseback, and on foot, we entered Cape Town in torrents of rain; and passed on to government-house between the troops at extended order: whilst his excellency, on his return to the seat of his government, was received with salutes of cannon from Cape Castle.

APPENDIX.

APPENDIX.—No. I.

Conference with the Kaffir Chiefs of the 15*th of August,* 1835.

On this day Major Cox, 75th regiment, and Captain Warden, Cape mounted rifles, accompanied by Klaas Dirk as interpreter, left the camp on the Upper Keiskamma; and at one o'clock P. M. met the Kaffir chiefs, Macomo and Tyalie, who were accompanied by all their head men, and about six hundred armed Kaffirs. The following is what took place at the conference, as reported by Captain Warden:

Major Cox.	*The Chief Macomo.*
1. The governor having heard that the Kaffirs wish to send in a message, Captain Warden has come among you to hear what the chiefs have to say.	1. We have been long tired of this war; all our best men are dead; there are no more Kaffirs left. You have had some soldiers killed: but our loss has been very great.

Major Cox.

2. It was you, Macomo and Tyalie, who commenced war upon the colony.

3. As we have known you both for many years, we would advise you as friends not to lose this opportunity of throwing yourselves on the mercy of the governor. The great commando will again assemble: a much larger one than the last, because all the soldiers the king of England is sending out will join it.

4. It was the intention of the governor to drive you all over the Kye; and when the great commando again takes the field, it can be done in a few days.

The Chief Macomo.

2. Do not talk about what has been done: we have killed one another long enough; and all the chiefs and their people now wish for peace.

3. We wish to make friends of the English; we cannot hold out any longer; we have no home for our women and children; and have lived long enough like wild beasts. We hope the governor will take us under his care: Cox and Warden must tell the governor how we are suffering, and ask him what country he will give us to live in.

4. We hope the governor will not oblige us to live beyond the Kye. Tell him we will obey his orders; and our people shall never steal cattle again from the colony: but the Fingoes

APPENDIX. 337

Major Cox.

The Chief Macomo.
will give more trouble to the English than the Kaffirs ever did. The Fingoes are fond of stealing. Will the governor send back these people to live with the Kaffirs?

5. We do not know what the governor will do with the Fingoes: but we believe they will not be sent to live among you again.

5. When will the governor send his orders to us? We hope it will not be long; as we wish to hear what is to become of us.

6. If you agree to place yourselves under the governor's orders, he will give you land to live in: but we cannot say where.

6. We are afraid the governor will send us too far away, and give our father Gaika's country to the Fingoes: he must not do so; the Fingoes are a bad people. We will, however, do as the governor wishes.

7. We are satisfied that you are sincere in what you have to-day said; and our patrols shall not molest the Kaffirs without giving due

7. We are all to-day very happy, because we have Cox and Warden among us; and they will tell the governor how we long for

338   APPENDIX.

Major Cox.	*The Chief Macomo.*
notice to you both. You must send Platjie and two other men to Fort Cox in three days hence, and wait the governor's orders from Graham's Town.	peace. Warden must give these two assegais to the governor, as coming from Macomo and Tyalie.

8. The assegais shall be given to the governor; and all that has passed between us to-day shall be told him.

After shaking hands with the chiefs and their head men, Major Cox and Captain Warden returned to the camp; and the Kaffirs to the mountains, apparently much pleased.

(Signed)   H. D. WARDEN,
Captain, Cape Mounted Rifles.

APPENDIX.—No. II.

Conference with the Kaffir Chiefs on the 6th of September, 1835.

On this day Colonel Smith, Captain Warden, &c. met Macomo and Tyalie on the Keiskamma, near Fort Cox: when what follows took place, as reported by Colonel Smith:

Colonel Smith.

1. The governor is good; he is grieved at the miseries of the Kaffirs: he therefore sends me to have a conference of peace with you, if you are penitent.

2. I will therefore make peace with you in his great name, and on his great faith; and I will fire seven

The Chiefs.

1. We cry mercy, great chief.

2. We wish to be British subjects: we will be good and faithful subjects; and will obey your laws.

Colonel Smith.

guns for peace, that all our people may know it, and that we may respect the word of peace, loving one another as brothers. The governor will be kind to Macomo, and all the children of Gaika; we must forget the past, and look forward to the future. I will do all I can to help the governor to make you and your people happy.

3. British subjects must be good men: then they may and will become great men, and rich men; and have houses and towns and churches; and live a good life in the land of their fathers, guarding the tomb of the great Gaika, who once was a great friend of the English, and he died a great friend. His sons, his children shall bless the day they became British subjects.

The Chiefs.

3. We humbly pray we may not be expelled from our native hills, the Amatola, Tabendoda, and others; and we will live under such restrictions as the governor may impose on us.

APPENDIX.

Colonel Smith.

4. In the mean time, then, your people must not cross the line of the Keiskamma, nor the road between Fort Willshire and the great ford of the Kye, until you have personally come to a settlement with the governor. In token of the good understanding between us, the guns will now fire. [Seven guns were accordingly fired.]

You are now, then, our brothers; that is, all the Kaffirs of the tribe of Gaika. We do not know T'Slambie's people; they have not yet asked for mercy: I must make them ask for mercy; and I will then listen to them.

The Chiefs.

4. There now being an end of fighting, we will meet the governor any where, finally to settle our affairs, to know our country, to help the governor against his enemies. His enemies shall be ours, and we hope our enemies will be his. The fire-arms taken during the war we will give up: but we pray the governor's word for those that we bought. We will give up the names of all the white and black men who said they would help us in the war. We will also tell the governor where we got the gunpowder to continue the war. We again, in the name of all of the tribe of Gaika, cry for mercy: war is bad for nations; we ask for peace. Give us peace; trust us, and treat us well like your own subjects: we will be happy and obedient; making war for you.

Colonel Smith.   *The Chiefs.*

And this is *our word,* which we swear to God : all of us holding up our hands.

5. The word is now therefore peace.

(Signed)   H. G. SMITH.
Colonel.

APPENDIX.—No. III.

Minutes of a Conversation between Colonel Smith and Guania, the great counsellor of Macomo, on the 8th of September, 1835; as reported by Colonel Smith:

Colonel Smith.	Guania.
1. You are much in the confidence of Macomo, and were of Gaika also.	1. Yes. And I am come to thank you humbly for the mercy shown to us; to ask where we are to live; and to talk of nothing but peace.
2. Well! Now understand: in consequence of your unjustly and wickedly going to war with the colony, we have taken possession of all the country up to the Kye; and the governor had determined	2. We went to war. It was contrary to *my* advice: we have suffered; severely suffered. You have been kind to us; we asked for mercy; you gave it; *we wish to be British subjects, and to live under*

Colonel Smith.

to drive the tribes over it: but since you have begged so humbly for mercy, he will listen to your wishes.

Guania,

British laws, upon such ground as you can give. You say the governor is good: we pray therefore for our native hills, and the grave of Gaika. *We will live where you wish us:* put us where we may die, and not be driven out. The governor is our father.

3. The English laws are very strict: particularly against murder and robbery.

3. So much the better.

4. As you may become British subjects, at your conference with the governor, it will be arranged how your former laws can be assimilated to the British laws, for the general good of your people.

4. I wish to speak of this. I am an old man, of few words: but peace and good will I desire. There should be one great man over all the "English Kaffirs," the same as there is over the other British subjects: all should be under the same laws. The Kaffir chiefs should be magistrates of their tribes under the great man; Ma-

Colonel Smith.	*Guania.*
	como will do well (as a magistrate). I now wish to speak for Umhala of the T'Slambies: they are Gaikas.
5. Umhala has sent to me; and I have suspended hostilities: *but he must come, and at my feet ask for mercy.* I will then ask the governor to listen to him.	5. That is just. Macomo did so; and he is greater than Umhala. But he will come: I pray you, then, to regard him kindly.
6. I will. The way to have good people is to have good men as chiefs: if we are not satisfied with Umhala, we will deprive him of his chieftainship, and appoint a good man.	6. That is just; and for the good of the T'Slambies: but he *will* be good. Seyolo and Fundasi should be chiefs over the people; and Kabana also.
7. We will listen to them. Understand what I now say: I am now talking to you that I may lay your desires before the governor, who comes to meet you, and to listen to you.	7. We thank, we truly thank the governor. I will speak out my mind: nothing can restore us *but being good friends with the English.*

Colonel Smith.

8. How do you propose to locate your people, when the governor points out your land?

9. It will be necessary that military posts be placed throughout your locations, to enforce the laws. You have many bad men amongst you.

10. Do you think it would be of any advantage to have English magistrates at each post: that is, with each tribe?

11. You are a man of experience; and you are asked these questions, that we may avail ourselves of

Guania.

8. Each chief should have so much ground given to him, upon which he can live, and share it out to his people. But Macomo will himself talk to the governor on this subject.

9. That is very right; it is very necessary. The chiefs will do all that is right; and these posts will help them. We have bad men; their hunger, when they were assembled, made them worse; this hereafter will not happen, now there is peace.

10. Yes: it is much to be desired.

11. I thank you for what you say of me. I will contradict you if I differ from you.

APPENDIX. 347

Colonel Smith.

all information: you may disagree with me whenever you wish.

12. What the governor is now coming to do, is not a thing of a day, but that which will last for years; and therefore requires thought and consideration.

13. If the tribe of Gaika were driven from the country, it would only be the punishment they brought on themselves, by their transgressions in making war with us. But when you are admitted as British subjects, this will not happen again.

14. When the ground is allotted to you, have you seed-corn?

15. Macomo has been

Guania.

12. We have not seen such a bright prospect for many days; and we thank the governor for sending you among us; and also for such good hopes for our welfare.

13. It will not happen again. To be British subjects is what we desire, and have desired. It is a good word for us.

14. I fear not. [They had plenty.]

15. I feel grateful, very

Colonel Smith.

unfortunate in the world, and says he has now nothing. If he hold fast the good word he has spoken, it is the governor's intention to improve his condition; and he will do so.

16. Have your people lost all their cattle?

17. Your people being placed under British laws, are you of opinion that this will incline them to become civilized: that is, that by habits of industry they will learn to become rich, know the use of money, clothe themselves, build houses and villages, and leave off the inclination which they have to acquire property by stealing?

18. Will your people learn the use of the plough?

Guania.

grateful; my heart is full with thanks.

16. All, all: we have nothing; we starve. [This, like the pretended want of seed-corn, was untrue.]

17. I look forward to living under British laws with anxiety. I am fully persuaded it will do great good among the tribes. Hunger makes our people very bad men.

18. We hope to learn every thing that is useful.

Colonel Smith.

19. I see you are tired: but pray ask me any questions you please.

20. You see, now, what the war of horrors, which you made upon us, has brought upon you.

21. Is it the custom of your country to declare war before you make it?

(Signed)

Guania.

19. I have only two things to ask:—for mercy, for our children are starving; and for peace.

20. Yes: I see it; I feel it. Our country was never so punished before. I begged our people not to go to war.

21. It is customary: but in this war the young men began it, before the wiser people knew it.

H. G. SMITH,
Colonel.

APPENDIX.—No. IV.

Elucidation of the Cause and Manner of the breaking off the Treaties of Peace between his Excellency Sir Benjamin D'Urban and the border Kaffir Chiefs, from the 13th to the 17th of September, 1835, at Fort Willshire.

Extract of a letter from Lieutenant Moultrie, 75th regiment, commanding at Fort Peddie, on the Clusie, to his excellency the commander-in-chief, and dated September 12th, 1835:—" I have the honour to transmit for your excellency's information, an account of the proceedings of the Kaffirs, and of my own operations, within the last few days. Having observed their spoor (traces) in the Fish River, in different small bodies, and hearing also of several robberies which had been committed in the colony; I yesterday again went into the bush for the purpose of intercepting them. I lay in wait in one of their most favourite paths; and during the night I succeeded in killing three of them. Shortly after my return to the camp this morning, a man arrived from Jan Tzatzoe, to inform me that the spoor of a number of Kaffirs had been seen by some of the women in the direction of the Guanga, where the cattle of

the tribe usually graze. Although I had but faint
hopes of the Kaffirs putting themselves in our power,
I nevertheless ordered the Field-cornet Piet Uys, with
two and twenty of the burghers, to proceed in the direction alluded to; and if the information was correct, to
endeavour to cut them off. It turned out to be true,
that a body of fifty or sixty Kaffirs had come through;
but upon finding themselves discovered, they had retreated towards the Keiskamma. The field-cornet followed them; and on being joined by Tzatzoe and his
men, succeeded in surrounding them in a blind (dry)
river near the Line Drift. Seeing, however, that he had
them in his power, the field-cornet sent a message to
them to the effect,—that if they would surrender and
throw down their assegais, they should not be harmed.
The messenger, one of Tzatzoe's Kaffirs, was instantly
killed. The Kaffirs were then immediately attacked;
eighteen of them were killed, and a number were
wounded. The burghers received some assegais through
their clothes; and one Kaffir ally, exclusive of the
messenger, was wounded. Only one gun was seen
among the enemy; and they did not fire. The Kaffirs
proclaimed themselves Tyalie's men. I have no doubt
that their object was to carry off the remainder of Tzatzoe's cattle, having already once done so with impunity.
I think, also, that they were not aware of there being
an efficient mounted force upon this post; and thus got
themselves into a scrape, from which they were unable
to extricate themselves. Mr. Southey, who was here
this morning from the Gualana, informed me that, on
the road from Graham's Town, he took eighty head of

cattle from four Kaffirs. I have also myself seen traces of them entering the colony by the Fish River; and although they talk of peace, they seem still extremely active in plundering. I have therefore thought it right, without loss of time, to apprize your excellency of the above transactions."

     (Signed) G. B. MOULTRIE,
           Lieutenant 75th Reg.

Note.—On the receipt of the above despatch at Fort Willshire, the commander-in-chief caused Macomo, Tyalie, and Guania to be called together; and the above letter was read to them. They were then told that their treacherous proceedings rendered them unworthy to be treated with; that they had never ceased to break the boundary imposed by the truce granted them; that if *they did not* in three days cause all these parties to be recalled out of the colony, having themselves, the chiefs, full liberty to go to their people, they would be instantly attacked in the Amatola and its dependencies with the whole British force; and that the operations against them would not cease till they had been swept over the Kye, or destroyed. The chiefs were then dismissed; they recalled their people, and peace was concluded.   J. E. A.

THE END.

www.ingramcontent.com/pod-product-compliance
Lightning Source LLC
Chambersburg PA
CBHW021829220426
43663CB00005B/182